Dot.cons

For David Wright

Dot.cons

Crime, deviance and identity on the Internet

Edited by Yvonne Jewkes

WILLAN
PUBLISHING

Published by

Willan Publishing
Culmcott House
Mill Street, Uffculme
Cullompton, Devon
EX15 3AT, UK
Tel: +44(0)1884 840337
Fax: +44(0)1884 840251
e-mail: info@willanpublishing.co.uk
website: www.willanpublishing.co.uk

Published simultaneously in the USA and Canada by

Willan Publishing
c/o ISBS, 5824 N.E. Hassalo St,
Portland, Oregon 97213-3644, USA
Tel: +001(0)503 287 3093
Fax: +001(0)503 280 8832
e-mail: info@isbs.com
website: www.isbs.com

First published 2002

ISBN 1-84392-000-X Paperback
ISBN 1-84392-001-8 Hardback

British Library Cataloguing-in-Publication Data

A catalogue record for this book is available from the British Library

Project management by Deer Park Productions, Tavistock, Devon
Typeset by GCS, Leighton Buzzard, Bedfordshire
Printed and bound by T.J. International Ltd, Padstow, Cornwall PL28 8RW

Contents

About the Authors

Yvonne Jewkes is Director of Undergraduate Studies in Criminology at the University of Hull. Her research interests focus on the relationship between the mass media and crime, constructions of masculinities, and prisons and imprisonment. She has published extensively in these areas including, most recently, *Captive Audience: Media, Masculinity and Power in Prisons* (2002, Willan) and, with Gayle Letherby, *Criminology: A Reader* (2002, Sage). She is currently writing *Media and Crime: A Critical Introduction* to be published by Sage.

Rinella Cere lectures in Media and Cultural Studies at Sheffield Hallam University. She is author of *European and National Identities in Britain and Italy: Maastricht on Television* (2000, Edwin Mellen Press). She is currently researching the use of the Internet by transnational social movements and NGOs.

Andy DiMarco is Associate Lecturer in Sociology and Criminology at City College, Coventry. His current research interests include the sociology of food and culture, the social construction of identities and presentations of self in cyberspace.

Heather DiMarco lectures at Coventry University and has undertaken research for the Centre for Social Justice at Coventry University. Research interests include deviant identities in cybersociety and issues surrounding social exclusion/inclusion.

Sarah Earle is Lecturer in Health Studies at University College Northampton, UK. Her research interests include the sociology of sexuality and sex work. She is also interested in the areas of disability and women's reproductive health. She is co-editor (with Gayle Letherby) of the forthcoming title *Gender, Identity and Reproduction: Social Perspectives* to be published by Palgrave.

Emily Finch is Lecturer in Law at the University of Reading. She has published widely in the areas of stalking, harassment, socio-legal constructions of identity and identity theft. Her most recent book is *The Criminalisation of Stalking: the Construction of the Problem and an Evaluation of the Solution* (2001, Cavendish).

Janice Joseph is Professor of the Criminal Justice Program at Richard Stockton College of New Jersey. She publishes in the areas of delinquency, gangs, domestic violence, stalking, sexual harassment, victimization of women, and minorities and crime, and is the author of *Black Youths, Delinquency and Juvenile Justice*, and co-editor (with Dorothy Taylor) of *With Justice For All: Minorities and Women in Criminal Justice*. She is editor of the Journal of Ethnicity in Criminal Justice.

Gayle Letherby is Associate Head of Subject (Social Work, Health and Social Sciences) and Deputy Director of the Centre for Social Justice at Coventry University. Recent and forthcoming publications include *Feminist Research in Theory and Practice* (2003, OU Press); (with Sarah Earle) *Gender, Identity and Reproduction: Social Perspectives* (2003, Palgrave); and (with Yvonne Jewkes) *Criminology: A Reader* (2002, Sage).

Jen Marchbank is Head of Undergraduate Studies in the School of Health and Social Sciences at Coventry University. She writes on policy, gender, education and conflict, and is the author of *Women, Power and Policy: Comparative Studies of Childcare* (2000, Routledge) and co-editor (with Susie Jacobs and Ruth Jacobson) of *States of Conflict: Gender, Violence and Resistance* (2000, Zed).

Keith Sharp is Head of the School of Contemporary Studies at De Montfort University, Bedford. He has published many articles on social theory and methodology, and is co-author, with Sarah Earle, of a forthcoming book, *Punters in Cyberspace: Men Who Pay For Sex* to be published by Ashgate.

Paul A. Taylor is Senior Lecturer in the Sociology of Technology at Salford University. His main research interests lie in the politics and culture of the information age and he has contributed to several volumes on various aspects of cybercrime. In 1999 he published *Hackers: Crime in the Digital Sublime* with Routledge.

Chapter 1

Crime, deviance and the disembodied self: transcending the dangers of corporeality

Yvonne Jewkes and Keith Sharp

This is how it works. The thief gets hold of the three pieces of information that are needed to create an identity. In the US, these are: your social security number, your date of birth and your driving licence number. This information is all...on the Net [for] around $50...You, of course, have an excellent credit record which is available over the Net for $8.50...Pretending to be your landlord or employer, I do the research. Given your financial good conduct, you are 'pre-approved' for card, phone and hire-purchase accounts. I apply for gold and platinum in your name, supplying your details, but indicating a change of address for billing...Spending fast, I max out the cards, ignore the monthly bills and apply for more cards...I fall behind on the rent. To forestall eviction and car repossession, I file for bankruptcy – under your name. Given the law's delays, I can expect two years of *dolce vita* before moving on (the world is full of identities). You, meanwhile, know nothing of this until – several months later – debt collection agencies begin to harass you. Life becomes Kafkaesque. You inform the police – but they can't see that you are the victim of any crime...You have to prove you're you...Your credit rating is shot – probably forever. You now know what it means to be an untouchable.

(Sutherland 2000: unpaginated)

In an enduring ritual of nightly 'cruising', a crowd of people has gathered in a lonely-hearts club. A man musters up the courage to approach a woman and fires off a few of his best one-liners. She takes the bait and tugs the line with some sexy retorts of her own.

The chemistry is right; things heat up. They are soon jarred back to reality by the teasing of those around them who've caught on to their little game. Embarrassed, they quickly pass notes and plan a late-night rendezvous. Both show up punctually at the private place they have chosen. An awkward silence is broken by more provocative flirting, and then, finally, what they've both come for: sex. They quickly undress one another and begin making frantic love. The exchange is short but intense. When they've finished, they swap a few nervous pleasantries. As each of them chooses 'Quit' from a menu of options on a computer screen, a cheap digitized voice says 'good-bye'. The telephone link between their computers is disconnected. Tonight's disembodied tryst has cost each about six dollars.

(Branwyn 2000: 396)

Identities and the Internet

Cyberspace opens up infinitely new possibilities to the deviant imagination. With the right equipment and sufficient technical know-how you can – if you are so inclined – buy a bride, cruise gay bars, go on a global shopping spree with someone else's credit card, break into a bank's security system, plan a demonstration in another country and hack into the Pentagon – all on the same day. More than any other medium, computer-mediated communications (CMCs) undermine the traditional relationship between physical context and social situation. Place and time are transcended. When we sit down at our computers and sign on to the Internet we are no longer 'in' our physical setting but are relocated to a 'generalised elsewhere' of distant places and 'non-local' people (Morley and Robins 1995: 132; see also Meyrowitz 1985, 1989). Anonymity, disembodiment, outreach and speed are the hallmarks of Internet communication and, combined, they can make us feel daring, liberated, infallible.

Contemporary life has been described as a world of spectacle, narcissism and performance (Abercrombie and Longhurst 1998). The Internet creates spaces for all three, providing us with the opportunity both to *present* ourselves and to *invent* ourselves. Discourses about identity are a major currency of contemporary culture but in postmodern analyses identity is not inherent or 'fixed' (for example by biological or psychological predispositions). Identity is multidimensional and amorphous; we can be whoever, whatever, wherever we wish to be. And the Internet is the postmodern medium *par excellence*; the slate upon which we can write and rewrite our personalities in a perpetual act of self-creation. Whether choosing a nickname or email address, constructing a home page, entering a chat room, leaving our auto-biographical details on sites that connect people in new friendships or rekindle old relationships, or engaging in the kinds of activities highlighted in the quotations above, the Net provides a locus for creative authorship of the self. These activities might be spectacular, performative, narcissistic or all three, but they are, in the main, harmless and often humorous vehicles for self-presentation. At worst, the personal details that we present on home pages, on sites such as Friends Reunited, or to potential sexual partners in cyberspace, are conspicuous self-promotions; 'a fanclub to oneself' (Di Giovanna 1996). But because the Internet provides more opportunities for 'embodiment' than for physical interaction – in other words, the channel of communication is limited so that aspects of the embodied self can only be apparent if truthfully described by the sender (Miller 1995) – it can liberate its users from the usual constraints of corporeality. The Internet thus gives users a freedom of expression – a freedom of *being* – quite unlike anything they have at their disposal in the physical world. As Sherry Turkle (1995: 12) notes, cyberspace makes possible the creation of an identity 'so fluid and multiple that it strains the very limits of the notion'. Equally, it affords users the potential to conceal stigmatised aspects of their 'real life' identities while simultaneously facilitating the establishment of identities that are fantastic, fraudulent, exploitative or criminal.

But although the Internet facilitates multiple identities and apparently limitless freedoms of choice, expression and agency, at the same time it magnifies many existing inequalities split along racial, gendered and economic lines.[1] The subject of gender has dominated sociological discussions of the relationship between computer-mediated communications and their users. After 30 years when the dominant image of the Internet user was of a (white, university-educated) man, there has been a sustained attempt in the last ten years to reposition the Internet as a feminine – and feminist – technology. Some feminist writers have described cyberspace as a feminine space, a maternal matrix, a womb-like place (Smelik 2000; see also Taylor, Chapter 8 of this volume). But claims that the Internet is a masculine technology are hard to dispute given that the vast majority of those involved in the design, development and production of CMCs are male and that there remains a cultural dominance of masculinity in newsgroups, discussion lists and most other online spaces. Furthermore, the practices being facilitated by the Net that are described in this book – child pornography, prostitution, stalking, sexual harassment, human trafficking, hacking, etc. – are without doubt predominantly (although not exclusively) the activities of men, and the victims are more often than not women and girls. At the same time, the sexist and oppressive structural, social-psychological and cultural factors that have traditionally impeded women's relationship with information and communication technologies have been slow to break down and arguably have not changed dramatically yet (van Zoonen 2002).

Yet, as some of the chapters that follow will argue, the simplistic positioning of men as oppressors and women as victims is systematically problematised in cyberspace. Cyber-feminists have made much of the Internet's capacity to provide women with a network on which they can 'chatter, natter, work and play…a new tactile environment in which women artists can find their space' (Plant 2000: 325), but van Zoonen (2002: 12) goes further, suggesting that in cyberspace:

> There seems…as much evidence for the claim that the Internet is masculine and a male world, as there is for the claim that it is feminine and a female world. There is yet another claim to the gender of the Internet, and that is that it has no gender, or better that it is a gender laboratory, a playground for experimenting with gender symbols and identity, a space to escape from the dichotomy of gender and the boundaries produced by physical bodies.

Cyberspace thus allows participants to be multi-gendered, gender ambiguous or gender free. The notion that in virtual reality gender can be multidimensional, non-existent or irrelevant highlights the danger of making generalised or essentialist claims for the Internet being either a woman's medium or a man's. None the less, given that socio-cultural, moral and technological constraints tend to bind women more restrictively than men, it *is* interesting to note how women are utilising computer-mediated communications to transgress conventional expectations of 'acceptable' femininity and assert their agency in ways which, in 'normal' life, would submit them to accusations of deviance, depravity and perhaps worse. As Sadie Plant (2000: 325) puts it: 'there is more to cyberspace than meets the male gaze…women are accessing the circuits on which they were once exchanged, hacking into security's controls and discovering their own post-humanity.'

The 'democratic' *vs.* the 'perverting' role of the Internet: women's use of online pornography

A good example of the subversion of traditional gendered roles is women's consumption of online pornography. John Naughton (1999: 34–35) sums up the appeal of Internet porn to a general audience, but his comments arguably alert us to the particular attraction of such material to the female consumer:

> What makes the Net unusual is that it is the first conduit for illicit or disreputable publications which does not require the consumer to cross a shame threshold. If you want to buy a raunchy magazine or a smutty video, you have to run some risks of exposure or embarrassment. You may have to visit a sex-shop, for example, and be seen emerging from the premises by a colleague; or receive a parcel in the mail that could be opened in error by someone in your family or office; or undergo the humiliation of having to ask the newsagent to take down a particular magazine from the top rack.

This quotation illustrates the way in which the emergence of the Internet articulates with familiar debates around freedom, access and censorship. At one extreme it is possible to argue that in making pornography widely available, an important democratic end has been served. The same point would apply to any material to which access has traditionally been limited, either explicitly or *de facto*, to certain social groups: the fact that anyone with a computer can, if they choose, view the material, means that no group is excluded from whatever benefits or perils such viewing brings. If the traditional organisation of the pornography industry has indeed meant that women have effectively been excluded as consumers, and as a result of this, pornography has been allowed to develop in ways that fulfil essentially patriarchal ends, then it would seem to follow that technologies which allow women to be equal consumers with men must be both democratic and socially desirable. Just as opening up higher education to women was surely a prerequisite for the challenges to patriarchal knowledge which followed, so the emergence of Internet pornography could be seen as a prerequisite for the emergence of an inclusive erotica, in which women's libidinal interests are represented, equally, alongside those of men.

Alternatively, it is possible to regard the expansion of access to pornographic material in exactly the opposite way, as a dangerously unblockable conduit through which fundamentally harmful images can be transmitted to an exponentially growing population of Internet subscribers. The argument would run like this: pornography is harmful and degrading to whosoever views it. It is, moreover, harmful to *society* in exact proportion with which it is viewed by society's members. It follows, therefore, that any technology which increases the volume

5

of pornography viewed in society is a bad thing and should be discouraged.

This conflict mirrors the polarisation of views among earlier generations of writers on the social consequences of the mass media who argued, at one extreme, that media representations merely reflect audience views (an argument usually put forward most vigorously by media producers) and, at the other, that they are – cynically or not – involved in shaping and determining those views (Wright Mills 1956). So in one sense, the availability of material on the Internet, which promotes (intentionally or not) deviant or criminal activity, does not pose a qualitatively different problem for analysts than that posed by more traditional media. There are, however, a number of important differences between the Internet and traditional media which, at the very least, make this problem more pressing.

First, the Internet is virtually impossible to censor. While for those of a libertarian persuasion this is undoubtedly one of its greatest attractions, if we are to endorse one or other version of the view that people and societies can be harmed by having access to certain material, we must conclude that the potential for harm, at least, is increased by the existence of the Internet. Secondly, the Internet has the capacity to be interactive, in ways that traditional media are not. The distinction between the producer and consumer is blurred, such that the consumers of one moment become the producers of the next and *vice versa*. This could be further evidence of its essentially democratic nature – control over content no longer rests with one, powerful, interest group, but potentially with each and every individual user. Equally, the scope for subversion and, ultimately, anarchy could be considerable. Thirdly, and related to this, the boundaries between mass and individual communication are blurred. Individuals can make themselves and their messages available to a mass audience, just as readily as they can to individuals. No longer does access to a mass audience require the resources and power of the very few; a PC, a modem and a telephone line is all that is required. Taken individually these differences are significant; taken collectively, and in the context of debates about the democratic versus perverting role of the Internet in society, they are monumental.

It is this dichotomy – the democratic versus the perverting role of the Internet – that lies at the heart of discussions about its impact on crime and deviance. There can be little doubt that the Internet facilitates participation in previously inaccessible realms of knowledge and experience. But equally incontrovertible, as the chapters that follow will show, is the fact that the Internet has a dark underbelly. As the *Guardian* recently reminded us:

Almost every time another social tragedy comes to light now, it seems to have been Internet-assisted: from selling babies like commodities (the Internet twins), to fascism (Nazi memorabilia for sale on *Yahoo!*), and most disturbingly, paedophilia (Wonderland and Operation Magenta). The news stories invariably lead some people to blame the Internet as a haven for vice, abuse and illegal activity…[and] they may be right.

(Left 2002: unpaginated)

And if this were not sufficient to fuel a moral panic, the *The Observer* adopts an even more hysterical tone, claiming that the dark side of the web includes 'pornography, paedophilia, murder, snuff movies and drug-dealing' including a site that 'allows you to arrange your own death by fatal injection activated by your computer' and one which takes orders to 'execute homeless children in South America and then promises to send a video of the murder' (Kemp 1999: unpaginated). Of course, there is nothing inherently sinister in the technology itself. Most cybercrimes are reasonably common offences; computer technologies have simply pro-vided a new means to commit 'old' crimes, and it is clearly not the case that if the Internet did not exist, nor would paedophilia, pornography and other offensive material, although it has undeniably increased the visibility of human depravity and suffering (Slevin 2000). Furthermore, much of the debate about Internet regulation and censorship appears to be based on speculative notions of the anti-social and harmful impacts it may have at some point in the future. An indication of the level of hysteria that surrounds the Internet is the finding that of over 90,000 newsgroups in the UK, only about 60 – less than one-tenth of 1 per cent – are of concern to the industry's 'watchdog', the Internet Watch Foundation (Left 2002: unpaginated).

Another important point, illustrated by the aforementioned example of women's use of online pornography, is that the Internet has prob-lematised traditional notions of what constitutes acceptable and deviant behaviour. Becker's (1963) view that deviance is in the eye of the beholder has rarely seemed so apt, and its contested nature is illustrated in numerous ways in this volume. Women's consumption of Internet pornography also illustrates three further themes that have already been touched on but are worth reiterating as they run throughout this col-lection and provide a unifying motif. First, it demonstrates that the social meanings of the Internet emerge from particular contexts and practices of usage. Specifically, women's use of the Net to explore and satisfy various aspects of their sexual identities serves to highlight the slightly paradoxical fashion in which the technology impacts upon gender and, simultaneously, is itself shaped by gendered usage. In a broader context, it might be said that that online pornography was the very thing that propelled the rapid growth of the Internet and demonstrated its commercial potential (Di Filipo 2000; Wall 2001). Another important theme which, in some of the chapters that follow, is inextricably linked to the mutual shaping of the Internet and gender, is the notion that in cyberspace identity is not fixed but is an ephemeral, fluid entity, open to constant negotiation, change and manipulation. In the case of women's consumption of online pornography this disentanglement from the body allows the self to break free from the usual constraints of corporeality which, in the physical world, may prevent individuals from displaying aspects of their identities that would be discredited or disapproved of by others. This may be regarded as a positive characteristic of cyberspace: it liberates people from the shackles that bind them in the physical world. But when it comes to constructing identity, the line is increasingly blurred between 'playful' and fraudulent, inclusive and exploitative, accessible and extremist, 'deviant' and criminal. This leads us to the final theme that arises throughout this collection, which is the conclusion that the Internet's capacity to sustain multiple, anonymous, complex and contested identities – essential to the virtual sex-trade but equally important to all the other cybercrimes and deviant activities described in this book – clearly poses problems for would-be regulators of the Internet. Just as it might be said that pornography got people interested in the Net which, in turn, drove the development of the technology to deliver pornography as an electronic service, equally it was pornography – a subject that provokes fear and fascination in equal measure – that precipitated the establishment of some of the most high-profile organisations which police the Net.[2]

The book

The collection that follows is intended to cross the boundaries of sociological, criminological and cultural discourses in relation to the growth of crime and deviance on the Internet. It was born out of a recognition of the growing numbers of degree courses and modules which – while located within traditional subjects such as sociology and criminology – are concerned with the study of new information and communication technologies (ICTs) and their impact on social life and on constructions of identities, including criminal and deviant identities. The book is primarily aimed, then, at students and researchers who are familiar with the Internet and various aspects of 'cyberculture' from their own academic studies and recreational use of computer-mediated communications, but who are left cold by the level of technologically driven information and jargon contained in the majority of books about the Internet. Similarly, it is not a book that includes long lists of legislation affecting Internet use as the many books on cyber-law do. Essentially, then, this is a book *not* about computers, nor about legal controversies over the regulation of cyberspace, but about *people* and about the new patterns of human identity, behaviour and association that are emerging as a result of the communications revolution.

The collection continues with a chapter by Yvonne Jewkes on policing the Internet which 'sets the scene' for the remaining chapters as it outlines the kinds of crimes commonly committed in cyberspace, as well as the forms of regulation that currently exist to tackle such crimes. The chapter then moves on to a discussion of the somewhat paradoxical proposition that, while law enforcement and other agencies are finding it increasingly difficult to regulate the activities of criminals and deviants on the Internet, 'ordinary' citizens are finding themselves subject to greater levels of electronic surveillance than at any time previously. This dichotomy brings into focus one of the most interesting and controversial aspects of the Internet – its public/private nature – many facets of which are explored throughout the book. In this case, Yvonne Jewkes suggests that the anonymity afforded by virtual reality is the reason why so many users feel 'safe' engaging in 'private' behaviour (albeit in the public or semi-public spaces provided by the Internet) they might not dare to in 'real life', and why many law enforcers feel they are involved in a never-ending game of 'catch up' with the criminals and deviants who conduct their illicit business online.

The Internet, then, has privatised certain behaviours and activities that were previously conducted in a more public sphere and were consequently considerably more open to detection, public censure and legal sanction. But the Internet also brings together people with similar tastes and proclivities, providing a forum for sharing information and experiences and 'legitimising' (at least in the minds of those involved) interests that might otherwise be frowned upon. These factors are especially true of sites dedicated to sexual activities, which are the subject of Chapters 3 and 4. Both chapters apply a Goffmanesque analysis to their subjects, exploring the ways in which the Internet has not only opened up sexual mores, but has also provided a new forum for the presentation and management of a deviant yet acceptable self to like-minded others.

In Chapter 3, Keith Sharp and Sarah Earle investigate a group of 'deviants' who have traditionally remained hidden from sociological and criminological inquiry – the men who use the services of prostitutes.

Sharp and Earle provide a fascinating insight into the motivations of men who visit prostitutes and who then post reviews of the women and their sexual encounters on dedicated 'punters' websites. They suggest that the Internet has empowered a group of men who are usually characterised as morally weak, 'normalising' their activities and making credible other-wise discredited identities. This chapter clearly illustrates how the Internet exposes the activities of individuals who are usually invisible to the gaze of the researcher and makes accessible new fields of method-ological inquiry.

In Chapter 4 Heather DiMarco also sheds light on an aspect of sexual behaviour usually hidden from public view. She argues that since computer-mediated communications have further privatised people's leisure time and facilitated a level of interactivity not permitted by more traditional media, Internet users have been liberated to explore aspects of their sexual identities that, in many cases, have been suppressed in the physical world. Hence, while habitual swingers and sadomasochists have found a new outlet for their desires, others who are generally more inhibited in their sexual conduct are using the Net to 'discover' aspects of their sexual selves and embarking on sexual adventures that might other-wise remain outside their realm of experience. DiMarco is particularly interested in the electronic 'cloak' with which secret sexual deviancy is shrouded in cyberspace and the advantage to which it is used by women who are confused or curious about their sexual identities. She notes that the Internet has provided individuals with opportunities to 'try out' homosexual relationships in the virtual realm while retaining the 'heterosexual privileges' they enjoy in real life.

It is the heterosexual privileges of marriage and raising a family that are explored in Chapter 5 by Gayle Letherby and Jen Marchbank. If cyberspace is a playground in which participants can act out deviant roles with little of the sense of responsibility that may accompany such activities in the physical world, it is also a place of hard-headed commercial transaction in which the most emotional and intimate of decisions – choosing a partner and having a child – are commodified. Letherby and Marchbank provide an overview of the kinds of sites which provide brides and babies and argue that these arrangements endorse, perpetuate and further complicate established patterns of patriarchy and colonialism in which women and children from relatively poor back-grounds and/or underdeveloped regions of the world are seen as com-modities for purchase by wealthy men in the west. But the authors emphasise that the women involved in providing such services (i.e. themselves as brides, their children or their eggs) are not necessarily passive victims, but are often knowing agents exploiting a market economy. Furthermore, Letherby and Marchbank are not critical of the *means* of selection/adoption although they suggest that the suspicion and hostility that frequently surround the buying of brides and babies online are not simply explained by the characterisation of would-be husbands as social inadequates and would-be parents as selfish and tampering with nature. Like other mass media that are perceived to be predominantly American in origin and content, the Internet is subject to a cultural élitism which, combined with the sporadic moral panics that arise over online pornography, paedophilia, fraud and so on, make it – in the popular imagination – an unseemly and inappropriate channel for choosing a wife or a child.

The chapters introduced so far all point to the contested nature of deviance and pose questions about whether CMCs normalise activities that would otherwise be regarded as deviant. They also illustrate the transformative impact of the Internet upon users' identities – as criminals, 'punters', sexual adventurers and upholders of the normative heterosexual ideals attached to creating a family. As already discussed, identity is a key theme of this collection. The existence of cyberspace opens up new possibilities for the construction and negotiation of identities which are not defined in terms of nation, ethnicity, gender, culture, social 'position' and physical 'place'. People are no longer defined by what they *do* – or even, as has been claimed by recent cultural commentators, by what they *consume* – but are increasingly related to on the basis of what they *are* (Castells 1996).

Perhaps this is why identity *theft* has become the topic of a growing number of books, reports and newspaper articles. Chapter 6, by Emily Finch, introduces the problem of identity theft; an act that, since the advent of the Internet, no longer requires a stolen birth certificate or forged driving licence, but simply a smattering of technical knowledge. As we see in the earlier chapters on sexual deviance, the Internet is the ideal medium for those who wish to create multiple personalities because cyberspace is a place without 'physicality': when we 'enter' the virtual realm, we leave our bodies behind and are free to take on whatever personae we choose (Danet 1996). But, of course, this ability to operate without proof of real physical presence is the key characteristic that provides a way in for the criminal. Identity theft is not merely restricted to the 'borrowing' of other people's credit card numbers for bankrolling extravagant lifestyles (online transactions arguably reducing the risk of detection of fraud) although there are fears that such cases are reaching epidemic proportions, especially in the USA. There are, as Emily Finch explains, numerous other forms that identity theft can take, including the wholesale adoption of another's identity. While not all such cases involve direct exploitation of computer-mediated communications, there is a growing online economy in the buying and selling of *bona fide* personal details to individuals whose own 'spoiled' (to use Goffman's term) or discredited identity has caused them to be blacklisted by banks and credit organisations, in addition to software which generates other people's credit card numbers and PINs.

It is the unfathomable amount of personal information available on the Net which has arguably exacerbated the general problem of identity theft, and the same is also true of stalking, an offence where the Internet can be used for both collecting data about the potential victim and as a medium for actual harassment. Cyberstalking is the subject of Chapter 7 by Janice Joseph, whose overview of the problem underlines the blurring of distinctions between crime and deviance. She examines the nature of cyberstalking, the attempts to combat it in the USA, Canada, the UK and Australia, and the unique difficulties that some law enforcement agencies encounter because of its position in the grey area between social harm and illegal act. Many states and countries have yet to recognise stalking in law, let alone *cyber*stalking, and of the countries mentioned above, only certain states in the USA and Australia have introduced legislation specifically aimed at online stalking. Even where legislation exists, it can be problematic for victims to convince police and Internet service providers of the seriousness of the problem and, even if a case does proceed to court, it may be difficult to prosecute due to a range of legal loopholes relating to anonymity, privacy and jurisdiction.

Of all the criminal and deviant groups written about in this book, the most demonised (at least in terms of sheer volume of material written about them) are hackers. In Chapter 8, Paul Taylor eschews the usual representation of the hacker as a maladjusted rebel trying to bring down governments and intelligence agencies and repositions him as an adolescent boy acting out psycho-sexual fantasies or cowboy dreams. Taylor examines the domination of hacking by young men and considers possible reasons for women's non-participation in it. However, he goes on to argue that 'hacktivism' – a form of political activism that, *in some cases*, exploits the capabilities of computer-mediated communications to disrupt targeted sites with email bombs, web hacks, computer viruses, denial-of-service attacks, etc. – *is* attractive to women because it has an end result (and therefore is not simply technical mastery for its own sake), is 'conversationally' based and promotes an inclusive social agenda.

Rinella Cere takes up this theme in Chapter 9. Her focus is also hacktivism and, in particular, the role of the Internet in circulating information and gathering support for radical politics and alternative social movements (as opposed to the more militant brand of hacktivism which Taylor mentions). Cere concurs with Taylor that, although hacking is an activity still dominated by men, hacktivism is not only dominated by, but is increasingly reliant on, the participation of women. She considers the extent to which CMCs have assisted in struggles 'on the ground' via an assessment of three very different case studies which, according to Cere, are none the less united as part of a common global struggle against neoliberal economic forces. Her analysis also picks up on another important theme raised in previous chapters. Specifically, she argues (echoing DiMarco in Chapter 4 and Letherby and Marchbank in Chapter 5) that, despite the fact that patriarchy is as evident in cyberspace as it is elsewhere, new information and communication technologies at least provide an opportunity for the re-formation of established divisions and inequalities along gendered lines, and offer women the scope to assert their agency and subvert traditional notions of deviance.

We hope that the contributions to this book will inspire you to conduct your own Internet-based research and, with this in mind, the final chapter changes tack and presents some of the ethical dilemmas and practical considerations that you might face if you do so. It is a given that computers and the Internet are a basic and essential prerequisite for academic research, but we hope that *Dot.cons* will convince you that there are unlimited new realms of social experience to be discovered in cyberspace. The concerns that have dominated ethnographic research in the social sciences and humanities – identity, agency, human creativity, lived experience, cultural politics and so on – are the very substance of Internet communication, and in Chapter 10 Andy DiMarco and Heather DiMarco underline the fact that the openness and richness of the ethnographic enterprise coincide with the very same qualities inherent in the Internet spaces described in this book. However, DiMarco and DiMarco argue that social scientists cannot simply transfer the methods and ethics of 'real life' ethnography wholesale into a virtual environment, precisely because of issues such as the shifting or blurring of the boundaries between the 'public' and 'private' in cyberspace. They caution that a number of potential pitfalls await, but that if we adapt the professional standards that govern our research elsewhere, we will find that cyberspace can be a vibrant and innovative place in which to work. The focus of this last chapter is on chat rooms, but the points of discussion raised, and the advice offered, apply to research in many other computer-mediated spaces. Similarly, DiMarco and DiMarco have elected to concentrate on covert participant observation – although there are numerous other research methods that the Internet can accommodate. Their choice is interesting, however, because it brings our discussion full circle. It is precisely the disembodiment of self, and the anonymity behind which we can hide, that allows us to transcend the dangers of corporeality and makes the Internet such an exciting place to study, research, relax and play. But equally, it is this capacity for operating covertly that makes the virtual realm so attractive to criminals and deviants. Who knows whom we might be rubbing shoulders with in the shadows of cyberspace?

Notes

1. The development, growth and expansion of the Internet have been described as a new form of colonialism (Kolko *et al* 2000). Information poverty tends to go hand in hand with material poverty (Holderness 1998) and debates about the liberating or restraining properties of the Internet have little meaning in many regions of the world where telephone access may be restricted (it is estimated that less than one in five of the world's population has a telephone line – Hamelink 2000). It is in these (materially and informationally) poor regions that people are least likely to be able to afford PCs and Internet access, are least likely to speak English – the single most dominant language of cyberspace – and have low levels of literacy (Kolko *et al* 2000; Slevin 2000). However, there is evidence of change. For example, although English language sites have dominated the Internet since its inception, now 59.8 per cent of the world's online population are from non-English speaking zones (www.nua.ie/surveys/index.cgi).
2. The Internet Watch Foundation (IWF), Adult Sites Against Child Pornography (ASACP) and Cyberangels, among them.

Chapter 2

Policing the Net: crime, regulation and surveillance in cyberspace

Yvonne Jewkes

There is no question that new information and communication technologies (ICTs) have opened up opportunities that might be described as 'truly magical' in their ability to compress time and space. Like traditional media the Internet 'creates new possibilities of being: of being in two places at once, or two times at once' (Scannell 1996: 91). But unlike traditional media, the Net allows us to interact with others anywhere in the world, in real time, and on equal terms. It is a 'many-to-many' medium, whereby everyone who is online is 'in the same place' (Holderness 1998: 35). Physical location and all the usual markers of identity are irrelevant. We can be anonymous, or 'invent' an entirely new personality, or divulge aspects of our identity that would normally be kept hidden; we can 'connect' with like-minded individuals and groups, forming communities and alliances with others on the basis of shared interests rather than geographical proximity; we can enter worlds previously unknown to us and partake in events and experiences in contexts far removed from our own (Slevin 2000). And we can do all this with far less fear of surveillance, legal intervention or public retribution than would accompany such activities in other mediated spheres of life.

This inevitably raises questions about the regulation of content and behaviours in cyberspace. If the moral, ethical and legal boundaries that usually constrain our behaviour are indistinct or unenforceable in the virtual world, what forms of regulation exist to define and curb 'excesses' of behaviour? Is it a case that 'anything goes' in cyberspace? Or are there effective bodies patrolling the cyber-beat with a mission to protect the vulnerable and enforce the law? This chapter will address these questions in relation to three main areas of concern. First, it will consider the various means of regulation that are currently in place, and will consider the role of the police in the UK in fighting computer-related crime. Then, it will outline the various types of crime that are most commonly committed using ICTs, notably the Internet, and consider their impact on conventional understandings of crime. Finally, the chapter will discuss the jurisdiction and ethics of authorities' use of new technologies to monitor the behaviour and communications of people they define as potentially criminal or deviant. It will investigate issues of power, regulation and accountability in relation to fears that increased 'policing' of the Internet could extend the powers of the police, security forces and even employers far beyond the powers they normally have, and may compromise individuals' civil liberties.

Cybercops or technoplods? The role of the police

When commentators talk of 'cybercops' they may be referring to a wide range of different bodies or strategies encompassing those whose primary aim is to 'protect'; for example, authorities who use encryption and digital 'fingerprinting' techniques to protect copyrighted material (Tang 1997) to those whose primary aim is to 'enforce' – for example, the National Hi-Tech Crime Unit (see below). Discussions of policing the Net are frequently dominated by expectations that an international law enforcement agency will be established to patrol the electronic beat and hunt down paedophiles, pornographers and criminal masterminds. Although attractive to those who have been alarmed by recent moral panics concerning the apparent expansion and increased visibility of such crimes, the idea of such an organisation is probably unrealisable given the sheer size and scope of the Internet, the volume of electronic traffic it facilitates and the possibilities it permits for encoding messages (Langford 1998).

In the UK the police have largely been (and arguably still are) unwilling to get involved both in the patrolling of cyberspace and in the investigation of cybercrimes. There are several reasons for their reluctance. First, many cybercrimes might more accurately be described as 'harms' as they have – as yet, at least – no reference point in law (Wall 2002). As will be pointed out elsewhere in this volume (see, for example, Chapter 7), even where laws exist that can be applied to cybercrimes, a successful prosecution may be rare: in fact, only 10 per cent of computer-related crime is reported and fewer than 2 per cent of cases result in a successful prosecution (www.intergov.org). A second, and related, point is that a certain degree of hysteria has accompanied the development of cyberspace over the last decade, the result of which has been a failure to distinguish between *potential* and *actual* harms with the result that much of the moral 'panickyness' surrounding the appropriation of cyberspace by potential criminals, perverts and anarchists appears somewhat overblown in what is, contrary to popular belief, a 'remarkably ordered' environment (Wall 1999: 2). Thirdly, it is often claimed that efforts to police cyberspace are futile because the Internet's global reach and inherent pliancy allow individuals and organisations to evade authorities 'by slipping into anonymity and by retreating beyond the bounds of their jurisdictions' (Slevin 2000: 214). As Lenk (1997: 129) points out, the mindset related to jurisdiction has always been somewhat parochial: 'letting foreign police tread a square metre of their soil in hard pursuit of criminals is still anathema to European national governments.' The difficulties facing Internet regulators are compounded by different moral codes and divergent legal responses in different countries: for example, material that is considered mildly pornographic in the UK and Ireland may not be censured at all in Sweden or the Netherlands but may be subject to much stricter regulation in the Middle East (Langford 1998). This diversity in definition is brought even more sharply into focus in relation to communications between countries with a tradition of freedom of speech and those that are more repressive, or when an Internet connection may provide a link to 'freedom' for political dissidents. Fourthly, the traditional and rather conservative nature of police work and of the police themselves can impede both investigation of cybercrimes and initiatives to monitor the content of the information superhighway. Most UK police forces are still paper-based organisations and many officers do not even use the Internet internally; moreover, one detective superintendent with the West Yorkshire police has complained that most of his colleagues do not consider computer-based investigation 'normal' work, and that their ability to respond to Internet crime is 'haphazard and based on luck rather than a prepared and researched provision of a service to the public' (Hyde 1999: 7).

A visit to the UK police website (www.police.uk) reveals that it is possible to report non-urgent minor crimes online, but a foray into the regional police forces' individual sites (linked via the website) reveals a surprising discrepancy between different regions in their attitudes to computer-based crime. Of the 43 forces in England and Wales, the vast majority (36 in all) use their websites primarily as a public relations tool to promote themselves and to disseminate public information, ranging from appeals for help with solving crimes to pages containing job vacancies and advice on careers in the police service. Other information commonly found on police websites includes mission statements, annual reports and 'in-house' publications, advice on crime prevention, police station locators, children's pages and links to Crime Stoppers and other police-related organisations. Fifteen forces provide a search facility via which information can be accessed about Internet crime, but only seven forces actually provide advice on how to protect oneself from cybercrime or how to report it. Even among these seven, the approach is somewhat haphazard. For example, at the time of writing, Thames Valley and Lancashire police are offering advice on using chat rooms; Lancashire also provides information on hacking and shopping on the Internet; Merseyside's site contains information about fraud; and on South Yorkshire police's site one can report hate crime online. The most 'sophisticated' of the current police websites are those belonging to the Metropolitan police force, Avon and Somerset, and Surrey Constabulary. The Met's site has detailed information about computer crime and Internet-related crime and includes several useful external links; Avon and Somerset has an 'Internet department' which further provides guidance on children's use of the Internet, viruses, fraud and unwanted email, a real-time newsroom, video reconstructions and an email bulletin service; while Surrey's site reveals that the Surrey Police Computer Crime Unit has been established to investigate Internet fraud, offensive emails and viruses. In fact, several local and regional forces now have specialist units concentrating expertise in computer-related crime, but as Wall (1997) notes, such units are vulnerable to the practice of rotating key personnel, a policy designed to circulate ideas and prevent corruption. In practice, the movement of expertise reduces the residual knowledge base and impairs their effectiveness. But however disjointed the police's current response to cybercrime is, it does promise to become more rationalised and effective in the near future. In 2001, the Home Secretary announced that £10 million was to be invested in the development of local police force computer crime units to bring all forces to a consistent level of competence and service delivery – an investment that indicates the degree of seriousness with which the government views computer-related crime, but does little to reassure the many cynics who believe that legislation will continue to fall behind technological advancements and that cybercriminals will continue to play cat and mouse with an in-experienced and less technologically competent police service.

Because of the problems of jurisdiction and resistance on the part of the traditional police forces in the face of the near exponential growth of the Internet in recent years, it was further decided that a national police unit was required with powers to investigate computer-related crime across national boundaries. Hence, in April 2001, the National Hi-Tech Crime Unit (NHTCU) was established, comprising representatives from the

National Crime Squad, the National Criminal Intelligence Service, HM Customs and Excise and police officers from the regions. Its objectives are twofold. First, it aims to work in conjunction with local police forces, supporting, offering advice and co-ordinating investigations carried out at a local or regional level. Secondly, it will conduct its own national and international investigations, make strategic assessments and develop intelligence about computer-related crime. The NHTCU also aims to provide a dedicated link with business and the ICT industry, and a 24-hour point of contact for G8 countries, and thus professes to offer 'a "joined up" response to the growing threat of cybercrime' (www.nationalcrimesquad.police.uk/nhtcu).

The police, however, are not the sole (or even the primary) agents of protection and enforcement in the virtual world. So vast and borderless is cyberspace that governments and the police themselves recognise that those who use the Internet – the community of so-called 'Netizens' – must bear the primary responsibility for cleaning up cyberspace, resulting in what Slevin (2000: 222) calls an 'almost blind enthusiasm for self-regulation'.

Non-police regulation

Unsurprisingly non-police intervention, or self-regulation, is also favoured by Internet users and Internet service providers (ISPs), a stance that goes back to the early days of the Internet, betraying its liberal (usually characterised as 'hippy') public origins in the late 1960s and 1970s, and adolescence in the 1980s, when deregulation was the guiding principle for public policy:

> [I]t is essential to appreciate the very strong collective ethos of the Internet. From its inception Internet users have always been passionately in favour of internal control and against outside influence. In effect, for many years the Internet has operated as a fully functioning anarchy.
>
> (Langford 1998: 98)

Non-police regulation broadly encompasses self-regulation by individuals and by the industry and interest groups. For example, individual Internet users can monitor their own use and that of others, evict offensive participants from chat rooms, or report harmful or illegal material on websites. Parents and teachers of young Internet users can utilise software such as Nanny Net which deny access to material containing sexually explicit words, or restrict children's use of the Net on the basis of rating systems provided by independent bodies such as the Internet Watch Foundation (IWF).[1] ISPs can draw up codes of conduct which their members and subscribers must follow, monitor the content of their sites and remove offending content or take other appropriate action. Finally, there are a growing number of interest groups – such as Women Halting Online Abuse (WHOA), Internet Hotline Providers in Europe (INHOPE) and Cyberangels – who support a particular cause or aspect of regulation. Although in many cases these organisations are state funded, all forms of 'internal' or 'self' regulation are less costly than external regulation, and are usually regarded as a great deal more effective. However, the charge most frequently made against these groups is that they are non-accountable, and despite the conviction of established Internet users that individual netizens can, and should, be trusted to use the system appropriately (Langford 1998), the rapid expansion of the cyber-population (expected to rise from 70 million in 1996 to around one billion in 2005) has inevitably resulted in a breakdown of the collective ethos that characterised early and anti-authoritarian users. For example, while senders of offensive comments or material may be 'flamed' by other users – their machines bombarded with thousands of messages or even blank pages, disabling their telephone lines and computers – those who resort to such tactics are themselves not beyond reproach. The following two quotations illustrate the lack of consensus:

> The other day I encountered my first neo-Nazi on the 'Net'; a madman shouting hate. You know what happened? A bunch of Internet citizens ran him out of town. Chased him away, sent him packing. Gave him the big heave-ho.
> (Carrol 1995, cited in Whine 1997: 224)

> [Flaming is] a dangerous invitation to digital vigilantism and promiscuous computer violence. It turns cyberspace into a rude, lawless, frontier town in which everyone carries a six-shooter and exacts his [*sic*] own revenge.
> (Littman 1995, cited in Whine 1997: 224)

Cybercrimes: the nature and extent of the problem

So what are 'cybercrimes' and what kinds of challenges do they pose for regulators and law enforcement agencies? Broadly speaking, cybercrimes can be classified in two categories: new crimes using new tools; in other words, crimes that cannot be committed in any other way or against any other type of victim (for example, hacking and the planting of viruses), and old crimes using new tools; in other words, familiar or conventional crimes committed using new computer and information technologies (fraud, identity theft, stalking and so on). Additionally, there are a number of activities that are not illegal, but may constitute what most people would consider harmful to some users (such as some forms of pornography, unsolicited email, etc.). The following examples represent some of the most serious crimes and social 'harms' in so far as they represent threats unique to, or significantly enhanced by, computer technologies. Although presented as distinct areas of concern, many of the crimes identified below overlap, and the list is by no means comprehensive.

Pornography and the exploitation of minors

Probably the most high-profile form of Internet regulation thus far has been that targeted at content of a violent and/or pornographic nature, and especially material which exploits children. The dual problems of illegal pornography involving minors, and children gaining access to sites with pornographic content, were among the main drives behind the founding of the NHTCU, the IWF, and the European Commission's establishment of hotlines allowing people to report illegal content on the Net, and their introduction of rating and filtering mechanisms to aid parental control. These initiatives followed high-profile cases such as the arrest of 107 people and the seizure of around 750,000 computer images of children in a global operation in 2001 to smash the so-called 'Wonderland Club', one of the biggest Internet paedophile rings yet discovered.

But demands for tougher responses to such cases (in the shape of more draconian laws to deal with paedophiles, more punitive punishments to deter those who use the Internet to circulate child pornography, a greater degree of censorship to protect those who might inadvertently 'stumble across' such sites and so on) have divided Internet users. Two particular cases have caused concern to those who believe that Internet users' civil liberties and freedom of choice may be compromised by over-zealous authoritarian intervention. In 1995 the prosecuting attorney's office in Munich, Germany, ordered the ISP, CompuServe, to prohibit access to over 200 Usenet newsgroups – a move which caused outrage among users of those groups – while in 1996, the British police wrote to all ISPs instructing them to ban over 100 newsgroups that were believed to carry pornographic material (Slevin 2000). Most of the controversy has surrounded newsgroups, which offer users a forum for the exchange of ideas, stories and photos. One IWF board member, Malcolm Hutty, general director of the Campaign against Censorship of the Internet in Britain, resigned after the board voted to shut down newsgroups simply on the basis of their name sounding like a forum for illegal content. Such knee-jerk responses arguably return debates about censorship to a pre-Internet age and reveal much about the fear of technological advancement and about authorities' inclination to police *people* under the guise of policing crime (Hillyard and Percy-Smith 1988; Curran and Seaton 1991; Slevin 2000).

Hate crime

The promotion of racial hatred is unfortunately widespread and the Internet is a relatively cheap and accessible means of connecting similarly minded people across the world and coalescing their belief systems. The Net is a sophisticated tool for recruitment and unification, providing links between hate movements that were previously diverse and fractured, and facilitating the creation of a collective identity and empowering sense of community (Perry 2001: 177). Various groups on the political far right – neo-Nazis, skinheads and groups with ties to the Ku Klux Klan – are using the Net to target a youthful and impressionable audience with racist, anti-semitic and homophobic propaganda with little fear of the kind of legal sanction that might accompany the circulation of such material in more 'traditional' forms (Whine 1997; Zickmund 2000). Although Germany and many other European countries have criminalised the publication and distribution of hate propaganda, the Internet remains largely unregulated. It is estimated that there are thousands of websites propagating violence and intolerance and many contain practical guides to assist proponents of hate in their criminal endeavours in the physical world. For example, bomb-making instructions – such as those contained in *The Big Book of Mischief: The Terrorist's Handbook* – are readily available on the Internet (Whine 1997). But arguably more insidious than these sites which tend to attract those who are already involved in, or predisposed towards, acts of crime and violence, are those sites which purport to be 'mainstream' and are used to target the 'unconverted'. For example, in an effort to change the demographics of hate movements by recruiting young students and professionals, many sites feature audio excerpts of CDs, downloadable album covers and online lyrics – a blatant appeal to the 'MTV generation' (Perry 2001: 178).

The use of the Internet to promote hatred has also led to cases of vigilantism and threats to individuals in 'real life'. Following the decision made by the European Court that the juvenile murderers of 2-year-old James Bulger in Liverpool in 1993 should be released from custody shortly after their eighteenth birthdays and given entirely 'new' identities to protect them, there were widespread reports that the pair would none the less quickly become identified, resulting in vigilante attacks. Despite an injunction preventing any details that might identify the killers from being published by the media, it was commonly believed that there was little that could be done to prevent their photographs, descriptions or whereabouts being circulated on the Internet. This fear was augmented by the circulation of vigilante email and by threats issued by individuals associated with the 'Justice for James' campaign (www.jamiebulger.co.uk) who were seeking retribution for the toddler's death. In July 2001 the Internet Service Provider, Demon, won a change to the injunction protecting the identities of the released killers. The original form of the injunction was found to be 'inappropriate' for the Internet, whereby a service provider could potentially be found in contempt of court for unknowingly providing access to material about the pair or their whereabouts. ISPs are now compelled to take all reasonable measures to prevent this from happening and at the current time the identities and location of Thompson and Venables remain hidden. But stories about the killers – posted on sites in other parts of the world – still abound on the Net, and many contain factual inaccuracies and perpetuate dangerous mythologies about the case. As the 1997 moral panic over paedophiles living in the community demonstrated, media campaigns to 'out' demonised offenders can result in mistaken or indiscriminate attacks on entirely innocent parties (Kitzinger 1999).

Intellectual property rights

One of the most obvious consequences of the new information and communications revolution is its creation and distribution of unimaginably more information-based products which, in turn, pose new legal challenges to define and protect copyright: 'In the looming digital age, pundits have begun to attest that the dynamic and expeditious technological advancements are creating too many works, too many users, and too many uses…[Consequently] there is a growing irrelevance of traditional copyright law' (Tang 1997: 191). Put simply, the electronic transmission and reproduction of information have become so easy and so commonplace that many of those who routinely transfer, copy and store material on to their own machines may not even be alert to the fact that they are engaged in theft. However, 'digital piracy' also refers to the knowing and criminal use of the Internet to market or distribute copyrighted software. One of the key groups leading the global campaign for more effective regulation of software piracy is the Business Software Alliance (BSA), an organisation that represents many of the big software companies. The BSA works closely with law enforcement agencies to co-ordinate enforcement of copyright laws and operates global hotlines for the reporting of suspected incidents of software theft. One of the BSA's main areas of concern is Internet auction sites where, it maintains, a high percentage of software sold is pirated. As with all the crimes discussed in this chapter, piracy has been afforded a new global dimension with the growth of the Internet and reaches a target audience already predisposed to buying software online. Legitimate e-commerce sites can provide a respectable veneer for the online ordering of pirate CDs, counterfeit software and so on, and auction companies such as Yahoo! and eBay are becoming increasingly overwhelmed by the amount of piracy that is being conducted on their sites (Hopper 2000).

The industry's solution to the problem of Internet users downloading and circulating material illegally is to develop system-based methods of payment for copyrighted material. For example, one such program under development checks if potential customers have paid a royalty and, if not, electronic payment will be demanded or access denied (Tang 1997). Perhaps the most well-known case highlighting the disputes that can arise over copyright is that of Napster, the free music download service that was forced to suspend its operation in 2001 when the Record Industry Association of America took it to court for copyright infringe-ment. At the time of writing, Napster is still suspended, and its plans to return with a new service in late 2002 that will charge members a monthly fee to download music are looking increasingly shaky. While few would argue that creators of material should not be rewarded for the copying and distribution of their work, cultural pessimists maintain that the development of such technologies will simply result in higher costs of access to electronic information, further creating a society of information rich and information poor (Tang 1997). Others are confident that the numerous peer-to-peer file-swapping services that have emerged since Napster was forced to suspend its activities will continue to bypass copyright legislation and give consumers the opportunity to carry on thumbing their noses at 'big business'.

Invasion of privacy, defamation and theft of identity

The entitlement to security of person is regarded as a fundamental human right, yet the scope and pervasiveness of digital technologies open up new areas of social vulnerability. Electronic harassment takes many forms from 'spamming' (or UCE – unsolicited commercial email) to online defamation, stalking, extortion and violence. Spamming has thus far been considered little more than an extension of conventional junk mail, although it is increasingly being recognised as an insidious and frequently illegal activity. It can encompass electronic chain letters, links to pornographic sites, scams claiming that there are extensive funds – for example, from over-invoiced business contracts or a deceased relative's will – available for immediate transfer into the recipient's bank account if he or she just provides their bank details, fraudulent pyramid investment schemes, phoney claims for cancer cures and, following 11 September 2001, fake anthrax treatments and bogus test kits for the disease. The American Federal Trade Commission is trying to crack down on the problem, and has brought 63 mostly civil cases against alleged fraudsters in the 6 months to April 2002 (http://online.securityfocus.com). However, the sheer volume of spam – which, according to a European Commission study, will soon average 60 unwanted messages per day for every user (Schofield 2002) – obviously poses difficulties for those trying to stem the tide of unsolicited mail, and pressure is mounting on ISPs to do more to stop spam at source.

The law does, however, protect individuals whose reputation is threatened by defamatory Internet content. Teachers and lecturers seem particularly vulnerable to such attacks. In 2000, Demon paid over £230,000 to an academic at a British university who claimed that the ISP had failed to remove two anonymous Internet postings defaming him. In America, students at the City College of San Francisco set up an online database – www.teacherreview.com – inviting students to post reviews of their college lecturers and rate their performance. Although some lecturers at the college have defended such initiatives on the grounds that students have a right to share information about the capabilities of their teachers, and that a database simply organises opinions that were formerly passed round by word of mouth anyway (Lathouwers and Happ 2000), others have vehemently criticised the initiative. Indeed, one teacher at San Francisco filed a lawsuit against Teacher Review, claiming that the site is a 'disgusting, lie-filled, destructive force' (Curzon-Brown 2000: 91). Friends Reunited (www.friendsreunited.co.uk), the phenomenally successful British Internet site that allows people to make contact with old friends and reminisce about their school days, also has a facility to allow participants to share memories of former teachers – but in addition to the usual disclaimers, its creators are trying to protect themselves by urging users to report abusive messages, which instantly removes them and reports the incident to the site support team.

Another cybercrime related to privacy is the theft of personal identity, a practice that has dramatically increased in the last few years (see also Chapter 6 of this volume). The American Federal Trade Commission report that, of the 204,000 complaints it received in 2001, 42 per cent involved stolen identities. It further estimated that up to 750,000 US citizens will have their identities stolen in 2002 for the purposes of accessing credit card accounts, securing loans and cashing cheques. Identity theft can be successfully achieved by a variety of means from the relatively sophisticated – following an electronic trail from banks' computers, paying back-handers to Internet data providers and so forth – to the mundane and opportunistic – e.g. rummaging through people's dustbins for discarded bank or credit card statements, stealing mail from mailboxes or picking up receipts left at bank ATMs. Card details are also obtainable from an individual's personal computer, and software pro-grams have been developed to work out PIN numbers. Digital thefts of identity are simply more sophisticated versions of 'real life' frauds, but the scope and anonymity afforded by the Internet – together with the fact that increasingly money only exists in electronic form – are attracting organised cybercriminals to turn to computer fraud.

But although credit card fraud has been a major crime problem for many years and certainly predates the widespread ownership of PCs, it seems that the growing trend in shopping on the Internet has dramatically increased buyers' fears about card insecurity. According to figures released by the Association for Payment Clearing Services (APACS), only 2 per cent of 'plastic fraud' is connected with the Internet, yet American Express report that 73 per cent of consumers have doubts about giving their credit card number on the Net (Cloughlan 2000). The financial industry is taking steps to make online transactions more secure with the development of digital 'signatures' which will authenticate the identities of Internet shoppers and silicon chips that are inserted into cards to make counterfeiting more difficult. But the truth is that the dangers of identity theft and credit card fraud still lie predominantly within the 'real world' of shops and restaurants where cards are 'skimmed', or copied, and a counterfeit produced using the information. This cloned card is then used to buy goods until the real card-holder gets a bank statement revealing that he or she has been leading a double life.

Information security, personal security and cyber-trespass

Fears concerning unauthorised access to high-security or sensitive information have been paramount within government and commercial institutions since the birth of the Internet, an unease partially born out of its origins in American defence strategy. But increasingly, private individuals are seeking to protect the information held on their personal computers, investing in anti-virus software and taking out insurance policies against viruses and stolen data.

Collectively known as 'hackers', those individuals who seek to infiltrate computerised information systems can be driven by a wide range of motives from a relatively benign belief in freedom of access to information for all, to those who wish to perpetrate acts of vandalism, incapacitation, espionage or terrorism ('we infiltrate the Net as techno-geeks and then become the cyber-parasites that destroy it'[2]). Three acts of 'cyber-trespass' commonly occur (Wall 1997: 217). First is the deliberate planting of viruses which either act immediately to disable systems ('denial-of-service' attacks), or else are 'sleeping viruses' to be activated or neutralised at a later date when ransom negotiations have taken place or when the virus originator has long since disappeared from the organisation targeted. One infamous case in America concerned Timothy Lloyd, a senior programmer for defence contractor Omega Engineering, manufacturers of sophisticated measurement and control systems for, among others, NASA and the US Navy. Anticipating his imminent dismissal, Lloyd exacted his revenge by planting a software time bomb that was detonated 20 days after he left the company in July 1996, deleting critical computer programs at a cost of over $10 million to the company and 80 job losses.

Secondly, there is the deliberate manipulation or defacement of presentational data such as home pages – a practice which increased fivefold in 2001 to 22,337 cases, according to hacker tracker Alldas.de (Heikkila 2001). These frequently take the form of personal attacks against individuals, often well-known personalities. For example, following success at the Academy Awards ceremony in 2002, the black American actress, Halle Berry, suffered vandalism to pages on her website, including defacement of photos and the addition of racist messages. But this kind of malicious damage can equally be global in scope, with potentially thousands of unfortunate recipients of unwanted and abusive electronic graffiti. One recent case involved the identification by Italian police of six members of a hacker group (aged 15–23) who attacked over 600 websites in 62 countries, replacing official home pages with anti-globalisation slogans. The case was notable for the number and significance of the targets, which included the Pentagon, NASA, the Chinese government, US law courts, universities, media organisations, ISPs, political parties and celebrities.

Thirdly, acts of cyber-spying or cyber-terrorism occur whereby computer systems are infiltrated and access gained to specific secrets, classified information or systems of the armed forces, police, defence or intelligence agencies. Following the terrorist attack on the World Trade Center and the Pentagon in September 2001, the US government and its close allies responded by announcing a 'War on Terrorism', together with plans to introduce legislation which would make computer crime a terrorist act, the result of which could see convicted hackers facing life imprisonment with no chance of parole (Middleton 2001: unpaginated). Ironically (and in a classic case of a government wanting it all its own way) it simultaneously authorised the introduction of public service announcements in prime-time TV shows targeting hackers and hacktivists with the message 'Uncle Sam wants you to help fight the war on terrorism'. Sponsored by Cyberangels, the aim was to enlist politically motivated hackers to assist with online intelligence gathering to track down terrorist groups and computer criminals.

Among the potential consequences of deliberate acts of sabotage perpetrated by those with the skills and inclination to hack into a state's computerised systems are the capacity to disrupt water and electricity supplies, close all international communications, manipulate air traffic control or military systems, tamper with National Insurance numbers or tax codes and paralyse financial systems. However, many commentators believe that while these kinds of possibilities are terrifying to con-template, the likelihood of such calamitous events occurring through human or software error is far greater than the chance of malicious hackers or terrorists bringing down a country's infrastructure (Hamelink 2000) and, for the time being at least, they remain the stuff of Hollywood writers' imaginations.

Cyber-sabotage in the workplace

A great deal more prevalent than the incidents described above are the acts of sabotage perpetrated by employees on their employers; indeed four out of five of all Internet-related crimes are committed from within an organisation (McGibbon 2001). Although some of these infiltrators might define themselves as hackers, and many will be disgruntled employees who have a grudge against the company, many more are 'ordinary' office workers – usually women – who disrupt the rhythm and routine of work by sabotaging their computers. Often, the sabotage will be unwitting, the result of carelessness or ignorance of security pro-cedures (as when viruses are spread by people opening corrupted email attachments). But damage to company computer systems may be the result of more knowing acts of resistance. In a high-tech version of the women who, in post-war Britain, would relieve the mundanity of working on factory production lines by dropping their wedding rings into the machinery so that production would have to be halted while the ring was searched for, female office workers in the twenty-first century assert their agency in the face of depersonalised and routinised systems by slowing down or temporarily stopping the flow of organisational communications and work. In some cases, a coherent networking culture exists among computer operators who circulate and swap tips for sabotaging the systems they operate. While management are usually fully cognisant of the fact that such damage by their workforce takes place, and accounts for infinitely more computer downtime and information loss every year than is caused by the demonised figure of the hacker, corporations who are dependent on digital systems of communication and information storage are understandably reticent to admit the extent to which they are vulnerable to such attacks (Ross 1991). Many companies do not wish to publicise that sensitive information has been accessed from within, but privately admit that access to passwords, confidential data and knowledge of an organisation's information systems can make it relatively easy for employees to exploit their security loopholes (McGibbon 2001). In addition, the rise in numbers of employees working at home or on the road has led to a great deal more storage of company data on home computers, posing a significant security threat – especially when an employee moves to a job with a rival organisation.

Security and surveillance: who's watching the watchers?

Although most experts agree that thorough regulation of the Internet is impossible, there can be no doubt that the Internet has itself vastly extended the scope and efficiency of regulatory practices: '[T]he Internet is making possible more complex arrangements for monitoring, tracking down and identifying "miscreants". Long gone are the days when authorities had to rely on "a good eye and retentive memory" ' (Slevin 2000: 215). These characteristics raise important questions concerning the 'policing' of cyberspace: what are the implications – good and bad – of the Internet's capacity to allow wide-scale regulation and surveillance of its users? Because the technology *is* inherently democratic and is available to 'authorities' beyond the police and state, the issue of privacy has become increasingly salient, yet the carceral net is widening and surveillance technologies are creeping in to virtually all aspects of everyday life. Yet who defines and identifies 'miscreants' and with what consequences to notions of citizenship and civil liberties? Who watches the watchers?

Technology might give us a sense of freedom and opportunity but: '[T]he same technology also multiplies opportunities for monitoring nature, society and individual behaviours. Remote sensing and surveillance of all types are no longer the privilege of powerful military or civil state authorities...governments are losing their Orwellian privileges of information detection' (Lenk 1997: 130). But regulation by governments remains the greatest concern of civil liberties groups. Frequently defended on grounds of security, or with reference to notions of taste and decency, state intervention can range from legislation (such as the Obscene Publications Act in the UK and the Communications Decency Act in the USA) to the restriction of use (for example, in Singapore the number of ISPs is limited, they require a licence which forces them to conform to the same regulations governing broadcasting and they are legally obliged to use software that prevents access to 'undesirable' sites). Other approaches are even more prohibitive. In China all ISPs have to register with the police and all Internet users must sign a declaration that they will not visit forbidden sites (Hamelink 2000), while in Saudi Arabia the government has approached the problem of harmful content by allowing only one state-controlled provider of Internet access (ibid.). But perhaps most punitive of all is Burma where the authorities are so hostile towards the Internet (because of its potential for political dissidence) that even owning a computer with a network connection constitutes a criminal act (ibid.).

The state surveillance of citizens has been one of the most controversial (although, not surprisingly, under-reported) aspects of the debate concerning authorities' use of ICTs, an issue brought more sharply – and more sensitively – into focus by the events of 11 September 2001. In an article entitled 'Say good-bye to privacy', American writer Doug Barney puts forward a patriotic view of his government's response to the act of terrorism that, in the parlance of the mass media, 'changed the world for ever':

> Now most of us are thanking our lucky stars and stripes that our government has been spying on us. Western governments have repeatedly denied the existence of the Echelon network, but it was the 'nonexistent' Echelon that provided solid evidence (like bank transfers and phone conversations) to pinpoint the mastermind behind the terrorist attacks and justify the assault on the Taliban and Osama bin Laden camp.
>
> (Barney 2001: unpaginated)

The 'Echelon' system referred to here is a US intelligent search agent used to monitor the communications traffic (especially Internet and mobile phone communications) of European citizens, politicians and military personnel; a sophisticated 'eavesdropping' device that is justified on grounds of terrorism and crime, but has been found routinely to intercept valuable private commercial data (Hamelink 2000). In addition, listening devices called 'carnivores' have been installed at several ISPs to monitor email traffic. But not everyone feels secure in the knowledge that state authorities have this level of power to monitor the communications and movements of individuals – not least because they failed to identify and act on the threat in the first place. Furthermore, as Nancy Murray, Director of the Bill of Rights Education Project at the American Civil Liberties Union of Massachusetts, reminds us, American governments have a long and troubled history of defining deviants, miscreants and people displaying the 'wrong kind' of patriotism:

> The 'War on Communism' that got underway in the closing decades of the 19th century was fought in large part to smash the trade union movement and stifle dissent. The big fear then was of anarchist bombs, of radical ideas brought by immigrants, and above all, of trade union organising – anyone sympathizing with workers qualified as a 'communist'. By the end of World War I [when] the young J. Edgar Hoover…was asked by Attorney General A. Mitchell Palmer to draw up a list of radicals he hastened to oblige, and soon had a card index of 200,000 names of people who had at some point criticized the government.
>
> (Murray 2001: unpaginated)

The prolonged period of moral hysteria that accompanied the war on communism reached its zenith during the 1950s period of McCarthyism, by which time the FBI was spying on hundreds of organisations to see if communists had infiltrated them. In the 1960s and 1970s the FBI added to their files the names of anti-Vietnam War protestors, black nationalists, the so-called New Left, members of the women's liberation movement and numerous other groups, and surveillance permeated the activities of every police and military organisation in the country (ibid.). After a short period in the late 1970s, when the dismantling of the Soviet Union and the end of the Cold War saw calls for the protection of civil liberties take priority over concerns about communism, US foreign policy turned its attention to the War on Terrorism, and civil liberties once again became secondary to the zeal for rooting out dissidents and dissenters.

It doesn't take much effort to imagine who might be the primary targets of the current administration's War on Terrorism. But as increased powers are given to authorities to monitor the activities of citizens, the question is raised of why law enforcement agencies *need* new powers when they do not necessarily make effective use of the considerable powers they already have (ibid.). Murray asks why the American authorities would want to intercept *more* phone calls, when they didn't have the foreign language speakers to interpret the 2 million calls they intercepted last year. Meanwhile, David Rose (2001) suggests that the 11 September attacks might have been averted had security chiefs in America and Britain accepted the offer of Sudan's government (made over a six-year period prior to 11 September 2001) to 'acquire a vast intelligence database on Osama bin Laden and more than 200 members of his al-Qa'ida terrorist network', including material about their financial interests and plans. They also turned down the opportunity to extradite or interview key bin Laden operatives who had been arrested in Africa on suspicion of planning terrorist atrocities.

The conclusion to be drawn seems to be that the technology is only as good as the humans making use of it – or not. The limitations of electronic surveillance methods are further illustrated by the finding that the hijackers responsible for the attacks on the World Trade Center and Pentagon had organised their efforts via the Internet, co-ordinating their activities – unmonitored – from Internet cafés and libraries. Following 11 September, the man believed to be behind the attacks, Osama bin Laden, disappeared. US intelligence has intercepted email traffic from members of his terrorist group suggesting that he retreated to a remote area of Pakistan but, despite a sustained military and surveillance operation, they have (at the time of writing) been unable to locate him or even say with any certainty whether he is dead or alive. Meanwhile bin Laden has reportedly eschewed his laptop computer for the more 'reliable' method of using human couriers to communicate with other members of his network (Cornwell 2002: 3).

A more 'micro', but equally concerning, example of the potential uses and misuses of computer and information technologies is that of surveillance by employers of their employees, whereby monitoring and interception of phone calls and emails are becoming increasingly routine. In July 1999, 20 workers at a Cable & Wireless call centre in the UK were sacked or suspended, and a further 29 were told they faced serious disciplinary action, when managers at the centre concluded a six-week period of electronic surveillance during which they claimed to have uncovered thousands of pounds worth of theft in the form of 'stealing' extra cable TV channels (Bright 1999). Cases at other companies have included disciplinary action and dismissal for employees who have sent risqué emails internally, been caught taking unauthorised rests at work and booked holidays on the Internet during office hours. However, surveillance operations are frequently far from foolproof, and employers are themselves not above suspicion of using technology for immoral purposes. Indeed, the 49 Cable & Wireless workers referred to issued counter-accusations that the surveillance operation was an elaborate ruse by the company to avoid paying redundancy (ibid.). Potential or would-be employees are also vulnerable to electronic entrapment. Software maker, the SAS Institute, claims to have developed a lie detector program capable of sifting through any written communication and spotting when the writer is lying or confused about the facts. Although such software has numerous potential applications, much of the reporting of the story has concentrated on the advantages it would give employers in, for example, recognising embellished or false CVs (http://news.bbc.co.uk). Established software programs – e.g. 'Ascentor' – have been used by some employers since 1999 to read all electronic mail traffic in a company and check it against certain keywords to assess whether the messages are legitimate company business (Hamelink 2000). Other forms of surveillance that are being introduced in work environments around the world are toilet bowls that automatically check for drugs and CCTV cameras in cubicles that then film the people who test positive, sensors monitoring whether workers wash their hands after visiting the washroom, smart badges that track employees' movements and various 'Big Brother' systems that check the performance quality of staff in call centres and other telephone-based work environments – including the number of calls taken and the number of calls with a 'successful' outcome in a given time period (ibid.).

Cybercrime: the challenges for the future

Many people argue that criminal and anti-social activities on the Internet are analogous to similar behaviour in the physical world. Website defacement is just electronic graffiti; passwords or credit card numbers stolen off the Internet are simply theft and fraud in a new guise; those involved with Internet pornography and prostitution are simply utilising a new medium; stalking and harassment will continue to be conducted by mail and telephone as well as via Internet technologies; governments have always found ways of identifying and recording information about the 'enemy within'; and office snoops have been a constant feature of the workplace. But the Internet enhances the potential for criminal and deviant activities to take place in several important ways. First, there is the explosive growth in the number of people with Internet access. As John Naughton (1999) points out, it took the World Wide Web just three years to reach its first 50 million users; a feat which eluded television for

15 years and which took radio 37 years to achieve from its point of inception. This potential audience – which is now estimated at around 740 million – provides limitless opportunities for those who are criminally inclined and a vast marketplace for the (knowing or unwitting) recipients and consumers of their illegal activities. Furthermore, the degree of anonymity afforded by the Net creates a sensation of cybercrime being an 'underground' activity, despite the scale and scope of the activities it permits. Hence, the Internet offers a lower risk of detection than other crimes and also carries greatly reduced physical risks when compared to crimes committed in the real world. In addition to affording criminals anonymity, cyberspace also reconfigures time and space, so that offences can be initiated, and their consequences felt, in entirely different parts of the world. And where a 'traditional' bank robbery might take months of planning and involve the acquisition of accomplices, weapons and a getaway vehicle, breaking into a bank's financial database can take minutes, with none of the immediate physical risks to oneself or one's 'victims'. All these factors may elicit feelings of invincibility in many cybercriminals – and with some justification.

Yet while the police and government authorities express fear and concern about the potential of the Internet for illegal activity, they are increasingly opportunistic in their own use of ICTs. While admitting they are powerless to do anything about most cybercrimes, they are none the less keen to monitor the activities of increasing numbers of people, usually without their knowledge or consent. As this chapter has indicated, and the events following 11 September 2001 graphically illustrated, the distinctions between warfare, terrorism and criminal activity are frequently unclear – and are made even more complex by the feeling among some dissenters that these labels apply equally to the governments and law enforcement agents of the USA and its allies as they do the terrorists who hijacked those flights and flew them into the twin towers of the World Trade Center. But this event, like many other actions by political or religious extremists, also reinforces the impression of a society beset by risk, insecurity and unpredictability from the 'enemy within', and may augment public tolerance of the monitoring of individuals as they go about their business in cyberspace. The implications of this trend – but one element of the creeping normalisation of surveillance that embraces CCTV cameras, electronic databases, 'smart' identity cards, digital fingerprinting and all manner of other innovations presented in the name of technological progress – are still under contention. The application of such technologies by authorities promises much to a public seeking reassurances of order and control, but is of growing concern to individuals and groups who predict that the role of governments and the police in cyberspace is threatening to destroy civil liberties and dismantling traditional notions of citizenship.

Notes

1. The Internet Watch Foundation began as a hotline set up in 1996 for receiving and processing complaints about child pornography and other illegal material, but has grown into a more formal organisation advising, for example, the European Commission, on Internet regulation (Slevin 2000). Although it claims to be autonomous, some have criticised the IWF for its lack of independence from government and its favoured methods of regulation which some say amount to censorship of legal content and do little more than to lull parents and teachers into a false sense of security (Cyber-Rights and Cyber-Liberties 1998).
2. A quotation from Weinstein and Weinstein (1997, cited in Bell and Kennedy, 2000: 215).

Chapter 3

Cyberpunters and cyberwhores: prostitution on the Internet

Keith Sharp and Sarah Earle

Introduction

It is with some justification that prostitution is known as the world's oldest profession. Yet, although prostitution seems to be endemic in human societies of any complexity, the nature of the relationships involved in the selling of sexual services is undergoing a significant transformation, thanks to the emergence and near exponential spread of the Internet. Not only is the Internet transforming the relationships between prostitutes and their clients, but it is also altering the nature of the relationships which exist among both prostitutes and clients.

The emergence of Internet sites dedicated to prostitution has also meant that social researchers interested in commercial sex now have a rich source of data – often relating to hitherto invisible populations. For example, although prostitutes themselves have long been a subject of inquiry (for example, see Walkowitz 1980), very little research exists on the men who use their services. Little is known, for example, about the meanings which men attach to paid-for sex, or about what characteristics and activities they seek in these encounters. Importantly, while significant research studies exist on what prostitutes say about the safety of the sexual acts they practise with clients, virtually nothing exists on men's accounts of the safety of their encounters with prostitutes. All this has changed with the emergence of sites dedicated to men's 'reviews' of the prostitutes whose services they have used. Such sites allow researchers an unprecedented insight into how men give accounts of their involvement in paid-for sex.

In this chapter we begin by giving an overview of how the social relationships involved in paying for sex are being transformed by the Internet. We consider the emergence of a 'cyber-community' of 'punters', as well as how prostitutes themselves have exploited the Internet for the marketing of their services. We also explore the implications of these changes for how power relations between prostitutes and their clients should be conceptualised, and consider the extent to which these changes challenge feminist accounts of commercial sex in particular.

In the second part of the chapter, we outline some of our own findings from an analysis of over 250 'reviews' of prostitutes posted by men on a British Internet site. After a brief consideration of methodological issues, we focus on the issue of self-identity and explore the ways in which men who pay for sex use the Internet to manage discreditable self-identities.

Prostitution on the Net

As any Internet search will reveal, there are literally tens of thousands of websites dedicated, in one way or another, to prostitution, and this number is increasing all the time. Most obvious perhaps are sites dedicated to marketing the services of prostitutes. These can take several forms. First are the 'escort agencies' which tend to be regional, and operate at the 'upper' end of the market. Typically, escort agencies which advertise on the Net emphasis their exclusivity and the 'sophistication' and 'beauty' of the women they offer. Usually, these sites contain photographs of the women and typically they are photographed professionally in the sort of poses that would be found in glamour or 'top shelf' pornographic magazines. These sites frequently carry comprehensive details of pricing (which is usually by the hour) and availability. Interestingly, it is unusual for escort agency sites to make explicit reference to sexual services, but these are often implied by the presence of disclaimers which make clear that any payments made are for the escort's time only, and that any sexual contact between escort and client is purely a matter of consent between them.

Secondly, there are the 'independents'. These are women who advertise sexual services on the Internet, but do not work for or through an agency. This is a very broad category, both in terms of style of presentation and prices charged for services. On the whole, however, independents tend to charge less for their services than agencies – one might assume that this is, in large part, because agencies charge a fee. While the sites advertising independents vary considerably in quality and design, it is usual for them to contain photographs of the women concerned. These vary from the professional quality found on agency sites, to single photographs of an obviously amateur nature. It is on these sites, too, that one is most likely to find more explicitly pornographic images. Total or partial nudity is not uncommon, and on a minority of sites one finds very explicit or 'hardcore' images of the women concerned. Again, the site will usually contain information on pricing which is frequently time based but, unlike agency sites, will often contain much more explicit detail on the kinds of services offered. While these sites will usually carry a disclaimer of some kind, it is not at all uncommon to find a list of services offered, such as fully protected intercourse, protected/unprotected fellatio, anal sex or domination/ submission. Contact information is also given, and this may be by telephone, but in a substantial number of cases is by email only. Exact addresses are rarely given.

Thirdly are the massage parlours. These typically focus on the establishment and contain photographs of the facilities offered. They often also carry photographs of the women available, sometimes with an indication of which days each works. Often prices are not quoted on these sites and, if they are, it is generally for the basic massage, which excludes the price of any sexual services offered. Addresses and location maps are provided, and details of appointment systems (if they have one) are usually given.

Punters on the Net

Another significant category of prostitution-related material on the Internet are the various sites dedicated to reviewing the services of prostitutes. In the UK this is dominated by one site, Punternet which, at the time of writing, contains over 5,000 'reviews' of British prostitutes. As well as publishing reviews, this site also contains links to other sites which directly advertise the services of prostitutes, or which contain discussion boards aimed at prostitutes, clients or both.

The emergence of such sites seems to imply – potentially at least – a significant change in the social organisation of the world of the punter. Historically, punting has been a lonely activity. The considerable stigma attached to paying for sex has traditionally meant that men who do so are reluctant to reveal their activities to even their closest friends. The risks of being discredited as a man who pays for sex are considerable and multifaceted. First is the obvious risk to a core feature of heterosexual masculine identity – namely, that one is sexually attractive to women and capable of attracting women as sexual partners. An obvious implication of paying for sex is precisely that one is *incapable* of attracting women as sexual partners. Secondly, it appears that many men who pay for sex are married or engaged in long-term co-habiting relationships (McKeganey and Barnard, 1996). McKeganey and Barnard (ibid.: 56) report the following responses when they asked prostitute-using men about the likely reactions of their partners to discovering that they paid for sex:

> If I told my wife she'd kick me out, simple as that.

> She'd be hurt, horrified, she wouldn't understand and it would probably end our marriage.

Whatever the truth of these suppositions, it seems clear that many men believe their partner would react adversely to disclosure of their activities. Thirdly, and related to this, are commonly held beliefs about the risks of contracting sexually transmitted diseases from sexual encounters with prostitutes. It seems likely that this could be another factor in men's reluctance to disclose their 'punting' activities to others.

The emergence of the Internet, however, makes it possible for individuals engaged in discreditable activities to 'meet' – albeit virtually – and to exchange information and experiences about these activities while remaining anonymous, and continuing to conceal their activities from those around them. The Internet makes possible the existence of 'virtual communities' of deviants; cyberworlds characterised by sub- or countercultures, in which discreditable practices are accepted as the norm and are entirely without stigma, and in which one may participate without threat to one's 'normal' identity. At their most mundane, such communities allow the free flow of information to the deviant which is practically useful in practising his predilection (the whereabouts, cost, breast size, etc., of a given prostitute). More significant, perhaps, is the opportunity afforded for deviants to reveal themselves for what they are without threat to identity or status.

Prostitutes, punters and power on the Net

The question of power is central to an understanding of prostitutes and their clients. This chapter deals with what Scambler and Scambler (1999) describe as 'voluntary adult sex work'. It must, however, be recognised that other forms of sex work exist, including that which is coerced and that which involves children – neither of which are explored in this chapter. A distinction should also be made between 'outdoor' and 'indoor' sex work, as the experiences and perceptions of women (and clients) working within these contexts can differ markedly (Plumridge 2001). This chapter deals predominantly with 'indoor' sex work; that is, women who work either from their own homes or residential accommodation, a parlour, or those who visit clients at their home or hotel.

Questions of power and exploitation must be situated within the context in which women work and there is considerable debate as to whether we should use the term 'sex work' rather than the term 'prostitution'. There is an increasing tendency in favour of the term 'sex work', with the suggestion that this acknowledges it is simply just another form of labour in which women sell sexual services (Scambler and Scambler 1999). The term also acknowledges the vast range of services in which women (and men) can engage, for example: stripping, table-dancing, 'glamour' modelling and so on. However, as we shall see later in this chapter, when women sell sex, they sell more than just a service. Although women who sell sex become prostitutes in the commodity exchange for sex, 'sex work' also involves the commodification of human emotion. As Wilton (1999: 187) argues, prostitution takes much of its meaning from its position 'in relation to the emotion/commerce boundary [being] positioned firmly on the "emotion" side'. In other words, women sell them*selves*, as well as selling a service.

However, the term sex work is often characterised by the commercialisation of emotion and is frequently used as a means of acknowledging women's agency. For example, Scambler and Scambler (1997) suggest that an understanding of sex work necessitates the respectful attribution of agency to women who sell sex. The term has also been adopted by organisations seeking to promote the rights of women who sell sex and, in the extreme, by those wishing to represent sex work as a valid 'career choice'. There are some who maintain, however, that all forms of sex work – especially prostitution – are exploitative: 'Prostitution represents the interface of two arenas of power and powerlessness, gender and class. Rich men have always used, abused, insulted and exploited poor women, working-class women and black women. And bourgeois men have vociferously defended their privilege to exercise this power over all women' (Edwards 1993: 91). As others have identified, the issues are, in fact, more complex than this (Aggleton 1999) but the question remains the same: are women who sell sex being exploited by the men who pay for it? There are many different perspectives and many different explanations for why women sell sex and why men are prepared by pay for it. Some writers adopt a materialist perspective, arguing that poverty and other forms of social exclusion force women and young girls into prostitution; and suggest that the unequal distribution of economic means puts men firmly in control (Davis 1971).

In contrast, writers such as Krafft-Ebing (1901) and Ellis (1936) have subscribed to the notion of essentialism – explaining the persistence of prostitution by reference to men's sexual 'needs' and powerful sexual 'drive'. Others adopt a structuralist perspective, arguing that men have colonised the representation of women and the representations of male and female sexuality (Dworkin 1981). They suggest we live in a society which propagates 'a culturally sanctioned misogyny where male definitions of women prevail' (Edwards 1993: 96) and where there is a belief that men have a right to unrestricted sexual access to women. Empirical studies of women sex workers portray images of both power *and* powerlessness, and of choice *and* control, as well as exclusion *and* exploitation (Chapkis 1997; Scambler and Scambler 1997; Plumridge 2001).

Cyberspace has been heralded as an opportunity for change in the social order of late-modern or postmodern societies. The increasing presence of the 'cyberpunter' and the 'cyberwhore' suggests an opportunity for change in the power relations of paid-for-sex. Cyberspace offers prostitutes a new opportunity for representation. However, it is clear from the frequently pornographic images displayed that, in marketing their sexual services, women subscribe to the commonly prevailing representations of female sexual availability. Cyberspace has also offered the punter a new arena for representing himself. By definition, the punter has always been a lonely, stigmatised individual, but cyberspace now affords him a place in which to become credible. If anything, we would argue that cyberspace has further empowered the men who pay for sex through the creation of a space which allows men to share good and bad experiences of punting.

Punters in cyberspace

The remainder of this chapter focuses on a research study of the site Punternet. This research can be seen as a type of covert 'cyber-ethnography', as Fox and Roberts (1999: 650) suggest: 'just as a traditional ethnographer would document a community or other cultural form...so cyber-ethnographers will document a virtual social world' (see also Chapter 10, this volume). The first section provides a detailed account of the Punternet site itself and explores some of the methodological issues and concerns associated with this type of covert cyber-ethnography. The second section explores punting as a transgressive act and documents some of the ways in which punters seek to minimise the risks to social identity and the ways in which participation in this type of cyber-community serves to normalise what would otherwise be considered a transgression. The next section focuses on men's concerns with giving women pleasure during paid-for-sex. It particularly focuses on how women's pleasure, especially female orgasm, can be used to perpetuate the myth that women receive pleasure from men, in whose power this lies, and that commercial sex is sexually satisfying for the women involved. The last section describes the phenomenon of 'girlfriend sex' – the archetype of paid-for-sex.

Researching the punter

While there is a considerable body of literature dealing with the experiences of prostitutes and other sex workers – both male and female (Chapkis 1997; Scambler and Scambler 1997; Aggleton 1999) – there exists comparatively little research on men who pay for sex. The reasons for this are obvious: paying for sex remains among the most discreditable and potentially stigmatising of activities in which a man can engage. It has, therefore, been very difficult to find men willing to participate in research and the research which has been done has tended to rely either on self-selecting samples – such as men who answer newspaper advertisements – or recruitment through STD clinics (for example, see McKeganey and Barnard, 1996). The limitations of each of these approaches are readily apparent.

The availability and popularity of computer-mediated communication have provided an alternative source of data. Instead of relying on finding samples of men willing to talk about paying for sex, we have based our study on a sample drawn from more than 5,000 'reviews' of prostitutes posted by men on the British Internet site, Punternet, between 1998 and 2000. The site in question contained, at the time of our analysis, 5,067 'reviews' (or 'field reports') of 2,661 different women written by 2,554 different authors. Although the majority of authors had posted only one review, many had published several, the highest number for any one individual being 46. Similarly, while the majority of the women had been reviewed only once, many had been reviewed several times, the highest number being 32. We chose to sample the reviews by author, and selected at random 10 per cent of the authors (n = 255). Since several of these authors had published more than one review, we randomly selected one of their reviews to be included in the sample.

The reviews were comparatively highly structured. When posting a review, authors must complete an online pro-forma, which gives details of the 'lady's' name, the location of the encounter (town and, in some cases, actual address), telephone number and/or website address, price paid and length of time taken. Comments are then invited under three headings: 'her place', 'description' and 'comments'. Finally, reviewers are asked to indicate whether they would recommend the woman in question and whether they would visit the woman again themselves. As expected, the reviews vary quite considerably in length and level of detail.

Using this type of cyber-data presents us with a number of potential epistemological problems. Perhaps the most obvious is the possibility that the reviews are not authentic, but are either the products of fantasy or the work of the prostitutes themselves. While there is clearly no way of ruling these possibilities out altogether, we consider it unlikely that significant numbers of the reviews are bogus. Although some reviews may well be based upon fantasy rather than genuine experience, the sheer quantity of the reviews – over 5,000 – suggests that this is not the case. Also, the fact that reviews contain very specific contact details of the women concerned – such as telephone numbers and addresses – suggests that the reviews are generally based on genuine experiences. The reviews are also frequently critical in tone and some are overtly hostile; we feel that were most reviews based entirely on fantasy, this would be unlikely. Similarly, although it may be that some reviews are posted by or on behalf of prostitutes seeking to boost their business – and this is discussed below – the high degree of consistency between different reviews of the same woman, together with the critical and evaluative tone of many reviews referred to above, suggests this is not generally the case.

While we do not believe that the reviews are generally bogus, we do consider that these accounts need to be treated with caution; they cannot wholly be read as literal accounts of events, or as authentic reports of subjective experience. Indeed, we prefer instead to regard the accounts as 'presentations of self' – as projections of an identity by individuals engaged in a potentially transgressive act.

Punting: a transgressive act?

Although prostitution is commonly described as one of the world's oldest professions punting is, none the less, a transgressive act. Public images of men who pay for sex portray lonely, physically unattractive men who are also sexually and emotionally inadequate. Punting is therefore a risky and potentially socially discrediting activity. O'Connell Davidson (1998: 154) suggests that it is sometimes this risk, whether real or imagined, which provides an element of erotic excitement, arguing that 'to do something dangerous and get away with it...can be experienced as exhilarating and contribute to a feeling of personal power'. However, as O'Connell Davidson points out, the extent to which the risk of discovery contributes to, or enhances, sexual pleasure is variable and can also depend on the degree to which men's risk taking is combined with exhibitionism.

On the Punternet site, each reviewer is asked to comment on the place at which the sexual encounter occurred. The majority of reviewers specify whether they considered the location to be safe and/or discreet and, in contrast to the conclusions drawn by O'Connell Davidson, punters appear to prefer discreet locations, as the following accounts indicate:

the entrance not discreet at all but felt very safe.

(field report 48)

flat located behind some disused shops, apart from a few people milling about it all felt safe and discreet.

(field report 54)

Clean parlour with discrete [*sic*] entrance.

(field report 248)

Flat in discreet block...in a nice safe part of town near the centre.

(field report 255)

More specifically, punters highlight the importance of minimising the likelihood of being seen and seem to prefer punting locations that reduce this risk. For example:

Nice Quiet Area. House is opposite a field so no nosy neighbours across the way.

(field report 28)

First floor flat typical walk-up. Busy road but you can slip in unnoticed. Feels safe enough.

(field report 17)

Other punters reveal their feelings of nervousness and the potential embarrassment of being seen using the services of a prostitute:

This well established sauna is on a small industrial estate...is quite discreet at night time but you need nerves of steel during the day when local workers are hanging around.

(field report 93)

I felt very vulnerable and was pleased to see it was very discreet, just like visiting a friend (until I was inside).

(field report 143)

It's a busy walk-up...but if you don't mind coming out red faced, sweating and grinning like you've had a great time, then this one's for you.

(field report 77)

The public portrayal of commercial sex is often sleazy. Prostitutes are portrayed as unclean and punters as inadequate (Pheterson 1993; Scambler and Scambler 1997). However, the field reports often stress the very ordinary, almost homely, nature of some commercial encounters and of the women themselves who, as Scambler and Scambler (1999: 73) identify, are 'for the most part "ordinary" rather than "extraordinary" '. For example, one punter wrote: 'The flat was clean and warm. Felt just like someone's home' (field report 97). Another punter describes his experience with a visiting escort, whom he describes as: '31ish with shoulder length blonde hair, fantastic figure, sexy underwear with stockings, a shaved pussy and an upper-crust accent...dresses like the lady of the manor...For any punters like me, this was a safe personal experience that took the shady slezz [*sic*] out of punting' (field report 71). The Punternet site, and other similar sites, provide men who pay for sex with an opportunity to share their accounts of punting with other like-minded men. Within the context of this cyber-community, punting is transformed from a transgressive act into a socially acceptable pastime to be shared and discussed with similar others and, in this sense, fulfils Rheingold's (1994) notion of the 'gift economy'; an economy in which information is freely given.

Giving sexual pleasure: or definitions of a 'good punt'

Previous research has suggested that the giving of pleasure is often central to men's experiences of prostitution (Plumridge *et al* 1997). The data from this study certainly demonstrate a preoccupation with this, as the following accounts show:

[I] opted for the full service and spent a long time enjoying the full works which she seemed to enjoy as much as I did.

(field report 231)

She then laid back on the bed allowing me to proceed to give her a blow job and she also prompted me to finger her at the same time. She certainly sounded like she was enjoying things at this stage.

(field report 109)

She was very responsive and I like to think she enjoyed it also.

(field report 105)

More kissing was followed by me going down on her which she seemed to enjoy…wonderful BJ and very responsive to me going down on her with plenty of sighs and moans.

(field report 57)

Punters' perceptions of women's ability to experience pleasure during paid-for-sex also appeared to be a strong reason for recommending her as a 'good punt'. For example: 'excellent breasts – she seemed to enjoy them being sucked…I would definitely recommend her' (field report 110).

The reliability of reviews appears to be an important feature of this cyber-community. As noted by researchers of other types of computer-mediated communication (Fox and Roberts 1999), some form of 'netiquette' is usually applied to and developed by members of each cyber-community. Factually incorrect, or misleading, information is usually regarded as a serious ethical violation (McLaughlin *et al* 1994) often leading to reproach by other users. In the case of Punternet, the deliberate posting of a misleading or inaccurate field report is seriously admonished, particularly when a favourable review has been posted at the behest of the prostitute:

probably the worst woman i have been with and will remember this night for a long time for all the wrong reasons…she said that roaming was an old friend and submitted the reports to help her along, thanks roaming for a revolting recommendation.

(field report 49)

She gave me oral and then doggy. It was awfull [*sic*]. The write up from the previous chap encouraged me to go. He must have been blind. This lady is not classy or sexy. Just an average pro.

(field report 7)

Although the majority of field reports highlight men's desires to give sexual pleasure, we would suggest that this appears to have very little to do with a genuinely altruistic desire to give pleasure but more because women's pleasure serves as an indicator of men's sexual performance. As previous research has highlighted (Roberts *et al* 1995), while men's sexual pleasure is seen as 'natural' and needs-driven, men are expected to use their sexual skills to 'give' women pleasure. However, when the woman is seen to be 'unresponsive' (in spite of his best efforts) the responsibility for this lies firmly at *her* feet rather than his:

> [She] seemed rather nervous and immature…Not very interested or responsive either…Needs to get more interested and responsive.
>
> (field report 195)

> Toy show was not erotic, her covered BJ was useless, her bum was producing an unpleasant smell. I lost all my drive and erection…In summary she was doing it all by the numbers with no hint of enjoyment.
>
> (field report 97)

And indeed, one punter felt that it was he who should receive payment: 'maybe she should pay me for the pleasure I am giving her' (field report 25). A belief in the ability to give women pleasure is fundamental to the construction of heterosexual male sexuality. The data seem to show that having sex with a woman who is perceived as 'unresponsive' or 'not interested' undermines men's sexual identity. Paying for sex also undermines male sexuality, since it implies (whether true or otherwise) that the man cannot acquire consensual non-commercial sex. The belief that women experience pleasure during paid-for-sex is, therefore, an important way in which men can preserve their sexual identity intact.

Uncertainty surrounding the genuineness of women's pleasure frequently appears in men's reviews, particularly in relation to the genuineness, or otherwise, of women's orgasm. Although the possibility that women are 'faking it' is entertained, on the whole punters appear to believe that the woman's orgasm is genuine:

> I am not going into the sexual side of things, suffice to say I went home a happy and very satisfied man, the crowning glory being, bringing her to orgasm on the second evening (no faking moans and groans here this was for real!).
>
> (field report 55)

very sensual and responsive. kisses and genuinely comes (BIG TIME).

(field report 156)

If she was faking her enjoyment and climax she is a talented actress, but I feel she really enjoys what she does.

(field report 185)

This appears to be generally consistent with men's perceptions of women's pleasure. For example, in a study of consensual non-commercial sex (Roberts *et al* 1995: 523), it was shown that very few men said that they had ever been in bed with a woman who faked orgasm. In contrast, almost all the women interviewed in this same study mentioned that faking orgasm was something they did, at least occasionally. Punters' perceptions of the genuineness of women's orgasm also contradict what is known about women's experiences of selling sex, as Edwards (1993: 99) clearly states: 'Contrary to an archetypal belief about prostitute women, there is little job satisfaction.'

Can't buy me love? The phenomenon of 'girlfriend sex'

Summary: Lady = attractive and sexy, Lady's emotional input = Good, Service = excellent, Value for Money = Good.

(field report 171)

The above comments were provided by one helpful punter; it provides a good summary of what it is that punters are looking for, as well as what it is that women provide. At the beginning of each review, punters are asked to describe the woman. Commonly described features include weight and figure, skin, hair, bust size, a description of the woman's vagina and pubic area, and approximate age. Sometimes punters also refer to the woman's country of origin, or ethnic origin, and whether or not she speaks English. More often than not, descriptions are flattering:

what can i say, she is blond, petite and nice and soft, just like your favourite fruit (peaches), good enough to eat.

(field report 17)

Dark hair, tanned olive skin. Early 30s but in very good condition. Very slim figure but busty, 36B/C.

(field report 3)

They are often complimentary, yet frank and critical: 'Sandy was a very sexy young lady. Lovely long blonde hair, although obviously out of a bottle…What a body!!! Mind blowing…Got a feeling her boobs came from a clinic…though…Nevertheless what a pair' (field report 26). Other field reports offer more negative descriptions and, in these cases, the women would not be recommended as a 'good punt':

> Eastern European quite dark skinned and dark hair. Basically fat and ugly, but to make matters worse did not speak English.
>
> (field report 21)

> She said 36–24–36 on phone and sounded really nice. Reality is 36 yes but more likely 36 and 40. a chubby size 16–18. OK tits didn't get to see anything else apart from loads of cellulite on thighs – Ugh!
>
> (field report 88)

Overall value-for-money and the type and quality of service provided were also important, as the following accounts indicate:

> Great fun and great value for money. She seem to genuinely enjoy her work. Will see her again.
>
> (field report 126)

> I definately [sic] didn't leave with a smile, complete waste of money.
>
> (field report 199)

Many punters identify their desire not to be 'rushed' and women who were regarded as 'clock watchers' were unlikely to be either recommended or visited again. For example:

> She started ruching [sic] me to come as soon as I started thrusting (mish). I suggested we try doggie only to be told that would cost an extra £10. I paid and she stuck a great arse at me. Again she was rushing me as soon as got started. She told me my time was up and I hadn't even come. Very disappointing.
>
> (field report 130)

> Gave a half-hearted covered blowjob only. Doesn't encourage any touching and to be honest the sex was below average, because she just lays there. A pity as she could become very popular if she wanted. I'm afraid she just wants your money…
>
> (Field Report 147)

In contrast: 'She really enjoys her work and is not a clock watcher' (field report 22). What has been described as the 'lady's emotional input' is also a characteristic of paid-for-sexual encounters and one which is clearly desired by many of the men who reviewed on the Punternet site. Here, the notions of the hardened 'whore' and the 'tart with a heart' are juxtaposed, as O'Connell Davidson (1998: 151) suggests:

> 'Hardened prostitutes' are not 'proper' women since they use their sexuality in an instrumental way, but the prostitute with a 'heart of gold' is a feminine, caring, almost 'mumsie' figure. She listens to the client's woes, allows him to rest his weary head on her ample bosom, and then takes care of his bodily 'needs'.

Prostitution is both physically and emotionally intimate. 'It involves, not only the sale of the body, but also, the 'fundamental sale of self' (Chapkis 1997: 71).' Hothschild's (1983) study of emotional labour is also useful here since it could be argued that punters are buying into the 'commercialisation of human feeling' and not just a physical sexual service which meets their bodily 'needs'.

The phenomenon of girlfriend sex appears to be the epitome of such commercialisation. In some cases, girlfriend sex is defined by some punters as an experience during which the woman has been given genuine sexual pleasure:

> She came for real (you can tell by the pulse) more than once. Great girlfriend like sex…She is one sexy lass. Hands off.
>
> (field report 72)

> She very much enjoyed receiving oral and judging by her moans and quivering of pelvic muscles, she did come…This is the closest I have ever come to girl-friend sex in a paying environment.
>
> (field report 155)

Girlfriend sex is also about feeling 'special' and 'unique', rather than just another punter. There is clearly some scepticism within the Punternet community but this type of paid-for-sex does appear to be something that some punters aspire to: 'Can't really do her justice just saying what we did. The atmosphere she created and the way she made me feel were wonderful. Truly now I can understand that some guys say that they can find girlfriend sex. WOW!!!' (field report 87). More commonly, punters tend to describe girlfriend sex as the type of sex which they would expect to have within a consensual non-commercial relationship. Punters also make the distinction between 'having sex' and 'making love', a narrative often associated more with women's descriptions of non-commercial sex (Roberts *et al* 1995):

> I suppose the best I can say that it was more like making love than having sex.
>
> (field report 69)

> The sex was fantastic, she makes you feel like a lover not a punter.
>
> (field report 134)

> Wow it was like making love to a girl friend of a kind she was so passionate and involved. I do not wish to go on in detail but suffice to say I had a real good time.
>
> (field report 247)

While men's sexuality is seen to revolve around the notion of a sexual drive and the application of his skill upon a woman's body (Waldby *et al* 1993), women are perceived as valuing emotionality and the development of relationships. Women who sell sex for money are, therefore, as O'Connell Davidson (1998) suggests, not 'proper' or 'natural' women. Punters cannot seem to reconcile the traditional perceptions of women's emotionality with the seemingly hard-hearted sale of sex for money. They do not appear deluded enough to believe that prostitutes are in it for love rather than money; nevertheless, prostitutes who provide 'girlfriend sex' are constructed as not solely being in the business for financial gain.

Conclusions

We have tried to show in this chapter that the emergence of the Internet has transformed, and continues to transform, the world of prostitution in a number of ways. Prostitutes themselves are increasingly making use of Internet technology to market their services, and to assume greater control than has hitherto been possible over the ways in which they represent themselves to potential clients and to the world in general. This development is open to a number of possible interpretations. On the one hand, we might choose to regard it as liberating, and see the greater control exercised by prostitutes over how they are represented as something of a redress in the balance of power between prostitute and client (or, perhaps, more globally, between men and women). On the other, we may see this development as a further insidious refinement in an ever-increasing drive to reduce women's bodies to mere commodities.

We have also considered the implications of the Internet for the relationships between men who pay for sex. For the first time, men who pay for sex are able to communicate with one another, to share practical information and to inhabit a virtual world in which paying for sex is the norm. This has a number of possible consequences. First, it may have the effect of actually increasing the level of commercial sex which takes place, by virtue of the general increase in information and access to sexual services which sites like Punternet generate. Secondly, it allows men to inhabit a social space (for some of the time, at least) in which paying for sex carries no social stigma. It thus has the potential to reduce the threat to self-identity which is inherent in the act of paying a prostitute for sex, and therefore, perhaps, to allow men who do so a certain freedom from the conventional forms of self-censorship which prevailing attitudes to prostitution generate. In this way, we could again predict that Internet developments will make paying for sex more, rather than less, common. We have also explored some of our findings from an analysis of reviews posted on the Internet by men who pay for sex. We have considered what these reviews tell us about men's motivation in paying for sex, but also how their accounts of encounters with prostitutes need to be seen as part of a process by which they manage their identities as punters. This also has methodological implications, for it warns us that all such accounts need to be seen not simply as unvarnished descriptions of events, but as active presentations of self, in the face of potentially discrediting information.

Chapter 4

The electronic cloak: secret sexual deviance in cybersociety

Heather DiMarco

Given the opportunities the Internet provides for secrecy and anonymity it is of little surprise that many users are increasingly exploring aspects of their sexual identities and experimenting with their sexuality in ways that may be precluded in 'real' life by a variety of social and personal impediments, constraints and repressions. It is the very anonymity of the Net that raises the question of what constitutes 'normal' and 'deviant' conduct and blurs the lines between the two. Many have argued that in a society dominated by the socially constructed norms that accompany a heterosexual paradigm, any behaviour that falls outside the confines of the heterosexual 'norm' is deviant and is open to sanction (Plummer 1975; Epstein 1997; Ault 1999). But the growth of the Internet and the spaces it provides – email discussion lists, newsgroups, chat rooms, websites and so on – have allowed individuals to experiment privately with their sexuality in the relative safety of their own environment and away from the prying eyes of those who might censure such behaviour. As the identity of the user is concealed, his or her 'real world' social position is maintained and his or her deviance remains secret for as long as the user chooses to keep it that way. With no fear of exposing themselves to stigma, ridicule or physical harm, Internet users can negotiate new sexual identities, engage in secret sexual deviancy and acquire numerous sexual partners, while all the time protected by the 'electronic cloak' that is virtual reality. Furthermore, evidence suggests that our lives in cyberspace are encouraging us to become comfortable with new ways of thinking about relationships, sexuality, politics and identity (Turkle 1996). This chapter addresses these issues and calls for society and sociology to recognise and respond to the influence of new computer-mediated modes of communication when discussing the concepts of presentation of self, sexual identity and deviance.

Recent research (e.g. Sagan 1995; Kaloski 1997; Zizek 1999) indicates that the use of virtual environments for experimenting with sexual identity and fulfilling erotic fantasy is widespread. Although not in any sense exclusive to women, this chapter will concentrate on the experiences of women, for whom the Internet is arguably especially empowering in providing a space to explore sexual boundaries in a society dominated by patriarchal definitions of sexual norms. Worldwide, the proportion of women using the Internet is growing (most sources agree that the female online population stands at just over 40 per cent of all users). For many women who are bound by the norms and conventions of traditional patriarchies, the disembodied nature of cyberspace has arguably afforded them greater levels of self-esteem and personal fulfilment than the reality of everyday life (Ravetz 1998) and has opened up new opportunities to explore their sexual identities.

As Tsang (2000) notes – after Foucault – we can reinvent our sexualities and over time can have more than one. In a rebuttal to what he calls the 'protestations of the latest adherents to gay ideology that they were born gay', Tsang tells us that the online environment illustrates that 'our sexualities are ephemeral, to be changed with a stroke of a key' (ibid.: 433). For example, this chapter is predominantly concerned with 'heterosexual' women who use chat rooms to meet other women and 'experience' a same-sex relationship. In a real-life situation, such women might be deterred from engaging in same-sex relationships because of their personal circumstances or by the societal sanctions that accompany identities such as 'lesbian' and 'bisexual'. However, as their encounters are taking place anonymously in a virtual realm they can maintain their heterosexual identity and its accompanying status as 'normal' and 'respectable' in their real lives. Furthermore, individuals who are unsure of their sexual orientation, or who simply want to experiment sexually in relative safety, are using chat rooms as 'practice grounds' for learning the required scripts, rules, language and behaviours in preparation for intended real-life encounters. Finally, Internet chat spaces and web communities are used by individuals who have constructed 'deviant' identities and wish to make contact with others who share their sexual proclivities but whose activities may be censured by society. For example, swingers, sadomasochists, gays, lesbians and bisexuals use such spaces to find willing participants for real-life encounters. For all these groups, the Internet provides a means of meeting like-minded people but from behind a mask of anonymity. Questions can be asked and requests made which, in real life, might cause embarrassment, ridicule or offence. The total anonymity of Internet services provides a cloak behind which sexual experimentation can take place.

Cybersex is a curious blend of phone-sex, computer dating and high-tech voyeurism (Branwyn 2000). It can take many forms, from individuals who do not act out sexual encounters online but like to talk openly about their sex lives and sexual problems using online discussion groups as forums for informal counselling, to the creation of group fantasy scenarios in MUDs (multi-user domains) and MOOs (multi-user domain object-oriented), where each participant's erotic fantasies are tailored to fit a collective story being created by all the players: a kind of sexual Dungeons and Dragons (ibid.). In addition, 'adult only' BBSs (bulletin board systems) are used to exchange computer-based pornographic images, swap erotic descriptions of what the participants are wearing and doing for masturbatory stimulation or arrange face-to-face encounters. Alternatively, 'tele-operated compu-sex' may take place where an individual or couple gives actual love-making instructions to another individual or couple ('Jim, I want you to slowly undress Carol') – a format popular with online swingers (ibid.).

It seems, then, that the Internet is at the forefront of changing attitudes to sex and sexuality. In an ever-evolving world, the way in which some individuals are exploring and experimenting with their sexual identities in cyberspace is contributing to a gradual but significant shift in attitudes regarding what is considered to be 'normal' heterosexual behaviour in the real world. This in turn raises questions about the kinds of attitudes and behaviours that belong within the remit of what is considered to be a 'heterosexual' identity. For example, Roseneil (2000a) argues that we are currently witnessing a change in the way that sexual identities are categorised and understood. She suggests that modern sexual experiences are blurring the boundaries between what is viewed as 'heterosexual' identity and what is regarded as 'homosexual' identity. She argues that we are currently witnessing an emergence of what she terms 'queer tendencies' in the characterisation of heterosexual relationships in modern western societies and that certain behaviours which were once viewed as specifically homosexual are beginning to appear within the realm of heterosexual experience (Roseneil 2000b). Equally, lesbians are using Internet spaces to initiate sexual relations with men, and gay men are using them to initiate sexual relations with women, thus supporting Tsang's (2000) challenge to sexual essentialism, and contesting the idea that sexual identities and practices within lesbian and gay communities are fixed (Roseneil 2000b).

This blurring of traditional, consensual understandings of sexual behaviour makes it increasingly difficult to establish a distinct sexual identity which precisely fits any of the labels that have previously been applied. However, it equally means that it is possible for both gay and straight people to cross the boundaries of their usual sexual behaviour while maintaining a consistent identity and status among their peer group in the real world. A temporary foray into sexual 'otherness' does not threaten their everyday selves. As Plummer (1975) argues, the way an individual views his or her own actions determines the status he or she accords it within his or her own mind. If individuals see their experimentation as an acceptable part of their sexual development, in their own minds their established sexual identity remains intact.

More recent social commentators (e.g. Ault 1999; George 1999; Roseneil 2000a, 2000b) have similarly explored the legitimacy of constructing two distinct and, superficially at least, conflicting sexual identities. They argue that sexuality is frequently more fluid than any normative expectations that may arise from the labelling of a specific sexual identity as heterosexual or homosexual. For example, George (1999) explores the question of whether married lesbians or lesbians who find men attractive can legitimately sustain a lesbian identity, and whether a woman can maintain a heterosexual identity if she has had (or has thought about having) a sexual relationship with another woman. Her conclusion is that 'the prevalence of other scenarios clearly make a mockery of definitions of sexuality which posit an absolute either/or for hetero/homosexuals' (ibid.: 104). Similarly, Roseneil (2000b) argues that even though today's society still largely views heterosexuality as normative, natural and to a large extent compulsory, the bases of intimate relationships are rapidly undermining such conventions and becoming more individualised and detraditionalised. For the modern woman, the traditional, domestic, heterosexual relationship may not only fail to satisfy her emotional and sexual needs, but may increasingly be regarded as the thing that constrains and limits her quest for individual fulfilment: a shift in consciousness that has arguably led to the displacement of the married, heterosexual couple with children as the basic unit in society.

Yet despite individualism and the pleasure principle arguably being at the top of many young women's agendas, and notwithstanding the opportunities that are increasingly being presented to individuals to 'play' with their identities (including their sexual identities) in the postmodern consumer culture, there is no denying that long-term heterosexual partnerships remain the dominant, hegemonic norm in contemporary western societies. Many people may fantasise about adopting new sexualities or engaging in sexually oriented behaviour with strangers, but dominant social ideologies will prevent them from acting out their fantasies. Yet the World Wide Web permits individuals *virtually* to be whomever they want to be, say whatever they want to say and do whatever is suggested by their fantasy life, without the practical and emotional problems that such interactions might generate in real life. Cyberspace provides a cover for people to discuss their sexual desires, exchange erotic messages or have virtual sex with other members of the 'community', either as a precursor to an actual meeting or as an alternative to contact in the physical realm. But more than this, cyberspace provides individuals with an opportunity for self-expression and for the continual creation and re-creation of 'new' selves. Web spaces can thus be seen as 'laboratories for the construction of identity', where individuals frequently feel more like their 'real' selves than in the physical world (Turkle 1996: 7).

The potential ethical problems that are raised by a technology that permits 'false' presentations of self have been much debated in recent years, particularly in relation to paedophiles who may use the Internet to procure their young victims, posing as teenage boys or girls and gaining the confidence of the victim over a period of time. But that aside, it is generally found that individuals who engage with others in an 'adult' (although not necessarily sexual) chat space will present an image that is consistent with the nature of that specific community, albeit that it may be an enhanced, altered or idealised version of themselves, constructed to make them more attractive to others in that chat room (Sannicolas 1997).

Zizek (1999) discusses further the idea that women who chat in 'virtual' spaces may be experimenting with their sexuality in an environment safe from physical risk (i.e. of assault, non-consensual activity or sexually transmitted diseases). But for Zizek, Internet chat spaces provide much more than a forum for recreational play, and their safety aspect extends to the preservation of the user's sense of 'ontological security' – or elemental sense of psychological well-being and trust in others (Laing 1960; Giddens 1990). In other words, individuals can construct a personal narrative about themselves, which allows them to assume certain characteristics and conceal others, depending on the context and 'audience' at the time. Whatever elements of 'authenticity' or fantasy are present in this ontological narrative, the adoption of a virtual self can act to preserve the individual's 'real' self-image. To illustrate this, Zizek (1999: 137) offers a personal testimony: '[in a chat room] I can present myself as a promiscuous woman and engage in activities which, were I to indulge in them in real life, would bring about the disintegration of my sense of personal identity.' The suggestion once again, then, is that the screen self is a sort of 'cloaking' device for the real-life self, keeping the virtual image external and separate from the 'real me'. Zizek (ibid.) states that in online virtual interactions:

> We maintain an attitude of external distance, of playing with false
> images: 'I know I'm not like that…but it's nice from time to time, to
> forget one's true self'…this way you can relax. You are delivered
> from the burden of being what you are, of living with yourself and
> being fully responsible for it.

This method of self-disguise enables individuals to act out their fantasies
without worry of exposure. The notion that the individual can do
whatever he or she wants – while knowing that he or she is not 'actually'
doing it – side-steps the feelings of shame, stigma and deviancy that
usually accompany such activities in the physical world. It is because of
the fear of stigmatisation that real-life deviancy is commonly kept
hidden, yet fear of physical harm may, paradoxically, force deviant
behaviour into open, public or controlled areas, one of which is the World
Wide Web which provides a forum where deviance can occur, yet 'no-one
notices or reacts to it as a violation of the rules' (Becker 1963: 20).
Consequently, not only are the individual's identity and status protected,
but social consensus remains unchallenged and social stability is
(seemingly) preserved.

Goffman (1959) argues that the risks involved in presenting a deviant
self-image in real life are maximised by dominant, socially constructed
norms. With regard to sexuality, the concept of 'heterosexual privilege'
(Ault 1999) grants certain rewards for those who maintain a heterosexual
identity, while those who are seen to be breaking the heterosexual 'norm'
may be subjected to peer condemnation. In order to prevent the acquisition of stigmatising labels, many individuals engage in 'impression
management' in order to place their interactions within the confines of
socially constructed expectations. One group for whom the presentation
of an acceptable sexual identity may be rendered especially problematic
is bisexuals. Although Ault argues that ambiguous sexual identities such
as bisexuality and bi-curiosity pose less of a challenge to the heterosexual
paradigm than overtly homosexual practices – as there is always the
possibility that the individual will 'come to their senses' and revert back
to the expected behavioural norms (ibid.: 175) – it is perhaps they more
than any other group who experience greatest animosity from others.
Although there is comparatively little literature on bisexuality and bi-
curiosity, those that *have* written in this area have highlighted the
problems experienced by bisexuals in relation to revealing their sexual
identities to dominant, 'powerful' groups. Both heterosexual and
homosexual communities may be hostile to the individual who wishes to
identify herself as 'other' than heterosexual but who is not 'totally' gay
either (Sansam 1992; Ault 1999; George 1999). This means that for women

who are curious or think that they might like to have a relationship with another woman, announcing these desires to a world where one is supposed to be either one thing or the other is problematic. As Sansam (1992: 210) states: 'the way society is structured...it's much easier to opt for one fixed identity or the other.'

There has been much recent media speculation about the apparent rise of bi-curiosity and bi-try as a phenomenon which serves to maintain heterosexual hegemony while at the same time leaving women free to experiment with their sexuality. Both Brooks (1999) and Theobald (1999, 2000) have written pieces in the *Guardian* discussing the idea that some women are experimenting while 'play[ing] safe with their sexuality' (Theobald, 2000: unpaginated). They suggest that as women are indulging in sexual acts with other women under the guise of mere 'curiosity' there is little, if any, threat to heterosexual hegemony. This has led many to challenge conventional notions of 'deviance' and argue that activities once regarded as deviant (e.g. same-sex relationships) are becoming increasingly acceptable and 'normalised' in today's society to the extent where lesbians and gay men are effectively *beyond* the closet (Seidman *et al* 1999).

But even if sexual barriers are beginning to crumble for some sections of the population, the majority of heterosexual people still view non-heterosexual acts as taboo. Furthermore, other aspects of sexual desire that diverge from conventional definitions usually remain either entirely hidden from public view, or else individuals induce strategies to 'neutralise' what might otherwise be regarded as deviant behaviours. 'Bi-curiosity' is one such technique, whereby individuals who 'manage' their identity as heterosexual in normal life can explore covert desires without threatening the hegemonic heterosexual paradigm and risking social marginalisation.

I have recently conducted research into the ways in which some women are engaging in bisexual practices in virtual chat rooms, while maintaining a heterosexual front in the real world. Many of them referred to these different personae on numerous occasions, and the fear of being exposed as something 'other' than that which they were presenting in real life emerged as one of the most dominant themes. Several women expressed serious interest in having a relationship with another woman, but suggested that social constraints made relationships with women only possible in the virtual reality of the chat room. Here they could be who they wanted to be without fear of stigma, persecution and loss of respect from their friends and families. An illustration of this anxiety can be seen in the following extract from a chat-room conversation:

I think I am bi, but I've never done anything about it...I can't really...if my parents found out they would kill me, they are very religious...they would see it as a sin...and my friends would probably never speak to me again, even though I am sure some of them feel the same as me...they all think I'm totally straight, the only person that knows about this is my brother.

This would seem to correspond with Goffman's suggestion that those who are engaging in behaviour that could be seen to be 'other' than the prescribed societal norm are most concerned about their closest relatives discovering their 'secret' or 'shameful' activities (Goffman 1963: 71). It also illustrates a finding of my research that many of the women who expressed an interest in having a same-sex relationship had never actually had sexual relationships with other women in real life, stating that the only such encounters they had experienced had been in chat rooms. This would seem to be compatible with Tsang's (2000: 435) view that some individuals come out 'genitally but not cerebrally' and Branwyn's (2000: 396) suggestion that these same-sex encounters rarely carry over into face-to-face meetings but that participants are 'content to return night after night to explore this odd brand of interactive and sexually explicit storytelling'.

It seems, however, that despite the fact that many of the women in my study had not experienced a same-sex relationship in 'real life' it was frequently suggested that a number of them would like to 'do it for real' but were not sure how to go about it. Of these women, some expressed a concern about 'getting things right' should they eventually get together with another woman. Many indicated that they were anxious that they might do or say the wrong thing in a real-life interaction, and chat rooms provided them with the space to find out what to do, what to say, how to react and so on. Preservation of self is a key issue here: chat rooms provide users with the opportunity to explore new sexual environments without the potentially embarrassing or risk-laden pitfalls that such contexts usually give rise to. They can be regarded as a 'face-saving' device where users can 'rehearse' for later, physical encounters. Chat rooms thus provide an opportunity: 'for the instrumental examination of the actor's sexual identities and desires with the co-presence of other actors, within a supposedly safe, anonymous social setting...it is also a whole socially constructed arena, a computer-mediated rehearsal space, where he (or she) can learn scripts, rules and behaviours' (Pryce 2001: unpaginated). As an illustration of this, one conversation I witnessed in a chat room went as follows (see glossary in Chapter 10 for meanings of acronyms):

'So where do u go 2 find women who feel like us then?'
'I dunno that's what I'm here 4...lol'
'me 2. Lol'
'Have u been 2 any gay bars or anything?'
'Not yet, I daren't'
'y'
'I wouldn't know what 2 expect, or how to act or anything?'
'mmm I see what u mean'
'and I've never tried anything, what if I decide it's not what I want?'
'Yeah...like what if someone comes on 2 u...what would u do?'
'like I said...that's what I'm here 4...lol'
'Me 2. If I try it here first I won't look a prat will I?'
'That's what I thought'

This interaction highlights the fear of being discovered as something other than they are presenting themselves in the real world. For example, if someone were to enter a gay bar without being versed in the 'rules' of expected behaviour they may fear being ridiculed, ignored or even exploited. Some women voiced concerns about openly declaring that they may be bisexual for similar reasons. This anxiety is reflected in Sansam's (1992) suggestion that some women do not wish openly to declare themselves to be other than either totally straight or totally gay, as to do so may provoke criticism from both the heterosexual and lesbian communities. As discussed earlier, while the straight community view being 'bi' or 'curious' as a temporary condition that will revert to the heteronormative ideal, lesbian communities often view this stance as a 'cop out' that allows women to maintain their 'heterosexual privileges' (Ault 1999).

The anonymity of chat-room encounters mitigates the effects of any hostile reactions that occur in them. In a chat-room setting, screaming and shouting can only be expressed textually, and the recipient of such abuse can easily choose to ignore anyone who is aggressive towards them by pressing the 'ignore' key on the chat menu. Persistent aggressors can also be ejected (or flamed) from the chat room, which means that both the physical and the emotional safety of participants is ensured. The possibility of experiencing high levels of emotional distress as a result of a confrontation in cyberspace is thus significantly less than in a face-to-face encounter. In addition, chat rooms are easily identified by the themes listed and, in any case, the consequences of wandering into the 'wrong' setting are arguably potentially less embarrassing or risky than in real life. For example, many rooms are specifically set up for lesbian or gay people to interact with each other, while others welcome only bisexual and bi-curious women. Branwyn notes: 'By far the single largest theme represented in the [chat] room titles…is sex. On a given night, the list might include "Naughty Negligees", "Men for Men", "Hot Bi Ladies", "Women Who Obey Women", and so forth'. Instances of self-defined 'straight' women entering chat rooms for bisexual and bi-curious women were high in my research. Large numbers of women who entered one chat room I observed stated that they were 'straight' or 'just curious'. Frequently conversations began with the phrase 'I am new 2 this, what goes on in here?', which usually resulted in the response: 'whatever u want hun…' ('hun' is a shortened version of the term 'honey'). This response would seem to demonstrate an open attitude and an acceptance of any sort of interaction initiated. It may be that women entering these rooms simply wish to chat to other women without the intrusion of men, or they may want to experience virtual or cybersex with another woman, or they may want to try to organise a meeting in real life. But most want to try to explore or establish their own sexual identity by talking about how they feel to others in a similar situation. Examples of participants 'checking' their sexuality were witnessed in a number of chat-room inter-actions. One instance concerned whether a woman could legitimately define herself as bisexual. The conversation went like this:

'can u be bi if u've never actually been with another woman?'
'yes'
'course u can'
'cool. I feel bi but never done anything about it'
'I'm the same'
'me 2'
'how do u know u r bi then?'
'because I want 2 do something about it'

This interaction can be seen as a woman seeking confirmation of her 'bisexual' self-image from the reaction of others to her questions.

I observed another chat-room interaction on a similar theme, when a young woman asked the main chat room whether they thought that she was bi or straight as she had been having sex with another woman to please her boyfriend. The conversation went as follows:

'my b/f wanted me to have sex with another girl so I did…does that make me bi?'
'do you feel bi?'
'I dunno'
'well would u do it again if ur b/f wasn't there?'

'dunno, I might…it wasn't exactly horrible lol'
'lol'
'I think it would be a bit weird if my b/f wasn't there though'
'y'
'because if any1 found out then they would think I was a les. I wouldn't be able 2 say I was straight anymore would I…I mean I'd be doin it 4 me and not him?'
'don't let it worry u hun…u don't have 2 tell anyone u did it do u?'
'I suppose not…but it would be right confusin'
'so just do it when ur b/f is there then if it makes u feel better…opportunity knocks hehe…lol'
'thanx lol'

In this particular interaction it seems that everyone was happy for the woman to define herself however she wished. It would also appear to support Plummer's (1975) argument that the individual has to interpret her actions as non-heterosexual in her own mind before she is non-heterosexual in reality. In this instance the woman who had sex with another woman to please her boyfriend has interpreted her action as heterosexual and non-deviant. It seems that the presence of her boyfriend legitimises an activity that she might consider deviant if he was not there. This example also highlights the views of Seidman (1997) and Roseneil (2000a, 2000b) who suggest that behaviours cannot easily be categorised according to the homosexual/heterosexual dichotomy. What might otherwise be regarded as a homosexual activity (two women engaging in sex) is interpreted as a heterosexual act because of the 'neutralising' presence of a man. In fact a number of the women in my research suggested that their interest in having a sexual relationship with another woman stemmed from suggestions put forward to them by their male partners, and that they were using chat rooms to locate willing participants either for real-life encounters or for cyber ' threesomes'. One couple stated that they wanted to experience a virtual threesome as an experiment to try to assess whether either of them would be upset if they 'really did it'.

The majority of the women in the chat rooms I visited presented themselves as straight, bisexual or bi-curious, and most stated that they had a male partner. It became apparent that the only same-sex relationships that many of these women had encountered had been in chat rooms. Many had indulged in cybersex with other women and had not taken it further in the 'real' world, although several said they would like to. It was suggested by a number of women that having virtual sex in chat rooms could not be considered as being unfaithful to their partners, as the only people actually touching their bodies were themselves, a belief that may be regarded as self-delusional given a recent case in New Jersey, where a woman was sued for divorce after her husband discovered that she had swapped erotic fantasies with a man on the Internet. The allegation was one of adultery although physical consummation had not occurred – in fact, the couple had never even met (Ravetz 1998).

The women who tell themselves that virtual sex is not adulterous are attaching what Plummer (1997) terms 'subjective meanings' to their actions, so that they can be placed in an almost non-sexual (or certainly non-infidelity) category. It can also be assumed that many women who indulge in cybersex interpret their actions as either masturbatory or as a virtual sex aid to embellish their real-life sexual encounters. Also, different rules may apply in the case of same-sex encounters between women which are often presented as male fantasies and can thus be seen as unchallenging both to the participant's real-life male partner and to the dominant heterosexual paradigm in general. Even if the women go on to explore what they have done in a chat room in the real world, they do not necessarily see their actions as being deviant, but as forming part of normal heterosexual activity, in the same way as reading erotic literature or watching soft-porn films can be interpreted in this way. In short, most participants in these kinds of chat spaces are women experimenting with their sexuality and collecting experiences. Although a few use chat as a medium for meeting other women and establishing relationships in the physical realm, most of the 'action' falls into the category of casual sex, sexual discovery and adventure.

My research indicated that individuals frequently change their profiles when visiting different chat rooms. For example, on one occasion I was chatting to an individual about which rooms she had used before. She said she had been in many different ones, but that I probably wouldn't recognise her because she didn't always use her 'real' profile. In other words, she changes her profile to one that other people in that particular chat room will find sexy; sometimes entering the room as a woman, sometimes as a man. Turkle (1995) similarly notes that some individuals create multiple identities which they swap around depending on the sort of chat they are looking for. One of Turkle's respondents states: 'it is a complete escape…I have three handles I use a lot…one is serious… [another is] a bit of a nut…and [a third is] very active on sexual channels, always looking for a good time' (Turkle 1995: 179). This freedom to role play is often a crucial part of the turn-on and is one of the main reasons why cybersex is flourishing (Branwyn 2000).

The electronic cloak that is provided via computer-mediated

communications such as Internet chat rooms thus provides a mechanism to obscure differentials such as age, sex, gender, race, ethnicity and disability from others participating in virtual chat. Indeed, all the conventional signals of gender identity – intonation, voice pitch, facial features, body shape, non-verbal language, dress and demeanour – are absent (Danet 1996). In virtual reality individuals can change any aspect of their identities, their gender and their sexuality to suit themselves and their 'audience'. As one early commentator predicted:

> In the ultimate artificial reality, physical appearance will be completely composable. You might choose on one occasion to be tall and beautiful; on another to be short and plain. It would be instructive to see how changed physical attributes altered your interactions with other people. Not only might people treat you differently, but you might find yourself treating them differently as well.
>
> (Krueger 1991: 256)

The observation that different physical characteristics may alter your actions and others' reactions to you is borne out by Tsang (2000), who notes that cyberspace is not immune from the racism and xenophobia that permeates the physical world. He cites the example of a gay man from Taiwan who found that many more people wanted to chat with him when he described himself as 'Caucasian' than when he was 'Chinese' (ibid.: 434).

This experience counters the dominant over-romanticised view of cyberspace as a Utopian culture embracing an alternative, better reality. Of course, the person with whom this man is chatting at any given time will accept his description as 'Caucasian' and may too be presenting a 'false' image. Virtual relationships are thus a consensual hallucination through which individuals can manipulate their appearance to assume any form they wish to (Reid 1996). Cyberspace overturns socially constructed barriers, subverts (albeit temporarily) the inherent prejudices of the physical world and their resulting stigma, labels and stereotypes, and can overcome the normative prescriptions that are influenced by the rules of aesthetics and fashion. The technology provides the 'mask' that makes the impermissible permissible, and transforms what is socially unrealisable in the real world into something that can be accomplished in virtual reality. The creation of identities that are external to reality enables individuals to engage in aspects of their life that would have otherwise remained hidden, perhaps even to themselves. This 'decentring of identity' is often taken to be symptomatic of a postmodern world where 'formerly paradigmatic patterns of identity construction...lose sway

[and] they are replaced by a hodgepodge of lifestyle choices' (Epstein 1997: 154).

In summary, Internet spaces have many advantages over 'real' meeting places in the physical world, especially for women who are usually bound by more social constraints and conventions than men. Chat rooms provide a safe environment for women to indulge their fantasies and to collect sexual experiences. Cybersex may even be more satisfying for some women than real-life sexual encounters. In cyberspace, they can be their 'most outrageous self' (Sagan 1995: unpaginated) and take their wildest desires beyond anything they feel permitted to do in the real world. They can experiment with same-sex partnerships while simultaneously preserving their self-image as 'normal'/heterosexual in real life. Cybersex does not carry the same risks of contracting sexually transmitted diseases or discovering unwanted pregnancy that real-life encounters do. Furthermore, individuals can use chat rooms as a practice ground for rehearsing their later, real-life interactions. For some, chat rooms can initiate the discovery of their 'true' selves, or permit users to ensure their fantasy is something they would like to act out in reality. My research uncovered much discussion in this area, with many people asking questions about where to go to find certain groups of people, what to expect when they get there and generally how to 'do' bi-sexuality.

It is also clear that some individuals use cyberspace to reveal their 'real selves'. For example, several writers (see, for example, Chandler 1998; Slevin 2000) have noted that homepages (and sites such as Friends Reunited) are frequently used as a means for young people to 'come out' as gay or lesbian. Chandler (1998) cites Rob, who used his homepage as a 'very easy way to come out'. He could say 'check out my web site' knowing they would 'come across the gay part'. More importantly, he notes, 'they could find out in my own positive terms and think about it before reacting' (ibid.: 13). Similarly, James was 'out' in cyberspace long before he was out in daily life, enabling him to say to people, 'Oh, didn't you know?' as if the issue was old news (ibid.).

Alternatively, for those individuals who feel compelled to keep aspects of their identity or sexuality hidden from even close family and friends, the Internet may provide a welcome respite wherein they can suspend their usual presentations of self and restore their ontological reserves. To this extent, cyberspace might be said to be a key 'backstage' area (Goffman 1959) where individuals who are usually engaged in the 'frontstage' activity of impression management (e.g. of a 'normal', heterosexual woman) can put aside that 'front' and be themselves – lesbian, bisexual or simply an exaggerated, sexually promiscuous and uninhibited version of themselves. Even in an ever-changing social world where identity is open to endless permutations and revisions, and sexuality is arguably more fluid than the heterosexual/homosexual dichotomy suggests, not everyone feels able to suspend the social and sexual rules prescribed by the real world. Internet chat rooms thus provide the 'stage' for individuals to 'act out' their desires and fantasies, while preserving their real-life status behind a mask of anonymity and self-perceived hetero-normality. Although this 'mask' is frequently nothing more than a self-perpetuated delusion, it may be that, as Proust poetically puts it: '[The] lie is one of the few things in the world that can open windows for us on to what is new and unknown, that can awaken in us sleeping senses for the contemplation of universes that otherwise we should never have known' (cited in Sedgwick 1991: 67).

Chapter 5

Cyber-chattels: buying brides and babies on the Net

Gayle Letherby and Jen Marchbank

Introduction

Historically and cross-culturally women and children have always been seen as the property of men and, while the Internet arguably continues this pattern, it also provides opportunities to reinvent the discourses around such social attitudes. Oppression and exploitation are not un-problematic concepts and it is too simplistic to argue that women are inevitably oppressed and men the inevitable oppressors (e.g. see Annandale and Clark 1996; Jacobs *et al* 2000). Furthermore, definitions of normality and deviance are also relative and subject to the dominant interpretations and expectations of the society in which an act or behaviour takes place (Becker 1963). The issues of family creation and family composition are enduring topics for discussions in the press, politics and in society generally, but certain views dominate, creating a 'popular', 'common sense' discourse (or set of discourses) that favour certain methods of family form over others. In recent years the World Wide Web has become central to debates about, for example, arranged marriages, childlessness and adoption. In this chapter we focus on the increasing practice of buying brides and babies via the Internet and consider whether, as is stereotypically assumed, this is an exploitative and deviant activity.

We consider three related issues. First, in 'Women and children for sale' we explore the way in which the Internet positions women, children and potential children (as in eggs and sperm) as consumer items; that is, products to be purchased. Secondly, in 'Consumers or carers/victims or agents' we consider the construction of the buyers of these products as either caring and altruistic, or self-serving, exploitative, even 'desperate' individuals, and of the purchased as victims or agents. Our concern in relation to the first two issues, then, is the perceived deviant activities of buying brides and buying babies. After a consideration of the characteristics and representations of the products and the purchasers we turn to our third concern: 'Artificial or real families?' In this section we consider the construction of the practice of buying brides and babies as deviant through a discourse which positions the traditional western family form as the norm. Finally, we end with some 'Brief reflections' on buying brides and babies.

Women and children for sale

It could be argued that the use of information and communication technologies to buy brides, babies, eggs and sperm is simply a continuation of the power of existing social divisions, a system by which those with money, often those resident in the richer nations, can continue to maintain structures of imperialism, colonialism and patriarchy. The fact that the vast majority of sites are US based and offer brides not husbands indicates that the Internet has not acted as an instrument of social levelling as it is sometimes claimed to be. In the following we describe several sites (selected via an Internet search for 'mail-order brides', 'adoption' and 'egg/sperm donation'). We have changed the names of all sites referred to.

Internet brides

Where can you meet exotic Asian women?
www.address.com an international picture personals [*sic*]

Click Here   Foreign Brides, International Russian Women, Oriental Girls & Latin Ladies

ASIANDATE.COM
Meet 1,000 Single Asian Women online

There are several types of 'bride' sites. Scholes (1999) distinguishes between various aspects of Internet bride trading as follows:

1. International correspondence services which post women's names, photos and descriptions on their websites (which is free to the

women). Men seeking to make contact pay a fee of about $2–$5 for each mailing address.

2. Companies which promote, organise and sponsor group tours to countries where interested women may be found.

3. Email pen-pal clubs which are generally free of charge. Men and women provide a biography, email address and an indication of the type of relationship they seek.

Here we are primarily concerned with the first category, an example of which is Mail-OrderBrides.com which is, in its own words, 'A Directory of Online International Dating, Romance, Introduction Matchmaking Agencies and Related Services'. It claims to provide the world's 'largest quality index of links' to other sites providing lists of women seeking marriage. The adverts on the first page of this site entice the viewer to 'Click Here NOW – you could have this problem too! Exciting and rewarding foreign romance tours'. Once on a listings site customers are presented with women's photographs for perusal, and many sites provide search facilities which allow the searcher to browse by a particular feature such as age group. As the advertisements above indicate, a degree of exoticism is also at play and men are frequently encouraged to select women on the basis of their 'otherness'. Naked pictures may be available and descriptions of waist, height, breast size and so forth can border on the pornographic. As such, many of these sites produce degrading and exploitative images that objectify women as sexual and secondary beings and suggest that the men selecting brides from such sites are not seeking an 'equal' sexual relationship. Not only can the purchaser select the 'model' of woman he seeks in the same way he might buy a car, he can also access all the other necessary business information, in just the same way as he would select a dealer and car loan firm! But in contrast to the sexualised portrayals of women found in the majority of website marketing, many men who have used such services claim to be seeking other attributes. A 1988 survey by Jedlicka (cited in Glodava and Onizuka 1994) found that most of the American men who married women via mail-order bride services talked about seeking a wife who shared their desire for traditional values; that is, to be homemaker for a bread-winning husband. Again, this seems to be a desire for unequal relationships: in this case, relationships that assume dependency and ownership.

Those seeking a bride are offered a 'choice of women' who, according to Scholes (1999), can be 'broken down' into four categories – Asian, Latin, multi-ethnic and Soviet based. Our own searches showed that, by 2002, other regions of the world such as Africa had been added to the list. Asian women portrayed on mail-order bride sites tend to be younger than women from other areas: the analysis reported by Scholes showed that 61 per cent of Asian women were under 25 but for Soviet-based women just 31 per cent were under 25. It might be assumed that older women retain a greater degree of autonomy and agency, but as Phizacklea (1996) shows, all women – whatever their age, background or characteristics – are treated as nothing more than objects for sale in a quest for profit which, of necessity, upholds many of the aspects of competitive marketing normally employed on other 'products'. Hence prospective buyers are warned of the extra financial outlay attached to women of certain nationalities: 'Whereas a Thai is unprepared for cold German winters – one has to buy her clothes – a Pole brings her own boots and fur coat. And she is as good in bed and as industrious in the kitchen' (ibid.: 168). Mail-order bride agencies have rapidly adopted the medium of the Internet to promote their trade, due to the ability of the Net to reach a 'prime group of potential buyers – men from western countries with higher than average incomes' (Hughes 1998/9: 24) through a technology which provides quick, easy and up-to-date information. Feminist critics of such agencies have rightly pointed to the anti-feminism of such sites which classify the women online as untarnished by factors which might make women local to the purchaser 'undesirable': 'American women are thought not content to be wives and mothers but seek personal satisfaction through their own careers and interests, while the foreign woman is happy to be the homemaker and asks for nothing more than husband, home, and family. Again, true or not, this is the perception' (Scholes 1999: unpaginated). It is true that the mail-order bride trade has taken advantage of the Internet but trade in brides is itself hardly new. Historical evidence points to the fact that one solution proffered for the supposed 'surplus' of women in Britain detailed by the 1851 census was migration to become the wives of men in the British colonies often via proxy ceremonies (Worsnop 1990). None the less, what the Internet has provided is a medium through which more women can be put up on offer to more men in more countries. Such a growth has been of concern to feminist activists who fear that the increase in mail-order websites, which frequently contain links to pornographic sites (or are themselves porno-graphic in the presentation of the women), constitutes a major threat to women. In fact Butterworth (1993) argues that the web has facilitated the rapid publication of information enabling men to pimp individual women and as such advances the sexual exploitation of women across the world.

Buying babies

Just as there are a multiplicity of 'bride' sites, there are many adoption, surrogacy and 'gametes for sale' sites. Here we focus on the presentation of children on one site – which we will call Adopt.com – and on a number of gametes for sale sites offering ova, sperm and surrogacy arrangements.

Adoption

> Licensed in five states and eleven countries – working with families everywhere. *Babies are waiting in Vietnam, Cambodia, Romania, China and Kazakstan* [*sic*].

> New Families Inc. is able to provide prospective adoptants with assignments in weeks, not months. Placing healthy infants from Central America. No application fees.

Adopt.com provides prospective parents with much the same kind of information as bride sites (through databases referred to under the banner titles of 'Waiting Child Photolisting'). As with bride sites, legal and practical details such as how to adopt are provided, as are email lists for prospective and completed adopters to exchange information. Under their lists of 'waiting' children (which implies a degree of agency by the child which cannot possibly exist), children are identified by a code number and a brief description based on sex, age, medical status and country of origin. An example of the information supplied on the web about a child is as follows:

> A head and shoulder shot of child
> Child's ID number
> Gender
> Birth date
> Race
> Eye colour
> Hair colour
> Health condition

Although this implies that children from all backgrounds may be available, the reality is that most are from areas suffering from economic hardship. On one visit 208 children were listed (with 17 agencies) mostly as individuals but a very few as sibling groups. What was striking is the number of children from Kazakhstan – 92 in total. Others described as

Eastern European equalled 75 and Russian equalled 11 with the remainder containing 8 Guatemalans and the rest generically described as Asian. This appears to indicate that Internet baby traffickers assume adopters will prefer children who appear to be genetically European. So although 'exoticism' appears to be a plus when purchasing a bride, 'otherness' is rejected when buying children (although there are sites specialising in inter-ethnic adoption). This is not surprising given the findings of Freundlich and Phillips (2000: 13), who state that for inter-country adoption:

> The forces exerted by the competitiveness and individualism of the market in the context of adoption raise a host of ethical issues… Increasingly, children are available for adoption at a price, with some, for example white babies, 'costing' more than others. Arguably families with resources are exploited through high fees. Perhaps trade and payment are an inevitable part of adoption.

Yet the reality of inter-country adoption is that 'in the majority of cases inter-country adoptees are far less likely than children born in the UK to be adopted by families of similar ethnicity' (ibid: 12).

Searching for an adoption site on the Internet is very simple. Accessing children's details is also quickly and easily achieved. Given the proliferation of such sites, many of them mediated through US-based organisations, it is rather surprising to find that in the professional and academic literature on adoption little is made of such services. In fact, a search of such literature for this chapter uncovered no material specific to Internet adoption in conventional journals. However, many of the issues are related less to the means of locating and identifying a child to adopt than to the process of adopting from overseas – a practice which is not without its difficulties, problems and critics.

Strict rules apply to all inter-country adoptions. In Britain adoption via the Internet involves the same process as any adoption from overseas. The applicants go through an assessment (a home study) to determine suitability and increasingly this is being presented to local authority panels and not just agencies panels (Fiddy 2001). The recent well publicised case of the Kilshaws illustrates the cacophony of criticism which falls upon those who circumnavigate this process as they did. In brief, the Kilshaws, a married couple from the UK, paid a baby broker at the Caring Hearts Agency in California £8,200 to arrange the adoption of 6-month-old twins, Belinda and Kimberley. However, another couple, the Allens from California, had previously paid the same broker £4,000 to adopt the children who had been in their foster care for two months. The birth mother asked to spend two days with the babies before finally relinquishing them for adoption, but during that time she handed them to the Kilshaws who fled to Arkansas with the babies and their mother and completed fast-track adoption proceedings before returning with the twins to their home in North Wales. However the local social services removed the children from the care of the Kilshaws after an emergency protection order was granted under the Children Act 1989, and placed them with foster carers in the UK. The Kilshaws were then subjected to a hate campaign by the British media, who questioned their morals, their finances, their marriage and their mental stability.

Yet, as Fiddy points out, it is entirely foreseeable that people wishing to adopt a baby, or who fail the assessment process in their own country, will still wish to consider inter-country adoption. Presumably those who fail the assessment process seek such adoptions to avoid the restraints of assessment and refusal. However, this is not to say that the legal and social work professions condone such actions, as Fiddy (2001: 13) argues: 'the Kilshaws' case justifies the need for assessment procedures and the regulation of inter-country adoption.' All inter-country adoption presents particular problems regarding ethical practice, and the use of the Internet to facilitate the process is no different in this respect. Reporting on an international conference on the role of ethics in adoption held at the Evan B. Donaldson Institute based in New York, Freundlich and Phillips (2000: 9) pointed out that 'Inter-country adoption was seen as presenting unique challenges to children's and adopter's rights to accurate and truthful background information…Some US adoption agencies require prospective adopters to sign disclaimers for liability by agencies for concealing information about children'. This 'opt out' for responsibility is clearly disadvantageous to the child as the agency has no requirement to ensure accuracy of records and thus a child seeking information later finds not answers but deficits.

The conference criticised inter-country adoption agencies in several ways, not least for providing false information and documents about prospective adopters to government agencies in the child's home country and therefore circumventing the criteria determined by the child's country of origin. They were also criticised for acting in ways which are 'ethnocentric and a blatant disregard of that country's beliefs and culture' (ibid.). Our fear is that although the Internet may have many responsible agencies, it can also provide a forum for many which may not be so. However, we question whether those who adopt via the Internet are any more 'deviant' in societal terms than others who build their families in alternative manners. Where criminal activity may lie is if those seeking to adopt attempt to avoid the checks and restrictions of government agencies within their own countries, and/or individuals or agencies misrepresent adopters to government bodies in the child's country of origin.

Gametes

> We are proud to announce the arrival of our new Egg Donor database on the Internet! Our database offers color photos and profiles of over 300 Egg Donors

> [sperm] Donor of the Month

Given that adoption cannot guarantee a 'child like your own' some prefer (for example, if one partner is fertile or the woman can carry but not conceive) to get closer to having their 'own' child. This can be achieved through the purchase of gametes (that is, eggs and sperm) or surrogacy services. FamilyMaking.com is a site specialising in egg donation and surrogacy. This and other similar sites allow you to view the donor and to choose your donor by her physical appearance. There is recognition here that 'a physical match is usually required' but we would suggest that a donor's 'looks' (as in her stereotypical attractiveness) appear to be as important as 'a physical match': a possible case of improving on the 'natural'?

From this it would appear that the feminist concerns of the early 1980s were warranted. At this time a group called FINRRAGE (Feminist International Network of Resistance to Reproductive and Genetic Engineering) argued that the new reproductive technologies (NRTs) clearly expose the politics of male supremacy in that they represent the purposes of big business on a global scale and are therefore harmful, especially to women. As Spallone (1989: 2) argues: 'clearly the technologies were not invented to serve women's needs but the various needs and desires of medical science, research science and the state, to further technological progress and to aid population control aims, all of which requires the use of women to those ends'. Further to this, Corea *et al* (1985: 39) add that NRTs turn human reproduction into a 'brothel system' in which 'women can sell reproductive capacities (i.e. eggs and wombs) the same way old time prostitutes sold sexual ones'. As Wajcman (1991) notes, embedded in this approach is a conception of science and technology as intrinsically patriarchal.

What then of sperm donation? The first thing to note is that it is a lot less traumatic in terms of physical and emotional trauma to donate sperm than to donate eggs or to act as a surrogate. Yet some common factors are to be found on sperm donation sites as on egg/surrogacy sites. In the case of all gamete donation we found that Internet sites provided information, and even search engines, through which it is possible to select specific genetic characteristics, permitting potential purchasers to create a physical match to themselves and/or their partners. Interestingly, although the producers of sperm donor sites are aware of the need for 'a physical match' in the same ways as are egg sites, no egg donor/ surrogate site we found allowed the purchaser to specify intelligence whereas 'high-achiever' sperm donors are the highlight of several sites.

Clearly, the presentation of eggs and sperm for sale does little more than reproduce existing societal values with regard to male and female attributes and adds weight to Hanmer's (1997: 372) view that women need to organise to '[R]efuse the new eugenics and the racism, anti-semiticism, heterosexism and able-bodiedism on which the new reproductive and genetic technologies are built; to resist the extension of the division of women into body parts, objectified and reduced to the carriers of male genetic material'. Evidence from the Internet suggests that it is precisely the forces against which Hanmer argues that are being promoted. There is certainly a long way to go before society employs the Internet to ensure that the 'star-like potential of information technologies is directed towards enhancing human well-being rather than strengthening existing power monopolies' (Arizpe 1999: xv). The differential values ascribed to the genetic material supplied by women and by men, and the information supplied about such material, indicates a continuation and a representation of existing values regarding gender. None the less, it is not technology per se that is at issue here. The Internet, like NRTs, is not itself a danger; what is dangerous is the use of such technologies in ways which can increase social and economic inequities. Stanworth's (1987: 35) argument regarding reproductive technologies is also relevant to information technology in that 'It is not technology as an "artificial invasion of the human body" that is at issue – but whether we can create the political and cultural conditions in which such tech-nologies can be employed by women to shape the experience of repro-duction according to their own definition'. The current presentation of gametes for sale does provide some opportunity for women to purchase the genetic material they require and to increase their autonomy with regard to reproductive choices. However, the presentation of female gametes for sale, with its majority focus on the physical attributes (i.e. conventional 'attractiveness') of the donor compared to the choice of intellectual or high-achieving (as well as physical) attributes of the donors of male gametes (sperm), merely belies the value judgements associated with male and female. As such, those involved in the purchase of gametes to create their families can be seen to be conforming to societal norms more than deviating from them. What is construed as deviant in popular discourses is the active seeking of gametes, yet this is surprising given that sperm donation has a long-established history and a degree of acceptability, as Pfeffer (1993: 158) points out:

> During the 1970s, heterosexual intercourse posed a far greater threat to the institutions of marriage and the family than the syringe of donated semen wielded by a doctor. The former was out of control and its effects unknown, whereas certainty and morality were assured in the latter by the doctor responsible for its arrangement. A now famous study had suggested that six out of every twenty babies born to married women had been fathered by someone other than their mothers' husbands.

Consumers or carers/victims or agents?

We now turn to a consideration of the social construction of the purchaser as caring and altruistic or self-serving, exploitative and even desperate, and alongside this consider the socially constructed status of the purchased as passive victim or active agent. Interestingly notions of true femininity and womanhood operate in discourses surrounding the woman as purchased (as in 'brides') and as purchaser of child or potential child. Domestic and sexual availability to men and biological and practical motherhood are key aspects of historical and contemporary conceptions of 'ideal womanhood' (Smith 1989; Letherby 1994; Ussher 1997). Hegemonic masculinity, closely linked as it is to the institution of marriage and to genetic procreation, is also significant to any understanding of the buying of women and children via the Internet (Connell 1987; Katz Rothman 1994).

Husbands and wives

The popular discourse surrounding men who buy brides is that they are pathetic and inadequate, unable to attract a woman by the more accepted routes of western courtship. However, Jedlicka's survey of American men seeking mail-order brides found that 94 per cent of the men were white and 50 per cent were college educated. Most were economically and professionally successful, with 64 per cent earning more than $20,000 a year and 42 per cent in professional or managerial positions (Jedlicka 1988, cited in Glodava and Onizuka 1994). So, stereotypically at least, it

77

would appear that these men were likely to be 'eligible' to women in their own communities and country. However, if we look again at Jedlicka's study it is possible to argue that the issue is not whether the men themselves are appropriate husband material but, as noted above, that they themselves are rejecting contemporary western marriage and partnerships.

Popular discourses surrounding women who offer themselves as brides are frequently judgemental and disapproving, often positioning the women as victims of their husbands and the agencies. While we would not argue against this view in general, we present an alternative interpretation of the situation of women. That is, rather than viewing all women on mail-order Internet sites as victimised and exploited, we argue that, for some, seeking such a marriage may be an act of agency. Admittedly it may be interpreted as an act of *limited* agency, for truly free women would not need to seek such a marriage, but it may be the only kind of agency available to women who are entrapped in social and economic structures which limit their life opportunities. Evidence from the USA supports the conclusion that women are seeking improved life chances by offering themselves on 'bride' sites, for they 'for the most part, come from places in which jobs and educational opportunities for women are scarce and wages low' (US Government Report on the Mail-Order Bride Industry, at www.wtw.org/mob/mobappa.htm). None the less, when representing themselves, the women avoid economic and social arguments preferring to use discourses of attraction and personal taste: 'When the women themselves are asked this question, the answer generally indicates an attraction to American men (they look like movie stars) and an aversion to native men' (ibid.).

The actions of mail-order brides can be construed as simply another form of women's migration with the same driving forces: 'poverty, displacement from the land, debt, and many other external constraints over which they have little control. These problems are shared with men, though their impact is always gendered' (Kofman *et al* 2000: 21). Yet migration is an act of agency and resistance (ibid.) and the forms of agency chosen are also often gendered. Men may migrate to urban or industrial areas and work in public spheres whereas women may seek positions as domestic servants or maids, or as wives, as a means of escaping oppressive structures. As such existing migration theory, which situates migrants as passive, has been criticised: 'once agency is put firmly in the same frame as structural context, we can begin to analyse in a rather different way migrant women's economic contribution and their efforts to improve their own (and their family's) standard of living' (ibid.: 25–26).

This highlights the danger of seeing all such women as lacking agency for it is all too easy to classify women who migrate to work as maids or to become brides as victims. Yet for some it is an active choice through which they can improve their own life chances and those of their families. Of course, this is not to say that mail-order brides are not imaged as sexualised, exotic and available, and as such we agree with Kofman *et al* who conclude that 'Thai women in Germany, many of whom have entered as mail-order brides, have become totally sexualised and regarded with utmost suspicion. Yet we should be wary of categorizing all mail-order brides in the same way' (ibid.: 70).

But even if we characterise Internet matches as an act of agency, that is not to say that they are necessarily without danger for the women involved. Danger can exist purely in the unequal power dynamics such arrangements establish. Given that it appears that the men seeking such unions have traditional views of marriage, what conflicts might arise if the women whom they marry – women who have had the strength of character and resilience to place themselves in the mail-order bride market in the first place – continue to act in an assertive and self-determining manner? A further consideration has to be the influence of immigration procedures which permit aliens to remain in the 'host' country only as long as their marriage continues. British immigration rules apply a 'one year' rule which places many women who enter the UK to marry (be they mail-order brides, arranged marriages or love matches) to remain with their husband for at least one year or face the penalty of deportation. Evidence gathered by feminist groups such as Southall Black Sisters shows that this law can be a licence for violent men to abuse, for if their wife seeks to leave she faces deportation[1] (Dunne 1997). Such legislation *removes* agency from migrant wives and positions them in a situation of legally imposed passivity. Thus, the situation for mail-order brides can be one of contradiction and danger; their own agency can result in outcomes which also have the potential for victimhood. An Australian example illustrates the gamble some women take:

Many Filipinas married to Australian men bitterly resent those who see them as mail-order brides, a stereotype that encourages their treatment as exotic/available Asian women, or as passive victims… Some women did enter Australia as part of the trade, seeking an Australian husband for better opportunities for themselves and their children and resources for family at home, including sponsorship of others to migrate. In this they were acting as agents and making what they could of arrangements…However, compounding male domestic power with being out-of-place and isolated makes these marriages deadly for some women and difficult for others.

(Pettman 1996: 194)

Agency exists in a variety of degrees and it seems logical to conclude that women involved in 'pen-pal' correspondence which may lead to more intimate relationships (Scholes' third category) have a greater opportunity to 'control' their contacts. However, this agency is limited to those who already have some social advantages, since these services require access to computers. The women thus tend to be older and better educated than those listed on agency bride sites and are more likely to reside in more developed countries such as Japan and Russia (Scholes 1999).

This fits neatly with observations regarding other uses of the Internet by women. Agustin (1999) points out, in response to the exhortations to women to empower themselves through the use of ICTs, that empowerment can only be enacted by those who are already empowered to some degree as 'to use the World Wide Web and even the simplest email programme, after all, requires a very high level of literacy' (ibid.: 151). Thus, the women who might have some degree of control over how they are presented on the web are likely to be those who already have some advantage. The most vulnerable women remain the most vulnerable.

Parents and children

In considering the presentation of potential parents and children on the web it is necessary to consider the social categories of motherhood and fatherhood and the value judgements they contain. Academic analyses of societal views of childlessness indicate that childless women have been frowned upon as not 'real' women:

A woman's capacity to create, bear and nurture a child is the very essence of her womanhood…When a woman has a child, she confirms for herself and for others that she is a complete woman, fertile and capable of the biological task of creating and perpetuating life.

(Ashurst and Hall 1989: 97)

As one of us has argued elsewhere, women without children still represent the 'other'. Thus:

For many people, 'childless' implies a person with something missing from her life, whether she is described as being 'childless' in a 'voluntary' or 'involuntary' manner, although the former women are more often viewed as selfish while the latter frequently incur pity. Either way, mothers are seen as 'proper' women, while women without children are perceived as 'improper' and treated as 'other'. They are also treated as childlike rather than fully adult...Thus, women who have no children are considered to have no responsibilities and thus to be like children themselves.

(Letherby and Williams 1999: 723)

Arguably fatherhood does not have the same significance to manhood as motherhood does to womanhood. However, male 'infertility'[2] is linked to masculinity as the man without children is often subject to cruel humour about his surmised lack of sexual performance (see, for example, Exley and Letherby 2001). It is interesting to compare this discourse of 'inadequacy' with the one directed at the man who purchases a bride. The first implies that one can get a woman but not get her pregnant, while the second suggests that one may be potent but cannot get a woman through 'normal channels'. The man who falls into the latter category – with his unchallenged potential to procreate – better fits the image of a 'real' man than does the former.

Franklin (1990) notes that the discourses of social loss, biological identity and medical hope that predominate in contemporary popular academic and 'scientific' publications all operate to give us a picture of 'infertility' and 'involuntary childlessness' that supports the dominant social order. Thus, it is possible to argue that the public exposure given to these issues over recent years has added to the stigma of the condition (e.g. Petchesky 1987; Franklin 1990). In particular, the media presents a stereotypical image of infertility. As Franklin (1990: 218) notes: 'The typical description of the infertile is one that emphasizes their "desperation", "anguish" and "suffering" and refers to them as the "victims of childlessness", or "unwillingly childless", "involuntarily childless" or as the "sufferers of infertility".' From our observations of the various websites offering male and female gametes for sale, the views expressed above regarding the desperation and anguish of the 'infertile' are reflected in the manner in which services are marketed and these presentations are very gendered. Sites offering eggs and/or surrogacy present a 'tasteful', sensitive and empathetic approach to the issue of female infertility whereas our research uncovered sperm donation sites that were less romantically presented and provided a faster route to the basic factual information regarding the genetic attributes of the sperm on offer. We suggest that this is due to the fact that those seeking eggs or surrogates are primarily couples where the woman is infertile whereas those seeking sperm are either couples where the male is infertile or single women and, as such, reflects a perceived need to be sympathetic to the 'unfortunate' infertile woman but not to discuss a man's inability to produce sperm (or adequate sperm) for that would challenge his manhood. As such, it appears that dominant ideologies of gender and family affect women's and men's experience of the pursuit of a baby via gamete purchase.

In contemporary western society, issues of kinship and the biological tie (Strathern 1992) and the fear of 'genetic death' (Houghton and Houghton 1984) are important, a fact demonstrated not least by the rise of surrogacy, the posthumous use of sperm to 'father' children and gamete purchasing. Arguably, it is not just the lack of babies available for adoption that leads more individuals to attempt to create a family through medically assisted conception but the fact that biological (and if at all possible genetic) motherhood/parenthood go alongside dominant discourses of 'true motherhood' and 'proper' families (Wegar 1997; Letherby 1999). Therefore, if a genetic link to at least one parent (i.e. when buying sperm or eggs) is possible, the couple can 'legitimately' present the child as their 'own'. Here we see the difference when buying brides and babies; an exotic wife is presented as an asset (though given discourses of inadequacy this is somewhat surprising) whereas if feasible, a child should look as much like his or her parents as possible.[3]

Whereas it is possible to argue that the women offering themselves as brides are acting through their own agency, this is obviously not the case for children (or potential children) who are acquired via the Internet. Given the high profile of the aforementioned Kilshaws, it is instructive to consider this case as an illustration of the use of the Internet to make a family. It appears to us that it is often the process of *constructing* a family rather than letting one 'emerge naturally' which is criticised. Using the Internet to find potential family members – be they actual or potential children – has added to this critique, as illustrated by the following quotation: 'The sad case of Belinda and Kimberley, the "Internet twins", has highlighted the stark reality that, with the aid of the Internet, money can buy virtually anything – even babies' (Fiddy 2001: 12).

In the West the private sector caters for the majority of patients undergoing treatment for assisted conception. Not surprisingly, then, the discourse of consumerism has invaded the medical literature and popular culture (Pfeffer 1993). For example in the UK *The Independent* newspaper has published guidelines on 'How to choose a test-tube baby clinic' – a guide to cost, accessibility, convenience and 'take home baby rates'. Yet, there is still a prevalent view that children are a 'gift from God' and that no one has the 'right' to that gift, a broadly conservative argument that coincides with the traditional right-wing view that media in general, and new media in particular, are of weak cultural status and appeal to the 'lowest common denominator' of society. The argument prevails, then, that women and men who pay for assisted conception and/or who buy gametes and children via the Internet are 'putting a price' on a priceless 'commodity', taking a decision that is not theirs to take through an inappropriate channel, and are thus unworthy and selfish parents. Yet, it is possible to argue that women and men who buy children or potential children on the Net are no more selfish than any other type of parent. Although Triseliotis (2000) suggests that compassion, humanitarianism and altruism are important aspects of international adoption all parenting could be construed as an act of altruism and equally all parents, genetic, biological, social, are likely to have non-altruistic reasons for raising children.

Artificial or real families?

All of us are socialised by societal views and culture. An aspect of western socialisation is the predominance of the traditional patriarchal nuclear family. Such dominance is both reflected in, and reinforced by, government policies. Although family forms vary extensively, with kinship links being both social and biological, the nuclear family is assumed by policy-makers to be the preferred form:

> Despite increasing rates of single parenting, divorce and alternative family groupings, economic, immigration and social policies are still shaped by this assumption. This results in public and social policies being both proscriptive and prescriptive...with fiscal benefits being accrued by heterosexual couples and child support policies ensuring a link of economic dependency between parents.
>
> (Marchbank 2000: 29)

As such, successive governments have provided strong messages about the image of the 'ideal' family. Even the current UK (Labour) government, the first to produce a consultation paper on the family, *Supporting Families* (HMSO 1998), still puts stress on the nuclear family as the most desirable type of family: 'Many lone parents and unmarried couples raise their children every bit as successfully as married parents. But marriage is still the surest foundation for raising children and remains the choice of the majority of people in Britain' (ibid.: unpaginated). There is a hierarchy of family forms, in which not only are 'created' families subject to societal judgements but so too are families created from different traditions, as shown in the negative presentations in western media regarding arranged marriages among communities originating from South East Asia. Even though arranged marriages also provide a patriarchal family they are considered less favourable than Judeo-Christian nuclear families which seem to be the most highly valued. In other words, it is the 'natural' as opposed to the 'created' patriarchal nuclear family which is depicted as the ideal both in politics and in society more generally. When wives and children are 'bought' rather than attracted or conceived in ways that are considered to be 'natural', their purchase is likely to attract hostility and moral censure. Individuals and couples who aim to create families by buying brides and babies via the Internet may be trying to find a way to meet the idealised 'norm', but society on the whole may view the buying of brides and babies as deviant activities. It is also necessary to consider for whom the family is ideal anyway. As Stanley and Wise (1993) argue, many women distinguish between the family as an institution and their own family. They argue that women often see the former as the desirable ideal while the latter is experienced as not meeting their expectations. Furthermore, the family is now recognised as a major site of physical abuse and male power over women and children (Dobash and Dobash 1980; Stanko 1985; Robertson Elliot 1986). The ideal of family that is held up by critics of those whose creation of family involves some kind of financial transaction is thus itself frequently a myth.

Brief reflections

Given the amount of pornography available via the Internet it might be expected that a search for literature on women and the web would primarily address issues of exploitation. However, this is not the case; in fact, the majority of published material about women and the web by feminists and non-feminists appears to be about women's use of the Net for liberational purposes. For example, Harcourt (1999) provides a range of articles addressing the ways in which women can use the web for their own advantage and for campaigning: 'women must now be active agents in experimenting and interpreting the new forms of communication that the new technologies offer us' (Arizpe 1999: xiii). Exceptions to this material include Butterworth (1993), Hughes (1998/9) and Gillespie (2000) who all write about Internet violence and exploitation. The work that we present here adds to this tradition. However, as we have suggested buying brides and babies online is not as simplistically deviant as may first appear, for the Internet both exacerbates and complicates existing power relations in society.

As well as having a place in a book concerned with criminal and deviant activity on the Internet we hope this chapter is relevant to discussion and debate about consumption in late modernity. Bostock (1993) suggests that the identities (including gender identities) of consumers are constructed through the items they buy which certainly seems to be the case for the husbands and parents represented here. However, as Bostock (ibid.) adds, consumption is increasingly related to desires rather than needs and is linked to lifestyle choices. As we have argued here, one's lifestyle choice is frequently influenced by the socially constructed 'ideal' and so-called 'deviant' behaviour may in fact be a person's only possibility of getting close to the myth of the ideal family.

Notes

1. Southall Black Sisters research showed that between January 1994 and July 1995, 755 women were threatened with deportation because of marriage breakdown. Some 512 of these were because of domestic violence. Only 3.2 per cent of the deportees were white (Dunne 1997).
2. We present 'infertility' in quotation marks to indicate the problems associated with this term.
3. We acknowledge that 'physical matching' is not always an issue: single and lesbian women use sperm donor sites and many people who adopt both 'at home' and through international links do not intend to present their social children as biologically their own.

Chapter 6

What a tangled web we weave: identity theft and the Internet

Emily Finch

Introduction

Following the news of the Paddington rail crash in October 1999, Lee Simm reported his flatmate, Karl Hackett, missing. According to Simm, Hackett had been due to return from a trip to Cheltenham on the train that crashed. No trace of Hackett's body was found and his family, from whom he had been estranged for more than ten years, were notified and attended a memorial service at the site of the crash. It later transpired that Hackett had not been killed in the train crash; he had not even been on the train. However, it was discovered that his flatmate, Simm, who reported Hackett missing, had been dead for 15 years. In order to escape his criminal record, Hackett adopted Simm's identity after his friend committed suicide. Hackett went on to live a blameless life using Simm's name and other personal details and would probably have remained undetected had he not decided to 'kill off' his former self in the rail crash (*The Sunday Times* 2000: 14).

Such a wholesale and enduring absorption of another's persona provides a relatively uncommon example of identity theft. The Hackett/ Simm case is unusual in that identity theft typically involves a partial and transient adoption of another's identity undertaken in order to facilitate criminal activity. Identity theft spans a wide spectrum of conduct that covers varying degrees of fraudulent behaviour. This chapter will begin with a consideration of the nature of identity, focusing on the disparity between individual, social and legal constructions of identity, and explore what it means for a person's identity to be stolen. Having outlined the various manifestations of identity theft, the chapter will go on to consider factors that have contributed to the growth of identity theft in recent years, with particular reference to the contribution of the Internet. The chapter will conclude by considering two means by which identity theft may be tackled; first, by technological advances that make the misuse of another's identity more difficult and, secondly, by the creation of a specific criminal offence to encompass conduct that has come to be known as identity theft.

Identity and identifiability

It is necessary to determine at the outset what is meant by 'identity'. From simplistic origins, identity has evolved into a complex and multifaceted concept that plays a central role in delineating the parameters of, *inter alia*, ethnicity, nationality and citizenship, thus generating an immense amount of debate across various disciplines (Gleason 1983; Williams 2001; Bendle 2002). In relation to identity theft, the concern is with identity as a means of ascertaining individuality and establishing person-hood rather than as a basis for establishing collective identity or group membership. Even within this narrower sphere, there are competing constructions of identity that jostle for supremacy (Perry 1975; Sider 2001). For the purpose of this discussion, a relatively straightforward tripartite categorisation of identity can be adopted based upon the categorisation used by Goffman, albeit using different terminology: individual identity, social identity and legal identity (Goffman 1963).

Individual identity can be seen as the sense of self that is based upon the internalisation of all that is known about oneself. For Goffman, the key characteristics of what he termed – after Freud – 'id' (or felt) identity are subjectivity and reflexivity. Hence individual identity is more than simply self-perception; rather, it is the subjective construction of the self that is modified by reflections on the views of others and the individual's interactions in the social world. As such, individual identity is not a static construction but one that is constantly evolving and readjusting in line with the individual's life experience. Although individuals do not remain the same, they retain a sense of sameness throughout their lives that is based, according to Locke's (1690) *Essay Concerning Human Understanding*, on the sense of continuity that arises from being able to remember being other than one is at present (in other words, unlike other animals, human beings possess a unique sense of themselves in the past as children or even babies, and can also project forward to envisage themselves in old age; they also understand that they are mortal). Individual identity can be encapsulated as being 'what most of us think of when we think of the deepest and most enduring features of our unique selves that constitute who we believe ourselves to be' (Williams 2001: 7).

To a certain extent, there is a symbiotic relationship between individual and social identity in that social identity is contingent upon the way in which individuals present themselves while individual identity can be influenced by the way in which an individual is received in society. For Goffman, social identity is based upon the categorisation of an individual to determine the acceptability of the membership of certain social groups. It is concerned with attributes of an individual that may be intrinsic but are not necessarily so. If individual identity is concerned with the question of 'who am I', then social identity is concerned with the question 'what is the nature of this person'. Having qualified for membership of a particular group, certain other characteristics may be ascribed to the individual by virtue of membership regardless of whether or not they are actually possessed by the individual. Social and individual identity will necessarily differ from each other for various reasons, not the least of which is that the internal and external views of the individual are based upon different information. Although both individual and social identity may be affected by identity theft, neither can be stolen. It is the third category of identity – legal identity – that has the potential to be adopted and abused by others; hence it is at the heart of concerns about identity theft.

By way of contrast to the other categories of identity, legal identity tends to be largely fixed and immutable. Goffman describes legal identity in terms of a set of characteristics that are unique to the individual thus providing a way in which one person can be differentiated from another. Similarly, the preoccupation of the law is to 'impose durable identities' (Torpey 2000: 166) in order to ensure that two inter-related questions – 'who is this person?' and 'is this the same person?' – can be answered. Therefore, it is clear that the legal construction of identity gives primacy to factual information regarding an individual; information that is largely unalterable. For example, birth certification is generally viewed as the foundation of legal identity as it records key pieces of information unique to the individual such as his or her sex, date and place of birth and details of his or her parents. Despite strenuous opposition, the English courts have steadfastly maintained that a birth certificate is a historical record of fact that cannot be amended retrospectively at the behest of the individual to whom it relates (*Cossey* v. *United Kingdom* [1991] 2 FLR 492; *Sheffield* v. *United Kingdom* [1998] 2 FLR 928). This illustrates the degree of permanence attached to legal identity and makes it clear that when legal and individual identity conflict, it is legal identity that prevails. As an individual progresses through life, the information on his or her birth certificate is supplemented by further details, thus contributing to the cumulative mass of facts that constructs the composite legal person. This is described by Foucault as a process that 'places individuals in a field of surveillance [and also] situates them in a network of writing; it engages them in a whole mass of documents that capture and fix them' (Foucault 1979: 189).

Foucault's reference to an individual being captured within a network of documents is particularly apt as it suggests that once an individual is enmeshed within this documentary web, it is virtually impossible for him or her to escape. As such, legal identity is more concerned with identifiability rather than identity as it seeks to make the link between a collection of facts and the person to whom they relate. The permanence of legal identity can lead to difficulties where there is significant conflict with individual identity. The clash of two polarised constructions of the identity of the same person can ultimately lead to identity theft if the individual concerned is desperate to escape from some unwanted aspect of his or her legal identity. This was the situation in the Hackett/Simm case where a new identity was adopted in order to escape the implications of an unalterable aspect of the legal identity – a criminal record. However, there are various manifestations of identity theft involving differing levels of absorption of another's identity and numerous motivations for engaging in this conduct. Having explored the nature of identity, the discussion that follows will consider what it means for identity to be stolen and examine the range of situations in which identity theft may occur.

A typology of identity theft

The previous discussion has established that there are different facets of identity that are constructed according to whether a person is viewed from an individual, social or legal perspective; hence it could be said that everyone is simultaneously endowed with three distinct identities. However, not all these identities are capable of forming the subject matter of identity theft. Legal identity differs as, although it lacks a tangible physical presence in the same way as other types of identity, it can be made manifest by the production of documents or the possession of knowledge that substantiates the claim to be the person in question. The tangible 'thing' that is 'stolen' is the personhood of another as manifested by the assertion to be that person, which may or may not be supported by documentary or other evidence. As such, it involves the misuse of information that is specific to an individual in order to convince others that the impostor *is* the individual, effectively passing oneself off as someone else.

This broad definition encompasses two distinct types of identity theft that can be differentiated on the basis of three inter-related factors: duration, level of immersion and motivation. The duration of identity theft ranges from a single incident lasting only a few minutes to the lifelong use of another's personal information – effectively, living life *as* the victim. Duration is often associated with the level of immersion as long-term identity theft characteristically involves a greater penetration into the victim's personal details than a one-off incident or a short-term impersonation. The level of immersion refers to the depth with which the impostor delves into the victim's life and to the range and extent of the personal details that are misappropriated. Identity theft can result from the possession of the most basic details about an individual, such as name and date of birth, to more complex cases involving a deeper level of immersion whereby the impostor researches the victim to ascertain a range of personal and financial details, such as employment history, education and bank account details in order to masquerade successfully as the victim. Whatever the level of immersion, all these personal identifiers can be found on the Internet, as we will see shortly.

A combination of duration and level of immersion provides a possible basis for establishing a twofold categorisation of identity theft. A permanent adoption of all the details of the victim could be classified as total identity theft while the temporary use of some of the victim's personal details could be more appropriately termed partial identity theft. However, a more useful categorisation is suggested by consideration of a third factor, which is motivation of the impostor. Typically, partial identity theft involves the transient adoption of the victim's identity to the extent that is necessary to facilitate the commission of a criminal offence. This is epitomised by the approach taken to identity theft in the USA where the Identity Theft and Assumption Deterrence Act 1998 makes it an offence to 'knowingly transfer or use, without lawful authority, a means of identification of another person with the intent to commit, or aid and abet, any unlawful activity' (18 USC 1028 (a) (7) as amended by the Identity Theft and Assumption Deterrence Act 1998).

This approach clearly limits the parameters of identity theft to the deliberate abuse of another's personal information in order to commit a criminal offence. Certainly, this would appear to be the most prevalent form of identity theft as it accounts for the vast majority of partial identity theft and a significant proportion of cases of total identity theft. The paradigm example of partial identity theft involves the temporary assumption of another's identity in order to gain access to goods and services in the victim's name; an offence that has been inflated by the growth of online shopping. In this way, the impostor gains the benefits of the transactions while the cost is attributed to the victim. Other examples of partial identity theft involve the impersonation of the victim in order to engage in criminal activity that does not give rise to a direct financial detriment to the victim. Examples of this include the motorist who obtained another driver's licence in order to continue to drive in defiance of a period of disqualification and the shoplifter who used various aliases when she was arrested, ultimately accumulating convictions in over 20 different names (Newman 1999).

The desire to engage in criminal activities may also be the motivation for total identity theft. By adopting a different identity, the offender increases his or her chances of avoiding detection by ensuring that his or her acts are attributed to someone other than him or herself. Even if the victim is able to establish that he or she has been impersonated, this generally leave the authorities with few clues to point them in the direction of the real perpetrator. For example, Terry Rogan was arrested and detained for robbery and murder on five occasions before the police were able to locate and identify the person who had committed these crimes using Rogan's identity (*Rogan* v. *City of Los Angeles* 668 F Supp 1384 CD Cal 1987). Cases in which the usurpation of another's identity (in whole or in part) is motivated by the desire to engage in unlawful activities in the victim's name can be termed 'criminal identity theft'.

The motivation for total identity theft is often more complicated than a straightforward determination to avoid the consequences of participation in criminal activity or to facilitate fraudulent behaviour (Marx 2001). Total identity theft provides a way in which an individual can escape from a life that has gone wrong and obtain an opportunity to make a fresh start (Newman 1999). This urge to reinvent oneself may derive from a general sense of dissatisfaction with one's own identity or be a way to escape from some particularly problematic aspect of life such as debt or a traumatic relationship. Identity theft provides both a practical and symbolic respite from a life that has gone wrong by enabling the individual to escape the problem and to acquire a legal identity that is in accord with his or her perceived or desired individual identity. For example, Karl Hackett no longer regarded himself as a criminal having reached a decision to lead an honest life but he was unable to escape his background due to the provisions of the Rehabilitation of Offenders Act 1974. For that reason, he resorted to identity theft and adopted an identity that was in accord with his view of himself as a non-criminal. Cases such as this in which the overwhelming motivation of the impostor is to establish a new identity in order to avoid any further association with some aspect of his legal identity can be termed 'escape identity theft'.

The extent to which individuals will go in order to purge themselves of undesired attributes of their legal identity demonstrates the pressure that can be created when a conflict occurs between individual and legal identity. This is exacerbated by the increased range of situations in which people are required to provide various forms of identification in order to access services that often bear no relation to the information that is demanded (Westin and Baker 1972). According to Clarke (1994), this 'information richness' has become an imperative in late modern society and individuals who decline to provide the information are presumed to have 'something to hide'. This can have an exclusionary, stigmatising impact as individuals sometimes feel compelled to avoid seeking access to services that require the disclosure of what might be deemed 'unfavourable' personal information. For example, Marx (2001: 323) concludes that individuals may now feel a need to lie about facets of their lives that in the past were unseen, overlooked or forgotten. The tightening of the information net generates structural pressures to fabricate personal information.

The tightening of the information net

As there appears to be consensus among writers that burgeoning demands for identification have contributed to the increase in identity theft, it is important to examine the genealogy of the state's obsession with recording information about its citizens. Historically, people tended to live in small, self-contained and relatively static communities in which one's character was a matter of public knowledge and identification was automatic. The localisation of assistance for the poor was a disincentive to mobility for many and an itinerant criminal population was not viewed as problematic as punishment was largely immediate and corporeal. Records were kept locally but the lack of a fast and efficient communications system meant that it was not practically possible to share information with other localities. It was accepted that offenders tended to leave prison, change their names and move to another area, presumably to continue offending. Methods were developed that enabled the authorities to 'fix' individuals with an identity, such as anthropometry (that is, measurements of the body, skull, etc.) and photography, but these were not wholly reliable, and storage and distribution of the information remained an impediment to effective enforcement (Torpey 2000: 19). These developments were paralleled by a trend towards removing the control of information from local institutions, for example, the centralisation of record-keeping introduced by the Births and Deaths Registration Act 1837 and the abolition of the Speenhamland system by the Poor Law Amendment Act 1834 that removed the administration of poor relief from local parishes. This move towards centralised administration was furthered by the creation of measures that contributed towards the evolution of the welfare state, such the introduction of compulsory education, pensions, welfare benefits and free health care. The greater involvement of the state in the lives of the populace led to a more unified and referable system of information that played a significant role in increasing the identifiability of individuals.

An inevitable corollary of this was a growth in the range of situations in which individuals were required to identify themselves in order to establish their entitlement to these various services and benefits. Greater mobility of workers led to rapidly fluctuating community membership which also increased the need for identification as did the expansion of licensing and administration by the authorities. These factors combined to create an ethos of identifiability in which it was commonplace to be required to identify oneself and where an inability or reluctance to do so was increasingly viewed with suspicion (Clarke 1994). As identification became the key with which to access a range of services and benefits, the adoption of fraudulent identity in order to access that to which one was not entitled increased, particularly as organisations rarely looked beyond the documents presented to ascertain their validity. The piecemeal development of the record-keeping system, in particular the absence of effective cross-referencing, meant that there were inadequate safeguards in place to prevent fraud. The growth of fraud put increased pressure on the state to introduce a means of controlling access to benefits that precluded fraudulent claimants, which effectively required the evolution of even more stringent means of establishing legal identity. This in turn made it harder for those with 'spoiled' identities (Goffman 1963) to hide the unfavourable aspects of their identities, hence creating a greater level of exclusion and generating pressure to fabricate a more acceptable self.

Identity theft and the Internet

The incremental growth of the requirement of identifiability undoubtedly contributed towards the escalation in identity theft as some sought to engage in fraudulent behaviour and others saw the theft as the only way to 'escape' their own identity. However, this alone cannot account for the massive upsurge in identity theft that occurred towards the latter part of the twentieth century, and led the Federal Trade Commission (2000: 5) to label identity theft as 'the fastest growing crime of our time'. As information about the victim is the lifeblood of identity theft, the increased ease with which information can be accessed on the Internet could provide an explanation for the increase in identity theft.

As has been discussed, the 'tightening of the identity net' has led to a situation whereby individuals who are unhappy with an aspect of their legal identity may face a stark choice between disclosure of sensitive, and potentially prejudicial, information or exclusion from the many activities that require identifiability. According to Gary Marx (2001: 323), with contemporary forms of data collection, storage and retrieval, 'elements of the past that tended to be forgotten are now preserved. For better or worse elements of the individual's past cease to be past and instead are passed on'. However, the desire to create a new and unblemished identity would not contribute to the growth of identity theft to such a significant degree if it were not for the relative ease with which the knowledge that forms the foundations of identity can be acquired. In this respect, 'escape' identity theft and 'criminal' identity theft share common ground. Whether the impostor is in search of a new identity in order to escape from his or her own life, to commit criminal offences with impunity, to defraud a victim or even as a means of causing harassment to a victim, it has become a relatively straightforward matter to obtain the information that is needed effectively to adopt the identity of another (Newman 1999).

The Internet provides unparalleled opportunities for those seeking a new identity to access the necessary information. One of the anomalies of Internet use is that although 'it is much more difficult to verify identity and sincerity online…many users appear to be more trusting of those met online than those they encounter in person' (Rowland 1998: un-paginated). This leads Internet users to be far less security-minded in relation to their personal information when they are online than they are in 'real life' situations. Certainly, there is evidence to suggest that many Internet users are cautious about the safety of Internet transactions that require them to provide their debit or credit card details but there appears to be an almost reckless disregard for basic security precautions in relation to publication of any other personal information on the Internet. Detailed information regarding individuals may be available on personal or workplace websites as well as via professional organisations of which the individual is a member. In addition to this, information may be posted about individuals by third parties for a range of reasons and many organisations include searchable databases on their websites that may yield valuable information about potential victims. Information has become a valuable commodity and some websites exist solely for the purpose of trading in personal information. This situation is more advanced in the USA where information brokers will provide data about an individual's medical records, bank details, credit rating, criminal record, driving licence and vehicle registration documents for a small fee. In short, everything that the impostor needs to select a victim and misappropriate his or her identity is readily available on the Internet (Newman 1999).

Not only is the information-gathering process facilitated by the Internet but the task of selecting a profitable target with a good credit rating and a high income is made easier due to the availability of such wide-ranging personal information. The speed and accuracy of Internet search engines ensure that all references to a particular individual can be accumulated in a matter of seconds, hence accelerating the selection process. It is clear that the Internet provides virtually instantaneous access to the sort of information that would not otherwise be available without conducting a meticulous search into the victim's background. Although it has always been possible to access much of this personal information, it tended to involve visiting various organisations and conducting time-consuming manual searches to obtain just a fragment of information about an individual. The process of researching potential victims and accumulating all the necessary information to adopt their identity was a long and painstaking process that would previously have taken weeks or months. This information is now only a few keystrokes away and can be accessed easily from the impostor's home or office. As the Federal Trade Commission (2000: 5) report on identity theft states: 'The Internet provides access to identifying information, through both illicit and legal means. The global publication of identifying details that previously were available only to a select few increases the potential for misuse of that information.'

The ease with which personal information can be accessed is only one way in which the Net has contributed towards the growth in identity theft. Businesses have responded to the expansion of the Internet by offering online services that provide impostors with the opportunity to engage in fraudulent conduct 'at arms' length'. The Federal Trade Commission has argued that this provides a sense of anonymity that encourages fraudulent activity in individuals who would not risk behaving in this way in person. Thus, for example, an impostor can make an application for a loan, credit card or even a mortgage online or make purchases using a victim's credit card details. This is surely a more attractive option than going into shops and businesses where the fear of detection must be felt more acutely. The opportunity to 'shop from home' in this way enables the impostor to remain within his or her own territory thus eliminating the perceived sense of danger that is attached to engaging in fraudulent transactions in person. Moreover, there may be a sense of unreality attached to the process as all that is required to escape from what has happened is to switch off the computer in the manner of exiting a role-play game – what Suler (1996) calls the 'disinhibition effect' of the Internet.

In this respect, the Internet provides a distance, both spatially and symbolically, that enables a differentiation to be made between transactions carried out online and the equivalent transactions in real life. The perception that there is a lower risk of detection stems from the commonly held view of the Internet as an enforcement-free zone in which there is minimal legal regulation. This may free users from the constraints that inhibit criminal activity in real life, as there is an appearance of an absence of accountability for one's actions. Moreover, the acceptability of the use of pseudonyms on the Internet and the ease with which users are able to construct multiple identities also contribute to a sense of freedom from the constraints and conventions of everyday life. Marx (2001: 323) considers that the relative anonymity of the Internet is a significant contribution to the rise in Internet-related fraudulent activity as 'individuals are freer to make and remake themselves than ever before'.

It would appear that opportunity is one of the key factors in explaining the growth of identity theft combined, in escape cases, with an incentive to fabricate engendered by the greater emphasis placed on identifiability in today's society. Although it has been described as the 'neoteric crime of the information technology era' (Saunders and Zucker 1999: 184), it is clear that identity theft is not a new type of behaviour but that the Internet has facilitated the construction of fraudulent identities by revolutionising the information-gathering process that is the foundation of identity theft. Ironically, Foucault's 'carceral network' of documentation enmeshing the individual is in some senses subverted by the Internet which promises the identity thief escape from his or her own personhood and offers a plethora of 'new' identities to 'try on'. Moreover, the Internet makes it easy to disassociate from the implications of one's activities. This increase in the prevalence of identity theft is likely to continue unless measures are taken to address these problems and protect individuals from those who would misuse their identity. Two important weapons in the war against identity theft are advances in identification technology that may prevent theft from occurring and the introduction of legal measures to ensure that appropriate penalties are imposed on those who commit identity theft.

Advances in identification technology

Fraudulent activity can place an immense financial burden on institutions and be devastating for individual victims. For example, in 1994, the UK's Department of Social Security suffered an estimated loss of one billion pounds to benefit fraud. On an individual level, victims of identity theft may suffer consequences beyond financial loss such as the problems posed by a bad credit rating or the difficulties of proving that they are not responsible for the acts of the impostor done in their name (Marx 1990). One solution to the problem of identity theft would be to introduce a system of identification that can be more effectively attached to the particular individual to whom it relates. The creation of an effective and accurate method of identifying individuals is essential in terms of increasing the administrative efficiency of institutions and preventing fraud. There are three categories of identification information. First is something that an individual has that is produced as a means of identification such as a security pass or a passport. Secondly, something an individual knows such as mother's maiden name or passwords. The final category of identification is based upon the physical characteristics of the individual. This is known as biometrics and includes such things as fingerprints, DNA and retinal images (Davies 1994).

Forms of identification that fall into the first two categories may prove to be unreliable and particularly amenable to fraudulent misuse. Documents and cards can be lost and information may be forgotten, hence inconveniencing both the individual concerned and the institution that has to issue replacements. Documents and cards are also vulnerable to theft or duplication. These forms of identification may be misused in a straightforward manner, for example, the use of a stolen credit card to purchase goods, or form the basis of a more complex fraud, such as the use of information on a birth certificate to obtain further identification in the victim's name as a basis for total identity theft. Equally, knowledge can fall into the possession of others and be abused, either alone or in conjunction with cards and documents, for example, the use of a bank card (something one has) and a PIN number (something one knows) to withdraw cash from the victim's bank account. Like biographical information, PINs and credit card numbers can be found on websites that randomly generate the sequences of numbers intended to protect genuine credit cards.

Even though many of these forms of identification would not be sufficient to establish a fraudulent identity in isolation, it is important to note that 'a relatively high-integrity identity is constructed by accumulating a collection of low-integrity evidence' (Clarke 1994: 10).

Clarke uses the example of the pensioner who defrauded the Australian Department of Social Security of $40,000 by exploiting the 'entry-point paradox' using 'seed' documents to create multiple identities for the purposes of fraudulent benefit claims. A seed document is one that contains facts relating to a certain event but has nothing intrinsic that associates it with a particular person. A birth certificate, for example, contains detailed information concerning the birth of an individual but there is nothing about it that relates it to the person using it as identification other than an assertion that he or she is the person to whom it relates. Copies of birth certificates are freely available to anyone who is prepared to pay the nominal fee with no restrictions placed upon the categories of person who may obtain a copy. It can be used to obtain various other forms of identification (the entry-point paradox). Hence its role as the seed from which a more complete legal identity can be grown. Unless safeguards are developed to control the misuse of basic forms of personal documentation and to implement more stringent checks when these documents are used to obtain other forms of identification, this type of abuse will continue.

Advances in technology have enabled institutions using documentary and knowledge-based identification systems to overcome some of these pitfalls. In particular, plastic cards have an increased capacity to store information that may make it easier to detect misuse and can carry images of the authorised user and even thumb-print identification. Card readers are able to make speedy checks to ensure that cards that are presented have not been reported stolen, and faster communications systems ensure that records of stolen cards are updated far more frequently than has previously been possible. However, just as advances in technology have assisted organisations to combat fraud, criminals have also gained the benefits of relatively low-priced sophisticated equipment that facilitates the production of high-quality duplicates (Carroll 1991). Even the standard of equipment that is readily available in many homes and offices can be used to make convincing duplicates of documents and cards by those with relatively limited technological expertise (Davies 1994). As such, technological advances could be said simultaneously to prevent and facilitate fraudulent behaviour.

It would appear that documents, cards and knowledge-based methods of identification are inherently vulnerable to abuse. Biometric systems avoid many of the problems encountered by these other methods of identification as they are inherently linked to a particular individual and are extremely difficult to reproduce. But what are biometrics?

The term 'biometrics' is used to refer to any and all of a variety of identification techniques which are based on some physical and difficult-to-alienate characteristic. They are sometimes referred to as 'positive identification' because they are claimed to provide greater confidence that the identification is accurate.

(Clarke 1994: 11)

Biometrics are based upon some physical attribute that is (usually) unique to the individual and which, as such, cannot be removed and misused by an impostor. The most frequently used form of biometric identification is fingerprinting. This has been used to fix identity on offenders since the end of the nineteenth century and has come to be used more recently by some countries for the purposes of controlling immigration (Torpey 2000). Computer systems that store and recognise fingerprints have made the process of identification faster and more certain with one Japanese system claiming to be able to match fingerprints in one second with a 99.9 per cent accuracy rate. But despite the clear potential for the expansion of the use of fingerprints as a means of identification, there is a general reluctance to extend their use for more general identification purposes, possibly due to the connotations of criminality (Clarke 1994).

Among other forms of biometrics being developed with personal identification in mind is hand geometry, a technique used to process frequent travellers to the USA using a system known as INPASS (Immigration and Naturalisation Service Passenger Accelerated Service System). It is a voluntary scheme that allows participants to bypass usual airport procedures thereby reducing processing time to a mere 20 seconds. Participants are required to establish their identity in order to register for this scheme. The palm of the hand is scanned and the image is stored on a smart card. At the airport, the passenger inserts the card into a terminal and places his or her hand on a scanner that compares this with the image stored upon the card. The system has a high accuracy rating and has the potential to be implemented in a range of other situations in which there is a need for a fast and reliable means of establishing identity.

Any system that links identifying information irretrievably with a particular individual has clear benefits for eliminating identity theft. Biometrics are, by and large, unique to an individual. Hence the potential for abuse would appear to be minimal. However, the reliability of any system of identification based upon biometrics could be thwarted by the weaknesses of a registration system based upon documentary identification. As has been outlined earlier, a collection of low-integrity forms of identification can be used to establish a convincing fraudulent legal identity and unless stringent checks are made there would appear to be little to prevent an impostor registering for a scheme such as INPASS that has the appearance of being a wholly reliable means of ascertaining identity. In this way, the weaknesses of low-integrity identification systems are inherited by high-integrity systems, and their apparent infallibility is undermined and eroded.

That said, biometrics have clear advantages over alternative systems of identification in that they appear to be incapable of being mis-appropriated by impostors as they are linked to a single individual. There is little scope for multiple users of the same biometric identity. Hence such a system has much to offer in terms of reducing the prevalence of identity theft. However, there are also significant disadvantages that require consideration. First, such schemes are expensive to develop and implement. This should not pose a serious impediment to their use due to the potentially immense financial benefits of reducing fraud but it is none the less important to appreciate that the costs of introducing these systems may prove to be prohibitive for smaller organisations. However, the potential for 'function creep', whereby forms of identification are adopted for a variety of originally unplanned purposes, is a more pressing cause for concern. As Davies (1994) acknowledges, the existence of a relatively high-integrity scheme might create irresistible temptations on the part of authorities to apply it widely, and inter-relate many hitherto separate collections of personal information. This can be illustrated by reference to the multiplicity of roles that have developed for the social security number in a range of jurisdictions where it is used in connection with taxation, welfare benefit, person entitlement, health care provision, access to education, financial services and even vehicle registration (Clarke 1994). It seems likely that the introduction of a seemingly unassailable biometric identification system could soon be adopted by a range of institutions until it became the default means of establishing identification.

One problem with this is that a system that has the appearance of providing a determinative means of establishing identity may engender a confidence that is not justified. For example, despite the reverence with which the social security number is viewed as a means of identification in the USA, it is estimated that 4.2 million people have managed to acquire alternative numbers. A system of biometric identification must be based upon a reliable registration system that is subject to stringent scrutiny in order to ensure that the potential for fraudulent abuse is minimised. It has been suggested that the most reliable system of identification would be compulsory DNA registration, which would create a foundation for legal identity that is unique to the individual and which would be immune from replication or adoption by an impostor. Specially developed equipment has increased the speed of DNA testing in recent years and it is likely that portable testing equipment for use at crime scenes is a possibility in the relatively near future. But despite the fact that DNA provides a unique identifier that cannot be transferred between individuals, it would appear that it has no role in combating identity theft because research has failed to establish an effective way in which DNA could be incorporated into a form of personal identification for everyday use. Moreover, public opinion views the introduction of a national DNA database with suspicion, at least outside the criminal justice arena. This is because DNA does more than establish identity; it provides a complete genetic profile that can identify up to 400 diseases, legitimacy at birth, etc., and there is a growing body of research claiming that specific genes can predict future substance addiction, sexual orientation, and criminal and violent tendencies. As such, a system of identification based upon DNA profiling could lead to the stratification of society, creating a Brave New World based upon genetic élitism that would exacerbate the exclusionary impact of an unavoidable system of identification. At the risk of combining dystopias, such a system would also engender opposition as it would risk giving the state a Big Brother-esque omniscience by facilitating the creation of a unified and comprehensive database of information about individuals that is linked to public fears concerning the creation of an Orwellian surveillance state. The extent of public opposition to a state-controlled multipurpose identification scheme is accepted as one of the greatest impediments to the introduction of the fully cross-referenced and rigorously validated system of identification that would be necessary to eliminate identity theft (Clarke 1994; Davies 1994; Marx 2001). Therefore, while DNA profiling remains an invaluable tool in the identification of offenders, it is unlikely to expand beyond that into everyday use, at least in the near future (Safir and Reinharz 2000).

One theme that has emerged during the course of this chapter concerns the irreconcilable interests that are at stake within the identity discourse. In order to eliminate identity theft, it would be necessary to reconstruct the whole system of identification that is currently in existence. Not only would this be a lengthy, complex and expensive procedure, it would also have unpleasant consequences for individuals who, for whatever reason, feel compromised by some aspect of their legal identity. It is important not to overlook the dichotomy that exists within identity theft in terms of motivation. While society may wish to detect and punish those who engage in fraudulent behaviour, there are also those who have resorted to identity theft in order to escape some aspect of their own identity with which they no longer wish to be associated. The creation of a widespread and reliable system of identification would increase the pressure on such individuals and force them to choose between disclosure/exposure and exclusion. Moreover, there is evidence to suggest that there would be widespread public opposition to the concentration of personal information in a single system of identification that would be controlled by the state. If the strengthening of the system of identification is not the solution, it may be that the answer to the problems of identity are to be found within the criminal justice system.

The legal response to identity theft

In response to concerns about the growth of identity theft, the Identity Theft and Assumption Deterrence Act 1998 was introduced in the USA. The objectives of this statute were threefold: to ensure that the individuals whose identities were misused were viewed as the primary victims of identity theft; to establish more stringent penalties for offenders; and to empower the Federal Trade Commission to introduce procedures for educating the public, receiving complaints and co-ordinating the enforcement of the law. This tripartite attack on identity theft provides a cohesive response to the problem and has been generally well received as a significant improvement in the law (Saunders and Zucker 1999; Buba 2000). However, one limitation to the scope of the legal protection available in the USA is that the offence of identity theft is only established if it is carried out with the intention of engaging in unlawful activity. It is likely that this excludes escape cases from the remit of the law as such cases would lack the requisite criminal intention. The issue of whether escape cases and criminal identity theft are equally morally reprehensible is a complex one that is outside the scope of this chapter. However, the differing motivations may be of little relevance to the victim of identity theft who has to deal with the inconvenience of reclaiming his or her identity.

Notwithstanding this lacuna, it is clear that legal protection in the USA is vastly superior to that of the English criminal justice system where identity theft is as yet unrecognised as a distinct criminal offence. The offences contained in the Theft Act 1968 are unlikely to cover identity theft per se although there are a number of offences that would encompass fraudulent activity using another's identity, such as obtaining property by deception (s. 15) or obtaining a pecuniary advantage by deception (s. 16). The difficulty of this position is that the law does not focus on the misuse of the identity but on the financial consequences of this misuse. Therefore, if the individual has not carried the financial loss of the fraudulent transactions, he or she has no status as a victim in criminal law. This fragmentation of identity theft into a series of composite transactions overlooks the harm that can accrue to an individual as a result of the misuse of his or her identity even if it does not involve direct financial loss. The exclusive focus on the pecuniary elements of the conduct also impacts upon the level of penalty that is likely to be imposed on conviction as the seriousness of the conduct is measured in monetary terms. Again, this is different from the position in the USA where the quantum of loss is only one of the factors to be taken into account when determining the severity of the crime for sentencing purposes. Other factors that are considered relevant are the level of planning involved, the level of sophistication of the role of the perpetrator, the number of victims and, crucially, the susceptibility and status of the victim. Although the provisions of the Theft Act 1968 can be used to address certain manifestations of the problem, the absence of a specific offence of identity theft that recognises the impact of the conduct on the individual whose identity is misappropriated is a significant weakness in English law. However, the absence of any recognition of the harm caused, both individually and to society in general, of identity theft suggests that any amendment to the law may be far into the future.

Conclusion

This chapter has outlined the various manifestations of conduct that has come to be labelled identity theft and has explored several explanations that could account for its increase in today's society. It has been suggested that the ease with which it is possible to obtain various forms of identification in another's name has played a significant role in the rising crime of identity theft. In particular, it has been argued that the expansion of the use of the Internet has led to virtually unrestricted access to personal information about other people as well as providing increased opportunities to engage in fraudulent behaviour. This chapter has not sought to engage with the debate regarding the regulation of the Internet (see Chapter 2, this volume), preferring to argue that it may be appropriate to consider placing limitations on the availability of personal information about individuals regardless of their source. However, any privacy-based argument is liable to be countered by an equally compelling assertion based upon the need for the free flow of information in a democratic society, hence illustrating the competing interests that underpin any discussion of identity theft. Suffice it to say that a continued escalation of identity theft may ultimately necessitate a thorough re-evaluation of the way in which access to personal information used for identification purposes is organised and controlled.

As has been seen, identity theft may also be committed so that an individual can escape his or her own legal identity and adopt another that enables him or her to have a fresh start unencumbered by some troublesome element of his or her past. This type of identity theft has received very little attention in the existing literature. It creates an anomalous situation in which any measures introduced to limit the adoption of another's identity actually increase the pressure on individuals who wish to abandon their own legal identity. This situation is a cause for concern as one way in which identity theft could be reduced is by the introduction of a more stringent system of identification that cannot easily be misappropriated by others. However, such a system would place increased pressure on those with spoiled identities and might ultimately lead to their exclusion from a range of social activities and benefits. The ubiquitous requirement of identifiability has created this tension and raises further questions concerning the individual's right to privacy that need to be addressed in a broader social context.

The chapter concludes by considering the legislative approach to identity theft in the USA and comparing that with the position in the English criminal justice system. Although the creation of a specific criminal offence to address identity theft appears to be a positive measure, it is likely that a criminal law response would not suffice in isolation to address the problem. Institutions engaging in financial transactions, especially Internet transactions, need to become more aware of the dangers of identity theft and may have to question the validity of identification that is presented to them. Individuals need to become more aware of the risk of identity theft and require education that would enable them to adopt sensible security precautions to protect their personal information. Until such a time as measures are taken to address identity theft in the UK, it appears that there is little to prevent an unscrupulous individual accumulating debt or even committing murder while claiming to be you!

Chapter 7

Cyberstalking: an international perspective

Janice Joseph

> When a woman in North Hollywood, California spurned Gary Dellapenta's advances, the 50-year-old security guard got back at her via the Internet. Using her name, he posted personal ads describing fantasies of a 'home-invasion rape'. Six men appeared at her apartment over five months to take her up on Dellapenta's offer. Sentenced to six years in prison in 1999, he was the first person jailed for cyberstalking [in the USA].
>
> (Cohen 2001: 49)

The rapid growth of the Internet and other computer-mediated communications (CMC) technologies is promoting advances in virtually every aspect of society and every corner of the globe. Most of these advances represent positive changes, but unfortunately the Internet has also become an attractive medium for criminals. With the increasing availability of computers and online services, more individuals are logging on to the Internet, and a growing number are falling prey to the 'cyberstalker'. Cyberstalking can be as frightening and as 'real' as being followed and watched in one's neighbourhood or home. It can take many forms, including unsolicited hate mail, obscene or threatening email, malicious messages posted in newsgroups, 'mail bombs', email viruses and electronic junk mail or 'spam'.

Because of the global nature of the Internet, legislators and law enforcement officers face serious challenges when dealing with the crime of cyberstalking. This chapter examines the nature of cyberstalking and responses to it. Specifically, the chapter examines different forms of cyberstalking; legal responses by governments in the USA, Canada, the

UK and Australia; the challenges law enforcement officers face when investigating the problem; and the control and prevention of cyberstalking. The chapter concludes with suggestions on how to combat cyberstalking.

The extent and nature of cyberstalking

While there is no universally accepted definition of cyberstalking, the term generally refers to using the Internet or other telecommunication technologies to harass or menace another person (National Center for the Victims of Crime 2001). Cyberstalking can, therefore, be defined as un- wanted, threatening or offensive email or other personal communication over the computer that persists in spite of requests by the victim that it be stopped. It can also include behaviour that is aimed at a particular person, but not sent directly to that person. It is analogous to traditional forms of stalking in that it incorporates 'persistent behaviours that instil apprehension and fear' (Ogilvie 2000: 1); it simply utilises a high-tech modus operandi to achieve its aims (Petherick 1999). In addition, the stalker can frequently trace the victim's phone number and address (Grafx-Specs Design and Hosting 1997), and cyberstalking frequently accompanies 'traditional' stalking behaviours such as threatening phone calls, vandalism of property, threatening mail and physical attacks (Laughren 2000).

Although online stalking can take many forms it shares important characteristics with off-line stalking. Many stalkers – online or off – are motivated by a desire to exert control over their victims and engage in similar types of behaviour to accomplish this end. As with off-line stalking, in many cases – although by no means all – the cyberstalker and the victim are acquainted or have had a prior relationship. Like off-line stalking, it appears that the majority of cyberstalkers are men and the majority of their victims are women (US Justice Department 1999). Given the enormous amount of personal information available through the Internet, a cyberstalker can easily locate private information about a potential victim with a few mouse clicks or keystrokes.

The extent of cyberstalking

The nature and extent of cyberstalking are difficult to quantify. It is perhaps more difficult to assess than physical stalking, given the anonymity and breadth of electronic communications. In addition, cyberstalking is difficult to assess in terms of its incidence and prevalence within any given population because some victims may not consider the behaviour to be dangerous; indeed they may even be unaware they are being stalked.

There is very little official data on cyberstalking because the majority of law enforcement agencies in the USA, the UK and elsewhere have not investigated many cyberstalking cases and, indeed, in many jurisdictions it may still be regarded as a social harm rather than a criminal offence. However, a few law enforcement agencies are beginning to investigate cyberstalking. The Los Angeles District Attorney's Office, for example, estimates that email or other electronic communications accounts for approximately 20 per cent of the cases handled by its Stalking and Threat Assessment Unit. The Sex Crimes Unit in the Manhattan District Attorney's Office also estimates that about 20 per cent of the cases handled by the unit involve cyberstalking. The Computer Investigations and Technology Unit of the New York City Police Department estimates that almost 40 per cent of the caseload in the unit involves electronic threats and harassment – and virtually all these have occurred in the past three or four years (US Justice Department 1999).

The American organisation Working to Halt Online Abuse report that, between 1 January and 31 December 2000, it handled 353 cases of cyberstalking. Eighty-seven per cent of the cases involved female victims; 68 per cent of the cases involved harassment by a male; 27 per cent of the harassers were female; and 5 per cent were of unknown gender. Fifty-four per cent of the victims were between 18 and 30 years; 27 per cent between 31 and 40; and 19 per cent were 41 years and over. Ninety-five per cent of the victims were Caucasian; 2 per cent were Asians; 0.5 per cent were African-American; 1.5 per cent were Hispanic; and 1 per cent were Native American. The data indicated that 53 per cent of the victims reported no prior relationship or contact with their harassers. Thirty-nine per cent of the cases involved emails; 16 per cent chat rooms; 13 per cent instant messaging programs; 9 per cent message boards; 9 per cent newsgroups; 7 per cent a website (other than message boards); 3 per cent a virus attack; and 4 per cent other ways. The highest percentage of cases came from California, followed by Pennsylvania, Florida, New York, Virginia and Canada. The organisation states that it receives nearly 100 cases a week and that stalkers meet their victims mainly via emails, chat groups, newsgroups and instant messaging. A common place for cyberstalking is at the 'edu' or educational sites for colleges and universities (Working to Halt Online Abuse 2001). Cyberangels – an international online safety organisation that assists victims and police, and provides information on all aspects of online safety, privacy and security –

estimates that as many as 80,000 Canadians are cyberstalked annually (Karp 2000).

The nature of cyberstalking

Email stalking

Electronic mail (email) is an electronic postal service that allows individuals to send and receive messages or information in a matter of seconds. This sophisticated use of telephone lines allows communication between two people who may or may not know each other but can 'speak' to each other using a computer and a keyboard. In general, email is an insecure method for transmitting information or messages. Everyone who receives an email from a person has access to that person's email address. With some online services such as AOL, a person's screen name is also an email address. In addition, when a person posts an item on a newsgroup, that person's email address may be available to anyone who reads that item. It is unsurprising, then, that email is a favoured medium for cyberstalkers (CNET Networks 2000).

Cyberstalkers often have a sophisticated knowledge of computers and the Internet, and can 'mask' their emails to disguise their origin. A hacker may gain access to an email account of an 'innocent' user and use this address to send messages that may be threatening or offensive. From his or her home computer in Toronto, for example, a person can hack into the computer server at the University of Australia. From the account at the University of Australia, he or she can hack into the University of Japan. From this new account he or she can then hack into the University of Arizona, choose a user name and send threatening messages to his or her next-door neighbour in Toronto. The message will appear to have come from Arizona, but in fact it is coming from their neighbour in Toronto. Email cyberstalking can also include unsolicited hateful, obscene, pornographic, threatening or harassing mail, or the cyberstalker might bombard his or her victim with electronic junk mail (known as 'spamming'). More technologically sophisticated email harassers send 'mail bombs', filling a person's mailbox with hundreds or even thousands of unwanted messages in the hope of making the account useless. Others send electronic viruses that can infect the victim's files (CNET Networks 2000; Ogilvie 2000).

Chat stalking

A chat room is a connection provided by online services and available on the Internet that allows people to communicate in real time via computer text and a modem. Cyberstalkers can use chat rooms to slander and endanger their victims. In such cases, the cyberstalking takes on a public rather than a private dimension. As live chat has become more popular among users of the Internet with tools such as Internet relay chat (IRC), it has also become more popular as a medium through which stalkers can identify and pursue their prey (CNET Networks 2000).

When a person enters a chat room, his or her screen name joins the list of names of others in the room. Depending on the nature of the chat software, that person can address others in the room (and vice versa) as part of the group discussion, form a smaller group in a private chat room or send private, one-to-one instant messages to others any time. During 'chat', participants type live messages directly to the computer screens of other participants. Chat-line users may capture, store and transmit these communications to others outside the chat service. When a person posts a message to a public newsgroup this is available for anyone to view, copy and store. In addition, a person's name, email address and information about the service provider are usually available for inspection as part of the message itself. Thus, on the Internet, public messages can be accessed by anyone at any time – even years after the message was originally written. Instant messaging, such as that found on AOL, is perhaps the most common form used in chat cyberstalking. The cyberstalker can use AOL's 'buddy' option to find out whenever a particular screen name logs on – and then monitor that person's activities (CNET Networks 2000). Chat stalking can take other forms as well. In IRC, a harasser may choose to interrupt a person's chat electronically or otherwise target a chat system, making it impossible for someone to carry on a conversation with anyone else. In other instances, a cyberstalker sends a person's message to multiple recipients (ibid.). The cyberstalker can engage in live chat harassment or abuse of the victim (otherwise known as 'flaming') or he or she may leave improper messages on message boards or in chat rooms for or about the victim (Ogilvie 2000).

Bulletin board systems

A bulletin board system (BBS) is a local computer that can be called directly with a modem. Usually they are privately operated and offer various services depending on the owner and the users. A bulletin board allows users to leave messages in group forums to be read at a later time. Often a BBS is not connected to a network of other computers, but increasingly BBSs are offering Internet access and so cyberstalkers are using bulletin boards to harass their victims. Bulletin boards allow an individual to publish or broadcast a message that a large group of readers can access. Some bulletin board services maintain forums that are restricted to users who have a password. While communications made in these forums may initially be read only by the members with access, there is nothing preventing those members from recording the communications and later transmitting them elsewhere. Online stalkers have been known to post insulting messages on electronic bulletin boards signed with the email address of the person being harassed. The cyberstalker can also post statements about the victim or start rumours which spread throughout the BBS. In addition, a cyberstalker can 'dupe' other Internet users into harassing or threatening a victim by posting a controversial or enticing message on the board under the name, phone number or email address of the victim, resulting in subsequent responses being sent to the victim (Gregorie 2001).

Computer stalking

With computer stalking, the cyberstalker exploits the Internet and the Windows operating system in order to assume control over the computer of the targeted victim. An individual 'Windows based' computer connected to the Internet can be identified, allowing the online stalker to exercise control over the computer of the victim. The cyberstalker can communicate directly with his or her target as soon as the target computer connects to the Internet. The stalker can also assume control of the victim's computer and the only defensive option for the victim is to disconnect and relinquish his or her current Internet address (Ogilvie 2000). An example of this kind of cyberstalking was the case of a woman who received a message stating 'I'm going to get you'. The cyberstalker then opened the woman's CD-ROM drive in order to prove he had control of her computer (Karp 2000). More recent versions of this technology can allow for real-time keystroke logging (the recording of every keystroke) and viewing the computer desktop in real time (Spring 1999).

Legal responses to cyberstalking

Cyberstalking is a relatively new phenomenon and many countries are only now beginning to address the problem. Stalking is defined by a list of prohibited activities and there is usually a requirement that the stalker's activities should present a 'credible' threat or a threat that can cause the victim to become fearful. It also results in a heavier sentence when the stalker is acting in breach of any form of court order. A few countries, such as the USA, Canada, the UK, and Australia, have passed legislation that can, in certain circumstances, deal with cyberstalking and stalking in general.

USA

In 1990, in response to the stalking and murder of Rebecca Schaeffer, California became the first state to pass anti-stalking laws. Schaeffer was stalked by Robert John Bardo who eventually murdered her at her home. Bardo had tracked Schaeffer using computer data banks that told him where she lived, her telephone number, what kind of car she drove and where she shopped. Bardo may have been physically distanced from his obsession but the computer electronically made him feel near to her (US Justice Department 1999).

Since the passage of the first anti-stalking legislation in California in 1990, 49 other states have enacted similar laws or revised old laws to encompass stalking. Of those states, 29 have statutes that either deal directly with cyberstalking or can be applied to cyberstalking. Twelve states have legislation against cyberstalking pending. To include cyberstalking in the anti-stalking legislation, states use terms such as 'electronic communication', 'electronic mail', 'electronic communication device', 'computer network', 'electronic form of communication' and 'electronic transmission' (National Center for the Victims of Crime 2001; Working to Halt Online Abuse 2001).

The federal government has passed a number of important pieces of legislation that can be used to prosecute cyberstalkers although, as we shall see, none are comprehensive and all contain loopholes. Section 18 USC 875 (c) of the federal statute makes it a crime, punishable by up to five years in prison and a fine of up to $250,000, to transmit any interstate or foreign communication containing a threat to injure the person of another. Thus, it includes threats transmitted via the telephone, email, pagers or the Internet. Certain forms of cyberstalking also can be prosecuted under s. 47 USC 223 of the federal statute. This statute makes it a federal crime, punishable by up to two years in prison, for a person who uses a telephone or telecommunications device to annoy, abuse, harass or threaten any person. Both these pieces of legislation are limited, however, in so far as they apply only to the communication, between perpetrator and victim, of actual threats. They cannot therefore be enforced in situations where a cyberstalker engages in a pattern of conduct intended to harass or annoy another, but makes no actual threat, or in a situation where an online stalker posts messages on a bulletin board or in a chat room encouraging others to harass or annoy an individual but where there are no direct threats (US Justice Department 1999). Congress has also passed the Interstate Stalking Punishment and Prevention Act of 1996. Under this Act, it is illegal to travel across a state line with the intent to injure or harass another person or, as a result of such travel, to cause that person reasonably to fear for his or her safety. The Interstate Stalking Act is limited because it requires that the perpetrator physically travels across state lines. The argument that Internet communication does cross state lines has not yet been tested (US Justice Department 1999).

The federal government has further passed an amendment (the Communications Decency Act 1996) to the Communications Act 1934, changing the language to include computers as a telecommunications device (where previously it referred only to the telephone). The legislation clearly targets activities that could be considered cyber-stalking, stating that anyone who commits the following is guilty of crime:

> [D]eliberately transmits any comment, request, suggestion, proposal, or other telecommunications which is obscene, lewd, lascivious, filthy, or indecent, with the intent to annoy, abuse, threaten, or harass another person or makes repeated telephone calls or repeatedly initiates communication with a tele-communication device solely for the purpose harassing another person.
>
> (US Justice Department 1999
> The Communications Act of 1996: Section 23)

In 1998, President Clinton signed a bill into law protecting children against online stalking. The statute, 18 USC 2425, makes it a federal crime knowingly to communicate (e.g. by telephone or via the Internet) with any person with intent to solicit or entice a child into unlawful sexual activity. But although this law can provide protection for children against predators, it does not cover harassing phone calls to minors in which there is no intent to entice or solicit the child for illicit sexual purposes (US Justice Department 1999).

A Just Punishment for Cyberstalkers Act 2000 was introduced in Congress by Senator Spencer Abraham. If passed into legislation, this new bill will revise stalking provisions of the federal criminal code to prohibit a person:

(1) from travelling across a State line or within the special maritime or territorial jurisdiction of the United States with the intent to injure or harass another person and place that person in reasonable fear of death or serious bodily injury to the person or a member of his or her immediate family; or

(2) with the intent to kill or injure a person in another State or to put such person in reasonable fear of death or serious bodily injury, from using or causing another to use the mail or any facility of interstate or foreign commerce to place that person in reasonable fear of death or serious bodily injury to the person, a member of his or her immediate family, or a spouse or intimate partner.

(106th Congress 2000: unpaginated)

Canada

In 1993, the Canadian government passed a bill making it a crime knowingly to engage in actions which cause someone to fear for his or her own safety or for the safety of someone else. Section 264 of the Canadian Criminal Code defines stalking – or criminal harassment – as repeatedly following or communicating with a person; watching or harassing a person at home or at work; repeatedly telephoning, writing letters, sending notes or gifts; issuing verbal or written threats; vandalism to, or leaving dead animals on, his or her property or work premises; and/or engaging in threatening conduct towards a person or his or her family. This crime is punishable by either summary conviction or indictable offence, as high as five years in prison (Ramsay 1998).

Despite the fact that Canada does not have any formal laws dealing specifically with cyberstalking, based on the above definition electronic stalking is clearly a criminal activity. The government has applied various traditional laws, with some success, to stalkers in Canada who send threatening emails to others. For example, in 1996, when various female students at a university were sent threatening emails the offender was charged with intimidation. While the Canadian government has been successful in cases such as this, various Canadian courts have stated that a 'reasonable person' must feel violated by such messages in order for a charge to be brought (www.victimsofviolence.on.ca/cyber.htm). The question then becomes – as with traditional stalking – whether the victim can prove that he or she was disturbed or threatened by the messages. This can be extremely difficult for victims of cyberstalking, as the offender may not even reside in their time zone.

UK

The term 'stalking' became popular after a number of well publicised cases in Britain in the mid-1990s in which the offenders repeatedly harassed their victims. The media labelled such incidents as 'stalking' and the term quickly fell into popular usage. Prior to such cases, stalking tended to be viewed as a phenomenon of celebrity, with obsessive fans following or trying to contact their idols (Budd and Mattinson 2000). However, the term 'stalking' has no legal status in the UK and although the Protection from Harassment Act 1997 is informally referred to as the 'anti-stalking law', it does not actually use or define the term stalking. Furthermore, the legal test as to whether a person is guilty of harassment is once again based on the judgement of 'a reasonable person' unlike most criminal offences which require some degree of intent (Budd and Mattinson 2000).

The 1997 Act created two specific criminal offences to deal with the problem of harassment. The first is an indictable offence involving fear of violence. This offence requires proof that the victim was put in fear of violence, regardless of whether or not the offender intended to do so, and carries a maximum sentence of five years' imprisonment (Protection from Harassment Act 1997, s. 4). The second is the summary offence of criminal harassment which does not require the victim to have been put in fear of violence, and could result in a maximum sentence of six months' imprisonment in jail (Protection from Harassment Act 1997, s. 2). A conviction on either offence could result in a restraining order, the breach of which carries a maximum penalty of five years' imprisonment. In addition to the two criminal offences, the Act also created a statutory 'civil tort', which gives the victim the power to seek injunction and damages. According to the Home Office, in 1998 there were 693 cautions and 2,221 convictions under the Protection from Harassment Act for the offence of harassment. For the offence of putting people in fear of violence there were 173 cautions and 522 convictions (Budd and Mattinson 2000). Although not concerned with stalking or cyberstalking per se, the Protection from Harassment Act can be used to address the problems of offensive or threatening communications, including emails. In addition, s. 43 of the Telecommunications Act 1984 makes it an offence to send by means of a public telecommunications system a message or other matter that is grossly offensive or of an indecent, obscene or menacing character. For the purpose of the Act, a telecommunications system is a system for the conveyance of electric, magnetic, electro-magnetic, electro-chemical or electro-mechanical energy of sounds, such as speech and music, and visual images.

Britain witnessed its first cyberstalking conviction in 1999 when a Cambridge graduate was prosecuted in 1999 for harassment by email. Nigel Harris, 23, a computer programmer, sent threatening and abusive messages to his girlfriend after she ended their two-year relationship. He was convicted for sending offensive emails to the children's charity where his former girlfriend worked and given a two-year conditional discharge (Born 1999). In another case, a cyberstalker who terrorised a teenager by setting up Internet sex sites and using her picture to lure strangers to her home received seven-and-a-half years in jail (Savill 2001).

Australia

The protection of free speech is the central concern of most Internet users (Slevin 2000) and the issue of electronic censorship is a hotly debated issue. Any attempt to limit freedom of speech on the Internet has therefore been challenged on the grounds that such action violates constitutional or civil rights. Recently, for example, Australia passed strict Internet copyright laws making it illegal to forward an email memo without the author's permission, punishable with fines of $60,000 or five years in prison. The Copyright Amendment (Digital Agenda) was intended to provide similar protections in an electronic environment as exists in a hard-copy environment. However, the action has been described as 'outrageous' and the Australian government was accused of censoring 'impure' thoughts and regulating the pleasure of others (Greene 2001). The fact that it may have implications for freedom of speech, however, does not mean that cyberstalking should not be outlawed. The challenge for governments is to find a balance between individual free speech and the protection of society.

Legislation covering stalking was introduced into Australia during the 1990s, with Queensland being the first state to introduce stalking legislation in 1993. Although many states in Australia have anti-stalking laws, Victoria and Queensland are the only states to include sending electronic messages to, or otherwise contacting, the victim in their legislation (Ogilvie 2000). Ogilvie argues that cyberstalking could be included in Australia's wider stalking legislation on the grounds that receiving violent email messages can cause the victim apprehension or fear, and that infiltrating another person's computer could be deemed to constitute interfering with property. The problem, however, is prosecuting such cyberstalking cases because of the absence of physical proximity between many offenders and victims and the requirement that the offender intended to cause serious apprehension and fear. Even where 'anti-stalking' legislation exists, its enforcement is not necessarily at all straightforward.

Enforcement of anti-stalking legislation

Establishing credible threat

Most existing laws on stalking and cyberstalking apply only to behaviour that constitutes a direct or credible threat and causes the victim to be fearful of his or her safety, which may make prosecution difficult. First, it can be difficult to establish 'credible threat' if no actual threat of violence from the cyberstalker is evident. Secondly, many cyberstalkers do not threaten their victims directly or overtly or in 'person'; they might post the name, address and phone number of their victim on the Internet, in newsgroups or advertisements, or may impersonate their victim in a chat room. Although these behaviours can be interpreted as harassment, it may be difficult to prosecute the perpetrators because they may not have made a 'direct' threat against the victim. It is even more difficult proving 'credible threat' when the online stalker and victim live in two different jurisdictions or countries. The issue of 'credible threat' was significant in the case of Jake Baker:

> Using the pseudonym 'Jake Baker', Abraham Jacob Alkhabaz, a student at the University of Michigan posted stories describing the rape and murder of a woman. Baker used the real name of a fellow student from the University of Michigan for the victim. Baker also corresponded with a reader of the story via email who used the pseudonym of 'Arthur Gonda' in Canada. In over 40 emails both men discussed their desire to injure women in the local area. Baker was arrested and charged with the interstate transmission and foreign commerce communications of a threat to kidnap and injure. A US judge dismissed the case against Baker, ruling that it lacked a specific intent to act or a specific target required under Michigan's stalking law.
>
> (*US* v. *Baker* 1995)

It is clear from the above that the judge did not believe that the emails posed any 'credible threat' to the victims.

Anonymity/identities

Another obstacle to the enforcement of legislation is the identity of the cyberstalker. Due to the sophistication of the technology, the Internet has created the possibility for anonymous cyberstalking. As discussed in many other chapters in this volume, Internet users – including cyberstalkers – can 'mask' or otherwise alter their identity in numerous ways. In most cases of online stalking, offenders use an Internet protocol (IP) address and anonymous 'remailers'; that is, mail servers that purposefully strip identifying information and headers showing where the message came from. By forwarding mail through several of these services serially, a cyberstalker can send emails that are virtually impossible to trace back to their originator. The presence of such services makes it relatively simple to send anonymous communications, while making it difficult for victims, Internet providers and law enforcement agencies to identify the person or persons responsible for transmitting harassing or threatening communications over the Internet (US Department of Justice 1999). Even if one country bans remailers, the service may be available in other countries.

Cyberstalkers can also create pseudo-anonymity by adopting an online identity which bears little or no resemblance to their true identity. Pseudonymity can be created by simply forging or 'spoofing' an email header so as to create an online persona. Cyberstalkers can also impersonate other users by faking the header of an email message to make it appear as if it originates from the victim's account (Ellison and Akdeniz 1998). Anonymity obviously leaves the cyberstalker in an advantageous position. The perpetrator could be in another state, around the corner, in another country or in the next cubicle at work without the victim knowing where he or she is located. The stalker could be a former friend or lover, a total stranger met in a chat room or simply a teenager playing a practical joke. It hardly needs stating that the inability to identify the source of the harassment or threats hinders police investigation of cyberstalking.

Given the enforcement problems, some people have called for the prohibition of anonymous communications while other have called for restrictions to be placed on anonymity. Opponents of anonymity argue that it facilitates illegal conduct and allows perpetrators to evade the consequences of their actions (ibid.). However, legislation that restricts anonymity on the Internet can be subjected to constitutional challenges. In the USA, for example, where anonymity has historically been recognised as valuable for free speech, attempts to control anonymity on the Internet have been ruled unconstitutional. The problem, however, is that this constitutional right can be abused by the cyberstalker.

Anonymity prevents businesses and the government from monitoring Internet users. However, some forms of anonymous communications can be eradicated. Internet Protocol Version 6 will improve the ability of law enforcement officers to track cyberspace communications through unique identifiers attached to every computer's IP number. Companies such as Microsoft, Apple, Sun, MCI WorldCom and IBM have already endorsed IPv6, and the Internet Assigned Numbers Authority, which is responsible for allocating Internet addresses, issued numbers based on the new standard for the first time in July 1999.

Issues of privacy

Even if the cyberstalker can be identified, the issue of his or her privacy is still problematic. In the USA, for example, the Cable Communications Policy Act (CCPA) 1984 prohibits disclosure of cable subscribers' records to law enforcement agencies unless the agency has a court order and has provided advance notice to the subscriber. Under the CCPA, a law enforcement agency investigating a cyberstalker has to provide the individual with notice that his or her subscriber records have been requested. This law was passed before the use of the Internet was so prevalent, and long before cable companies became Internet service providers (ISPs). The purpose of the law was to prevent the police from abusing their power by checking on the viewing habits of cable subscribers without the knowledge of the persons being investigated. The law was designed to protect privacy, but now that cable companies are ISPs it can hinder police investigation of cyberstalkers. Put simply, if the police give a suspected cyberstalker notice that they will be checking his or her ISP records, the cyberstalker has the opportunity to destroy evidence. Although it may be appropriate to prohibit the indiscriminate disclosure of cable records, there is a growing feeling among commentators that the government should allow law enforcement officers to have access to a person's file without his or her prior knowledge if that person is suspected of cyberstalking (US Department of Justice 1999).

Jurisdiction and statutory authority

Legislating against cyberstalking also presents inter-jurisdictional difficulties. The Internet links people around the world and the global nature of the medium makes it difficult for countries or even states to determine their jurisdictional responsibilities, especially in cyberstalking cases. Difficulties initially arise when the stalker and the victim live in different states or different countries. For example, if a cyberstalker sends a threatening message from a computer in Michigan, USA, to a computer in Seoul, South Korea, the dilemma for the law enforcement agencies is to determine in which country the investigation should take place: the country where the email originated or the place where the victim lives? The difficulties are compounded when the two countries or states involved have different attitudes and responses to the problem of electronic stalking. While some citizens who are victims of a cyberstalker may have legal recourse, others who experience exactly the same kind of victimisation, but are living somewhere that does not recognise cyberstalking in law, may not have any recourse at all. In other words, although the Internet may be borderless for the cyberstalker, law enforcement officers are constrained by geographical boundaries. This makes investigating and arresting a cyberstalker outside their jurisdiction extremely difficult. For example, Brian Andrew Sutcliffe, a 37-year-old man living in Victoria, Australia, was accused of stalking a Canadian actress by email. His lawyer argued that the tradition in Victorian law was that jurisdiction to hear a case depended not on where the crime originated but where the 'effect' of the crime was felt. The magistrate agreed and dismissed the charge, ruling that she did not have jurisdiction to hear the case because the effect of the alleged crimes occurred outside her jurisdiction – in Canada, not in Australia. However, a Supreme Court judge overturned the magistrate's decision stating that the case should be tried in Australia. In response, the alleged cyberstalker has appealed against the decision of the Supreme Court judge (Cant 2001) and, at the time of writing, the case is still pending.

Control/prevention of cyberstalking

Governmental response

A few countries are taking steps to control cybercrimes, including cyberstalking. In the USA, for example, the federal and state governments have created 'cybercrime units' (and similar initiatives have been implemented in the UK and Europe; see Chapter 2, this volume). The Federal Bureau of Investigation (FBI) has computer crime squads throughout the country, as well as the National Infrastructure Protection Center in Washington, to ensure cybercrimes are properly investigated. Additionally, they have computer analysis and response teams to conduct forensics examinations on seized magnetic media. In 1996 the Justice Department established the Computer Crime and Intellectual Property Section within the Criminal Division. These units have highly trained personnel who remain at the cutting edge of new technology and investigative techniques. In addition, each US attorney's office contains experienced computer crime prosecutors. These individuals – known as computer and telecommunications co-ordinators – assist in the investigation and prosecution of a wide variety of computer crimes, including cyberstalking. In addition, at state level, several attorney generals have established special divisions that focus on computer crimes (US Department of Justice 1999).

The European Parliament is currently studying a proposal that would limit the use of anonymous email in an effort to assist online surveillance of criminals across Europe. If the proposals are approved, anonymous email communications in all European countries could effectively be outlawed (Middleton 2000). In another initiative, and in accordance with a 1995 European directive, ISPs in the UK are currently obliged to store logs of all user activities for three months. Although service providers are under no obligation to hand over logs to the police, they tend to co-operate with police investigations. The European Parliament is presently discussing plans to give law enforcers legal rights to access these traffic logs. Some civil liberties groups have said that abolishing anonymous email is a gross invasion of privacy and that giving police access to ISP traffic logs is likely to spark an increase in the use of anonymous browsers and encrypted email (ibid.).

Industry response

The cyber-industries have made some efforts to inform consumers about ways to protect themselves online. Most ISPs have 'kill files' or 'Bozo filters' which allow a user to block email messages from a particular sender. Programs such as Eudora and Microsoft Outlook have filter features which can automatically delete emails from a particular email address or those which contain offensive words. Chat-room contact can be blocked as well. Most Internet 'chat' facilities offer users the ability to block, 'squelch' or ignore communications from individuals who are attempting to harass or threaten them. Some providers allow a subscriber to change his or her email address whenever he or she wants to do so. These approaches may be useful in situations where the communications are merely annoying but may be useless in situations in which threatening communications are not received by the intended victim. A victim who never 'receives' the threat may not know he or she is being stalked, and may be alerted, for the first time, when the stalker shows up to act on his or her threats.

The cyber-industries also recognise the need to co-operate more fully with law enforcement officers and have indicated their willingness to participate in training for law enforcement agencies. This is viewed as an important initiative because they can assist police departments in designing training programmes. Moreover, closer co-operation between law enforcement and industry would make investigation easier (US Department of Justice 1999). Internet groups have also been working with governments to provide more information on privacy protection and crime prevention on the Internet. In the USA, for example, there are the Federal Trade Commission and government agencies on Project OPEN (Online Public Education Network). Project OPEN provides information about fraud, parental controls and protecting privacy (ibid.).

Individual responsibility

The individual is an important component in the control and prevention of cyberstalking. If individuals are given clear direction about how to protect themselves against threatening or harassing communications, and how to report incidents when they do occur, both industry and law enforcement will be in a position to co-operate to conduct investigations. The following are some suggestions that Internet users can follow to prevent cyberstalking and to protect their privacy:

- Do not share personal information in public spaces anywhere online, nor give it to strangers, including in email or chat rooms;

- Do not use your real name or nickname as your screen name or user ID;

- Do not post personal information as part of any user profiles;

- Be extremely cautious about meeting online acquaintances in person. If a meeting is arranged, users should do so in a public place and take along a friend;

- Make sure that your ISP and Internet Relay Chat (IRC) network have an 'acceptable use' policy that prohibits cyberstalking. And if the network fails to respond to your complaints, users should consider switching to a provider that is more responsive to user complaints;

- Log off or surf somewhere else if a situation online becomes hostile;

- Block or filter messages from the harasser;

- Delete emails from a troublesome email address or those that contain offensive words;

- Report any form of cyberstalking to the police.
  (US Department of Justice 1999 paras. 105–114: unpaginated)

Cohen (2001: 48) has also suggested that users should:

- Clear the memory cache after they surf the Internet because the computer keeps a memory reserve, effectively a log, of the sites a person visits. Anyone with access to the computer can see what sites that person visited;

- Check the privacy policies of web sites because many reserve the right to share personal data with third parties, unless the user requests otherwise;

- Use dummy email or secondary accounts from free services such as Hotmail or Yahoo! and reserve your primary email address for friends and people you can trust;

- Consider using an anonymiser since web sites keep a record of your visits and may be able to identify you by name. The user can hide his or her identity with anonymisers like www.anonymiser.com. Anonymisers also encrypt the URLs that a person visits so that an Internet Service Provider cannot keep a record of them.

(Cohen 2001: 48)

Implications

Policy

Cyberstalking is expected to increase as computers and the Internet become ever more popular. Governments, ISPs, law enforcement officers and Internet users need to recognise that cyberstalking is a serious crime. Governments should review their existing laws to determine whether they adequately address cyberstalking. If they are found to be inadequate, they must enact appropriate laws to address cyberstalking. In addition, governments should develop legislation that would make the prosecution of cyberstalkers easier when it involves multiple jurisdictions. A law dealing with cyber-jurisdiction must address whether a particular act of cyberstalking is controlled by the laws of the state or country where the website is located, by the laws of the state or country where the ISP is located, by the laws of the state or country where the user is located, or perhaps by all these laws.

With the coming of the information superhighway, a cyber-community has been created without a police force and, at the present time, it appears that most law enforcement officials are ill-prepared to deal with cyberstalking. Proper training and understanding are required effectively to detect and investigate it, and a thorough knowledge of the relationship between online stalking and off-line stalking is essential for its effective regulation. Law enforcement officers must take prompt action when an incident of cyberstalking is brought to their attention, and must be enabled to develop networking with other agencies so that they can share resources and information about cyberstalking. There is a strong argument for the establishment of an international law enforcement agency to police the Internet, with officers being given special powers to investigate cyberstalking when it involves international boundaries. Countries could sign mutual legal agreements giving domestic law enforcement officers the procedural authority to obtain electronic evidence in other countries that have signed the agreement.

Many ISPs ask for almost no identifying information, and make little or no effort to verify the information they do request. It is much too easy for a person to establish an email account under a fictitious name and then use that account for cyberstalking or other nefarious purposes. ISPs generally have clauses in their service agreements prohibiting inappropriate use of the account. These clauses are rarely enforced, for two reasons. First, the service provider is often unaware that someone is using his or her service to engage in inappropriate activity. Secondly, even if the problem comes to the ISP's attention, the account might be registered under a fictitious name. ISPs need to make a greater effort to ensure they know who is using their services.

Industry should take the lead in protecting users' privacy. The US Vice President's *Report on Cyberstalking* reported that there were three common complaints regarding ISPs' polices and procedures: (1) the procedure for reporting a complaint was not well advertised; (2) the user service agreements were overly vague about what behaviour constitutes a punishable violation; and (3) the complainant was not kept informed of the steps taken to curb the problem (US Department of Justice 1999). Internet industries have a responsibility to keep their clients' information confidential as well as providing information for their clients on how they can protect their privacy.

Research

The lack of comprehensive data on the nature and extent of cyberstalking makes it difficult to develop effective response strategies. Any attempt to deal with cyberstalking necessitates a general understanding of the problem. Effective preventive measures or strategies cannot be developed unless there is adequate information on cyberstalking. There is, therefore, a need for more research in this area to determine the actual extent, nature and effects of the phenomenon. Future surveys should examine the effectiveness of the laws; the impact of punishment on perpetrators; the effects of preventive measures on the rate and extent of stalking; and effects of cyberstalking on victims. Cyber-industries should also conduct research to evaluate the effectiveness of their measures and strategies against cybercrimes, including cyberstalking. Since cyberstalking is a global problem, it is necessary to conduct comparative studies focusing on the international community. Such studies could compare the laws governing the Internet in various countries and their impact on cyberstalking, and law enforcement practices in various countries dealing with cyberstalking. Comparative studies would provide a more comprehensive and holistic overview of the problem of stalking.

Summary

Cyberstalking has become a very serious global problem and is expected to rise as use of personal computers increases. While some countries have enacted cyberstalking laws or anti-stalking laws that can address cyberstalking, other countries have no such legislation. In addition, most cyberstalking legislation is inadequate or unenforceable. The impersonal and global nature of cyberstalking poses problems for law enforcement officers. The anonymity of the Internet provides opportunities for a cyberstalker to hide his or her true identity, which can be concealed by using different ISPs and/or by adopting different screen names. The cyberstalker may be located in one country while the victim is in another country, making it more difficult for either local authority to investigate the incident. Even if a law enforcement agency is willing to pursue a case beyond its own jurisdiction, it may be difficult to obtain assistance from law enforcement officers in another jurisdiction.

There are several steps that can be taken by governments, cyber-industries and the individual in an attempt to deal with cyberstalking adequately. First, all governments need to enact new laws specifically written for electronic stalking activities. These laws should be effective and constitutionally sound and not subjected to constitutional scrutiny and challenges. Secondly, law enforcement officers need to be properly trained to deal with cyberstalking. By becoming technologically proficient and understanding cyberstalking in general, law enforcement agencies will be better prepared to respond to incidents in their jurisdictions. Thirdly, cyber-industries need to develop policies and procedures designed to protect their clients. Fourthly, governments and cyber-industries need to operate as partners and not as adversaries. Fifthly, the individual should take responsibility to avoid becoming a victim of cyberstalking. Individuals should be knowledgeable about the dangers of the Internet and ways to protect their privacy. Since cyberstalking is a relatively new phenomenon, there is still much to be learned about this crime. The challenge is for researchers to conduct studies which can gain a better understanding of cyberstalking and the cyberstalker and for policy-makers to establish effective policies and guidelines for ISPs and Internet users. In short, although the Internet is a wonderful place to work, play and study it can, like the real world, be a place of danger. Criminals use the Internet to terrorise their victims. Governments, businesses and Internet users will have to make a collaborative effort to combat cyberstalking. It is an activity of global proportions but it necessitates the willing participation of every nation, every cyber-industry and every individual to combat it.

Chapter 8

Maestros or misogynists? Gender and the social construction of hacking[1]

Paul A. Taylor

Does she Do the Vulcan Mind Meld on the First Date?
By Nick Herbert

I want your bra size, baby,
Fax number, Email address,
Modem com code, ID,
Phone machine access.

Give me your thumb print, password,
Blood type and credit check;
Give me your anti-body spectrum,
Your immune response spec.

Let's break bread together baby,
Exchange cryptographic primes;
Let's link up our parallel ports;
And go online in real-time.

Let's indulge in covalent bondage;
Let's communicate in C.
Let's merge our enemy bodies
And bob in the quantum sea.

I wanna swim in your gene pool, mama;
Snort your pheromones up close range;
Tune in your neurotransmitters,
Introduce you to Doctor Strange.

I wanna surf in your quantum potentia;
Mess with your thermostat;
Wanna tour your molecular orbits;
Wanna feed your Schrodinger cat.

Let's surgically merge our organs;
Our kidneys, our lungs and our hearts;
Let's read our physics journals together
And laugh at the dirty parts.

Let's Bell-connect our bellies
With some quantum-adhesive glue;
Let's do new stuff to each other
That Newton never knew.

I wanna feel your viscosity, honey,
Melt my rheological mind;
Let your female force-field vortex
Deform my male spacetime.

(Computer Underground Digest 4(17)[2])

Introduction

Women often feel about as welcome as a system crash.
(Miller, in Brooks and Boal 1995: 49)

Hacking, as guerrilla know-how, is essential to the task of maintaining fronts of cultural resistance and stocks of oppositional knowledge as a hedge against a technofascist future.
(Ross 1991: 82)

Published in an online hacking journal, the above poem's overtly sexual tone provides an illustration of the typically male timbre of the computer underground. This chapter explores the issue of gender in relation to the construction of the hacker persona and the wider culture of programming. The chapter starts with a brief description of hacking and programming's dominance by men and introduces some basic theories for the resultant gender gap. Since the term 'cyberspace' itself was first fully explored in the fictional context of William Gibson's *Neuromancer* it is perhaps not surprising that our understanding of programming has been disproportionately affected by rhetorical constructions and representations. Thus next, the chapter explores the psycho-sexual dimensions to the activity, asking why the act conveys a feeling of power that particularly appeals to young men,[3] and further explores how such feelings of power are projected into rhetorical constructions such as the comparison of cyberspace with the frontier land of the Wild West. This pioneer mentality is examined with reference to the political culture of technolibertarians or cypherphunks which are then contrasted with the rise of a new form of technologically fuelled political activism: hacktivism. The chapter concludes by arguing that although the early core values of hacking and its role as a site of 'cultural resistance and stocks of oppositional knowledge' were seriously undermined by the excesses of computer underground and technolibertarian groups, hacktivism is crucial in rejuvenating the hacking ethos. In an ironic twist, a culture initially deeply inimical to female participants now relies upon them for its future development.

Hacking the system

> Wherever computer centres have become established…bright young men of dishevelled appearance, often with sunken glowing eyes, can be seen sitting at computer consoles, their arms tensed, and waiting to fire, their fingers, already poised to strike at the buttons and keys on which their attention seems to be as riveted as a gambler's on the rolling dice. When not so transfixed they often sit at tables strewn with computer print-outs over which they pore like possessed students of a cabalistic text…They exist, at least when so engaged, only through and for the computers. These are computer bums, compulsive programmers. They are an international phenomenon.
>
> (Weizenbaum 1976: 125)

The above quotation is a 'seminal' description of the archetypal hacker who is stereotypically male and distanced from the rest of mainstream society through the obsessive nature of their hi-tech pastime.[4] The MIT (Massachusetts Institute of Technology) psychologist Sherry Turkle provides a thorough delineation of the main elements of hacking. She conflates the wider definition of illicit hacking with the general mentality of those who hack in its sense of seeking to manipulate any technology for unorthodox means. She refers to *the hack* as the 'Holy Grail' (Turkle 1984: 232), explaining that it is a concept which exists independently of the computer and can best be presented by using the example of another technology complex enough to support its own version of hacking and hackers (ibid.). The example she uses is that of phone-phreaking[5] and one of its main adherents, John Draper, alias Captain Crunch. The hack, in this instance, refers to such technological stunts as having two phones on a table; talking into one and hearing your voice in the other after a time-delay in which the original call has first been routed around the world. Turkle (ibid., emphasis added) interprets this type of hack in the following manner:

> Appreciating what made the call around the world a great hack is an exercise in hacker aesthetics. It has the quality of [a] magician's gesture: a truly surprising result produced with ridiculously simple means. Equally important: Crunch had not simply stumbled on a curiosity. The trick worked because Crunch had acquired an impressive amount of expertise about the telephone system. That is what made the trick a great hack, otherwise it would have been a very minor one. Mastery is of the essence every-where within hacker culture. Third, the expertise was acquired unofficially *and at the expense of a big system*. The hacker is a person outside the system who is never excluded by its rules.

It is only comparatively recently that the term hacking has come exclusively to relate to computers and the much more pejorative connotation of illicit intrusion.[6] In its earliest days, as Turkle shows, the activity referred to the ingenious manipulation of any technology or technological system. Thus, the basic definition of 'the hack' stems from exploration of phone, not computer, systems. In a similar fashion, Levy (1984) describes how early hackers at MIT – the institution where students built the first modern computer system and where the term 'computer hacker' was first coined – discovered their love of complex wiring systems while members of the Tech Model Railroad Club. Another example involves an arrested hacker calling himself Agent Steal who describes how to 'hack' the criminal justice system.[7] The common element to all these different technological targets of 'the hack' is the enjoyment hackers derive from identifying an artefact's place within a bigger system in order to manipulate that artefact more effectively. Technical knowledge of both the artefact and its wider system is closely associated, and is an end in itself. By contrast, we shall see in due course how hacktivism, while staying faithful to the notion of the ingenuity of 'the hack', uses that ingenuity not as an end in itself but rather as the means to a more outward-looking political end. The dominance of the end-in-itself mentality within hacking is arguably the single most important factor that has tended to exclude women from it, as will be explored further below.

The gender gap and pointless acts

A new study by the US Department of Commerce reports that only 9 per cent of engineers, 26.9 per cent of systems analysts and computer scientists, and 28.5 per cent of computer programmers are women. In 1984, 37 per cent of computer science degrees went to women; by 1998 that number was 16 per cent...And studies show that women working in IT now make 72 cents on the dollar when compared to their male counterparts. In the mainstream, above-ground, work-a-day world of high technology, women are becoming less visible rather than more so. Little wonder that they're downright invisible in the élite band of digital cowboys who call themselves hackers.

(Lynch 2000: unpaginated)

Girl hackers are as rare as Linux code in a Windows factory.

(ibid.)

This section looks at the possible reasons for early hacking's gender bias as illustrated in the above two quotations (for further evidence of this, see the Appendix to this chapter). Psycho-sexual theories suggest that hacking provides men (and especially young, pubescent men) with a cathartic outlet for their frustrations and biological urge to dominate. We will shortly look at this rationale in the context of the construction of male-orientated conceptualisations of cyberspace. The second type of argument is much more practical. It is based upon the social conditions that make it: (1) less likely for women to be involved in programming activities in the first place; and (2) a hostile environment for women if they do choose to get involved. It seems that hacking culture is disproportionately influenced by the values of pubescent, socially awkward boys. The combination of hacking's esoteric and hi-tech knowledge seems to provide a heady mix that produces manifestations of aggression in the form of pointless acts of destruction and sexist behaviour:

Jane Del Favero, the network security manager at New York University, has read the riot act to plenty of students caught for breaking into machines. Not one of them has been female. 'I'm not sure if there is much about hacking that attracts the average teenage girl. My impression is that they're not interested in the pointless glory of defacing a web site', she said.

(Segan 2000a: unpaginated)

The 'true hacker' would claim that pointless vandalism within computing is the work of crackers (usually defined as criminally motivated cyber-trespassers) not hackers. Leaving aside the contested nature of the terminology, however, it is possible that even though vandalistic activity can involve at least an element of technological ingenuity, it is very seldom an activity that appeals to female programmers who appear more concerned with the ultimate ends to which the technological ingenuity is to be applied:

> The female hackers say they're interested in technology for what it is or what it does, not so they can break it and watch people suffer. RosieX, editor of the Australian feminist technology magazine GeekGirl, said cybervandalism was a 'masturbatory' activity she'd prefer to leave to the boys. 'I really abhor most of the crimes. I find them petulant and, yes, more male than female. I find nothing clever about dismantling an individual's system', she said.
>
> (ibid.)

Such pointless and aggressive acts create an immediate mindset barrier to female involvement in hacker culture that is subsequently reinforced by a general level of sexism ranging from the low to high level: 'The experience of women at the entry levels of the hacking scene, mostly in online chat groups, is one of relentless sexual harassment. It is a hard battle for women to be respected in a culture dominated by teenage boys' (Segan 2000b: unpaginated).

Turkle argues that part of the explanation for both the disproportionate presence of men in hacking and its aggressive nature lies in men's predisposition towards 'hard mastery' whereas females, in contrast, tend towards 'soft mastery':

> Hard mastery is the imposition of will over the machine through the implementation of a plan…Soft mastery is more interactive…try this, wait for a response, try something else, let the overall shape emerge from interaction with the medium. It is more like a conversation than a monologue.
>
> (Turkle 1984: 102–103)

Turkle's concept of these contrasting forms of technological interaction reflects a stark difference in the way the two genders relate computing activity back into the real world:

> In our culture girls are taught the characteristics of soft mastery – negotiation, compromise, give-and-take – as psychological virtues, while models of male behaviour stress decisiveness and the imposition of will...Scientific objects are placed in a 'space' psychologically far away from the world of everyday life, from the world of emotions and relationships. Men seem able, willing and invested in constructing these separate 'objective' worlds, which they can visit as neutral observers...We can see why women might experience a conflict between this construction of science and what feels like 'their way' of dealing with the world, a way that leaves more room for continuous relationships between the self and others.
>
> (ibid.: 107, 115)

The subsequent analysis seeks to show how the maleness of the early hacking environment was reinforced by this tendency to create 'objective' concepts as distant as possible from the real world of messy contingencies. Such a project involves the use of both psychological and rhetorical elements that take two main forms: the pyscho-sexual and cyberspace as the Wild West.

Psycho-sexual theories of hacking

> The computer underworld is populated with young men (and almost no women) who live out their fantasies of power and glory on a keyboard. Most are single. That some young men find computing a substitute for sexual activity is probably incontrovertible. Just as a handle will often hide a shy and frightened fifteen-year-old, an obsession with computing to the exclusion of all else may represent security for a sexually insecure youngster. The computer is his partner, his handle is his real self...and the virus he writes is the child of his real self and his partner. A German virus writer once said: 'You feel something wonderful has happened when you've produced one. You've created something which lives. You don't know where it will go or what it will do, but you know it will live on.' He was talking about his new virus.
>
> (Clough and Mungo 1992: 8)

Technological endeavour has been portrayed as a sublimated libidinal process in various cultural expressions through the ages. This tradition ranges from the Greek myth of Pygmalion and Galatea (in which a sculptor falls in love with his sculpted figure of a woman which eventually is brought to life) to Mary Shelley's evocative and perennially resonant novel and warning to Enlightenment thought, *Frankenstein*. It is perhaps not surprising therefore that claims have been made about the purportedly erotic charge underlying computer activity and, by extension, hacking. Psycho-sexual perspectives provide further, if some-what more speculative, lines of reasoning for the general absence of female hackers. Men are represented as seeking either erotic fulfilment or an artificial shortcut to paternity through their non-human creations. A spokesman for a hacker group calling themselves Toxic Shock seems to add weight to the idea that hackers may hack in order to fulfil some subconscious sexually based desire to penetrate and violate, with his rather 'orgasmic' description of hacking:

> It doesn't happen like *Wargames* shows it. Oh no, it is so much different. The geek in the movie…he had it so easy. No real hackers would exist if it was that easy…No, we hack and hack at a system like a man on safari, clearing away the vines of the jungle with his machete, trying to forge ahead to a destination he cannot yet see. We keep on, torturing our brains and pounding our fingers on the keyboard until at last…oh at long, sweet last…we are in.
>
> (Toxic Shock Group 1990: file 4)

The popular perception of hackers as sexually inadequate, obsessive individuals who, lacking the social skills necessary to converse with other people and especially women, prefer the company of their computers to social interaction, is reinforced by characterisations such as the pre-viously cited assertion of RosieX that the activity is essentially a masturbatory pastime: 'In the sense that hacking is a solitary and non-constructive activity, it might be termed *masturbatory*. The pleasure or interest is confined to the activity itself, and has no object, such as a lover, and no objective, such as a demonstration of affection' (Keller 1988: 57).

Negative connotations of hacking as a masculine pastime also include the views that hackers suffer from too much testosterone, machismo or misplaced libidinal energy. In addition, one imaginative psychoanalytical explanation of the male predominance of cyberspace relies upon a reversal of the Freudian concept of *penis envy*:

The expression 'cyborg envy' has been used to talk about the inversion of the classical 'penis envy' taking place in the longing for cyberspace. Stone [1995] notes that the cybernetic mode 'shares certain conceptual and affective characteristics with numerous fictional evocations of the inarticulate longing of the male for female'. In 'cyborg envy' we long to become woman. In the cybernetic act, 'penetration translates into envelopment. In other words, to enter cyberspace is physically to *put on* cyberspace. To become the cyborg, to put on the seductive and dangerous cybernetic space like a garment, is to put on the *female*'.

(Moreiras 1993: 198)

The word matrix comes from the Latin root *mater* meaning mother or womb. From a Freudian perspective, the matrix becomes a womb-substitute where one can leave the 'meat' of one's body behind in a form of transcendent cerebralism that seeks at least partially to recreate the sense of security once enjoyed in the physically limited, floating environment of the amniotic sac. Cyberspace may have womb-like attributes so that one 'puts on the female' when one enters it, but in its recreation of Freudian womb-longing, it adopts a typically male form. Paglia argues that, historically, men have had a predisposition to creating the 'objective spaces' Turkle associates with 'hard mastery' within:

The realm of number, the crystalline mathematic of Apollonian purity, was invented early on by western man as a refuge from the soggy emotionalism and bristling disorder of woman and nature... Number is the most imposing and least creaturely of pacifiers, man's yearning hope for objectivity. It is to number that he ...withdraws to escape from the chthonian mire of love, hate, and family romance.

(Paglia 1990: 18)

The Apollonian aesthetic for Paglia describes a particularly lineal and clean-cut form of artistic representation that contrasts with its much more organic and materially orientated Dionysian counterpart.[8]

The relevance of this appropriately binary, but otherwise seemingly esoteric, aesthetic theory of gender relations to computing is illustrated by the real-world experiences of hackers and programmers. Thus, Amnon Zichroni, the defence lawyer for Ehud Tenenbaum, an Israeli hacker accused of accessing sensitive areas of NASA and the Pentagon's computer systems, couches his description of the activities of his client in terms of sublimated pubescent romance: 'In the past we used to boast about the girls we had. Nowadays kids boast about their ability to hack into computer systems' (quoted in *Guardian Online* 26 March 1998: 3). Meanwhile, a female programmer, Ellen Ullman, asserts that not only is programming culture strongly male, but also the act of programming itself is premised upon an escape from the corporeal complexities of the real world. In a meeting, when the end-users began to complain, she describes the shock of discovering the disjuncture between programming code and their actual needs:

> I started to panic. Before this meeting, the users existed only in my mind, projections, all mine. They were abstractions, the initiators of tasks that set off remote procedure calls; triggers to a set of logical and machine events that ended in an update to a relational database on a central server. Now I was confronted with their fleshy existence.
>
> (Ullman 1997: 11)

This seductive way in which code promises to deliver the programmer from the messy contingencies of the physical world underlines the previously encountered notions of hacking as essentially a sublimated form of masturbation or immature sexuality: 'We give ourselves over to the sheer fun of the technical, to the nearly sexual pleasure of the clicking thought-stream' (ibid.: 15). Ullman provides first-hand experience of the way in which programming encourages an escape from 'soggy emotionalism and bristling disorder', through the promise of its 'Apollonian purity'. She describes the almost drug-induced trance such a feeling of purity is capable of producing: 'I remember the feel of a system at the early stages of programming, when the knowledge I am to represent in code seems lovely in its structuredness. For a time, the world is a calm, mathematical place. Human and machine seem attuned to a cut-diamond-like state of grace' (ibid.: 21). She further explains the pressure this creates for adapting human requirements to those of the computer: 'human needs must cross the line into code...Actual human confusions cannot live here. Everything we want accomplished, everything the system is to provide, must be denatured in its crossing to the machine or the system will die' (ibid.: 15).

Ullman sees a direct relationship between the abstract world of code that programmers work within and a specifically male form of arrested social development. Cyberspace becomes the manifestation of a flight from adult interaction into an asynchronous world of pure code that allows free rein for puerile behaviour; a state which Ullman labels 'the cult of the boy engineer'. She describes, how 'they behave like children.

They tell each other to shut up. They call each other idiots. They throw balled-up paper…It's like dropping in at the day-care center by mistake' (Ullman, in Brooks and Boal 1995: 138). Such an environment is at best discouraging and at worst hostile to women, not only because there are few women present, but also because those women who do brave an appearance keep a low profile:

> We attend a convention of chip designers. Not a female person in clear sight. If you look closely, however, you can see a few young Chinese women sitting alone, quiet, plainly dressed, succeeding at making themselves invisible. For these are gatherings of young men. This is the land of T-shirts and jeans, the country of perpetual graduate-studenthood.
>
> (ibid.: 139)

To explore further how both the act and the culture of programming tend to adopt a strong male perspective, we now turn to the crucial constitutive role played by rhetorical narratives such as cyberspace being a Wild West realm for technological pioneers.

Cyberspace as the Wild West

> *Bobby was a cowboy*, and ice was the nature of his game, ice from ICE, Intrusion Countermeasures Electronics…Legitimate programmers never see the walls of ice they work behind, the walls of shadow that screen their operations from others, from industrial-espionage artists and hustlers like Bobby Quine. *Bobby was a cowboy*. Bobby was a cracksman, a burglar, casing mankind's extended electronic nervous system, rustling data and credit in the crowded matrix, monochrome nonspace where the only stars are dense concentrations of information.[9]
>
> (Gibson 1986: 197, my emphasis)

> Hackers are…the kind of restless, impatient, sometimes amoral or egocentric spirit that chafes at any kind of restriction or boundary, the kind of spirit (either 'free' or 'outlaw', depending on how you look at it) that bristles resentfully at other people's laws, rules, regulations, and expectations, and relentlessly seeks a way to get over or under or around those rules…In other words, very much the same sort of spirit that drove the people, who, for good and ill, opened up the American West, the kind of spirit that produced far-sighted explorers as well as cattle rustlers and horse thieves, brave

pioneers as well as scurvy outlaw gangs, and that built the bright new cities of the Plains at the cost of countless thousands of Native American lives.

(Dann and Dozois 1996: xiii)

The above two quotations vividly illustrate the close association between the metaphor of the 'Wild West', the concept of cyberspace and the culture of computing. At the beginning of *Neuromancer*, the first brief description of the cyberspace matrix is immediately followed by Case, the protagonist, bemoaning the fact he 'was no console man, no cyberspace cowboy' (Gibson 1984: 11) and such imagery does not simply remain within the pages of fiction. It encourages the projection of macho personalities by actual hackers: 'the actual natives are solitary and independent, sometimes to the point of sociopathy. It is of course a perfect breeding ground for outlaws and new ideas about liberty' (Barlow 1990: 45). Their very names – for example, the Electronic *Frontier* Foundation (EFF) – contribute to the macho, pioneer ethos.

To supplement the psycho-sexual issues already explored, Laura Miller (in Brooks and Boal 1995: 52) identifies the implicitly masculine sexual aspect of the frontier metaphor as crucial for developing an understanding of the gendered basis of cyberspace:

> The classic Western narrative is...concerned with social relation-
> ships...In these stories, the frontier is a lawless society of men, a
> milieu in which physical strength, courage, and personal charisma
> supplant institutional authority and violent conflict is the accepted
> means of settling disputes. The Western narrative connects pleasur-
> ably with the American romance of individualistic masculinity;
> small wonder that the predominantly male founders of the Net's
> culture found it so appealing. When civilisation arrives on the
> frontier, it comes dressed in skirts and short pants.

The 'skirts and short pants' Miller refers to captures the dismissive attitude the self-styled male pioneers of cyberspace have towards attempts at regulating their domain. Elsewhere (Taylor 1998) I have traced in detail the way in which, despite being fuelled by the rhetoric of cyberpunk rebelliousness, the initially counter-cultural qualities of hacking were increasingly co-opted into a more commercially friendly form of computer programming (when geek became chic); a process vividly portrayed in Coupland's *Microserfs* (1995). A remnant of active underground hackers still remains, but by far the most powerful and widespread articulation of the implicitly male anti-regulation approach to computing is the mentality that can be loosely covered by the terms *technolibertarianism* or *cypherphunkery* to which we now turn.

Cypherphunkery or technolibertarianism

[T]he most virulent form of philosophical technolibertarianism is a kind of scary, psychologically brittle, prepolitical autism. It bespeaks a lack of human connection and a discomfort with the core of what many of us consider it means to be human. It's an inability to reconcile the demands of being individual with the demands of participating in society, which coincides beautifully with a preference for, and glorification of, being the solo commander of one's computer in lieu of any other economically viable behavior. Computers are so much more rule-based, controllable, fixable, and comprehensible than any human will ever be. As many political schools of thought do, these technolibertarians make a philosophy out of a personality defect.

(Boorsook 2000: 15)

The terms technolibertarian and cypherphunk refer to those who ally their involvement in the computer industry with strong libertarian and free-market political principles. They provide a good illustration of some of the major gendered characteristics of computing such as a frequently articulated preference for a society as free as possible from regulation and the social ties and obligations that inevitably stem from community relations in the real world. With cypherphunks, the previously cited notion that hackers' technological prowess reflects a sublimated form of arrested sexual development takes the form of an arrested appreciation of social values and an accompanying preference for the predictability and abstract purity of programming: 'Cypherphunkery in a way pays weird homage to a Freudian view of the world – all base emotion and power drives and secret motivations – where higher brain functions such as altruism or empathy or trying to do what's right or mixed emotions are left out of the mix' (ibid.: 92). In a form of 'digital Darwinism', the merging of cyberspatial abstractness and instinctive power drives produces 'a view of human nature that reduces everything to the con-tractual, to economic rational decision-making, which ignores the larger social mesh that makes living as primates in groups at least somewhat bearable, when the weight of days becomes intolerable' (ibid.: 110).

In keeping with the previous psycho-sexual framework of analysis, the rhetorical excesses of cypherphunkery can be seen as an overcompensatory response to fears that increased regulation and socialisation will emasculate the pioneering ethos of the cyberspatial environment they have constructed and conceptualised. Cypherphunkery becomes an attractive ethos because it simultaneously provides an expression of virility ('It helps to get rid of the wimp within' – ibid.: 96), and an escape from real-world uncertainties. Both these qualities come together in the wholesale adoption by cypherphunks of the cult of the entrepreneur and the central tenets of laissez-faire principles. Thus, in a celebration of the 'proleptic inevitability' of the free market's dominance of other forms of social organisation Marx's famous opening to the *Communist Manifesto* is, in true hacking style, re-engineered to produce the *Crypto Anarchist Manifesto* and the claim that 'A specter is haunting the modern world, the specter of crypto anarchy' (cited in ibid.: 89). Confidence in the ultimate 'programmability' of the real world reaches beyond social organisation and down into close personal relationships as well.

'Nerverts' is the term used to describe the conflation of nerd culture and sexual perversion that, according to Boorsook, is a subculture within cypherphunkery and is characterised by the belief that the model of computer programming can be effectively reapplied to emotional ties. The potential confusions and vagueness of amorous cues and seductive interplay are replaced by the nerverts with a marked preference for much more structured forms of interaction. Role playing and consensual S and M create a much more predictable emotional environment where 'monogamy is viewed as emotional terrorism' (ibid.: 100). Robin Roberts, the founder of the nervert 'cultural edifice' for the acting out of sado-masochistic sex known as the Backdrop Club, highlights the close fit between sexual perversion and the nervert's working environment: 'the elaborate negotiations of S-M courtship are like network protocols…and handshaking [a system for two different pieces of hardware to establish communications connections]' (ibid.: 105). The fact that Roberts also teaches programmers how to read another person's body language leads Boorsook to make the acerbic comment that 'Using their brains to construct and act out a fantasy, reducing that most maddening and paradoxical and mysterious of human activities, sex and attraction, to codes – it's a magnificent case of making lemonade out of overcerebrated lemons' (ibid.).

Hacking to hacktivism

Hackerdom with all its failings and foibles, eccentricities and extremism is just a techno-nerd boys' club. Its membership is male not because men's biological urges drive them to sit in front of a computer screen and wangle their way through firewalls. Its membership is male because women don't possess the techno-logical savvy and depth that are the price of admission...Call it a testosterone problem. Call it a technology problem. Call it an economic, social, political, it's-those-darned-whining-feminists-again problem. But while we're pontificating and proselytizing about hacker danger and its threat to our national security and American way of life, let's also remember that those hackers are bound to be boys. Sophomoric, solipsistic, and scruffy. Techno-logically skilled, savvy, and successful boys.

(Lynch 2000: unpaginated)

The term *hacktivism* refers to the transformation of traditional hacking techniques and knowledge into a new form of political activism. It is a phenomenon that returns hacking to its roots in the manipulation of technological systems rather than any particular artefact. It seeks to use either automated hacker-type programs and/or mass co-ordinated web activity to disrupt targeted sites in order to make an explicit political point. Hacktivist activities make use of such technical activities as email bombs, web hacks and computer break-ins, computer viruses and worms, and denial-of-service (DOS) programs[10] to carry out virtual sit-ins and blockades. The latter types of activity are presented by such groups as the Electronic Disturbance Theatre (EDT) as *electronic civil disobedience*.[11] Since hacktivism has only arisen since the late 1990s, it is too early to say what its effects will be on the male-dominated aspects of computing described in the previous sections, but the early signs are that its much more inclusive roots in political and social activism offer considerable potential to close the gender gap and to reintroduce more real-world concerns to the Appollonian constructions of male pro-gramming culture.

In interview, the female hacktivist Carmin Karasic provided me with numerous insights about the changes that have occurred in the Computer Underground as a result of female participation:

Hacktivism isn't restricted to just hackers (conventionally defined) it is much more about bending the technology to suit your political cause and that's something that's not just interesting to men. Women are taking a bigger and bigger role and starting to be more influential. Women are much more about negotiation and consensus and as hacktivism involves more women, hacktivist tools are likely to involve more participation. The lone, male hacker tends to do things with their own little piece of code, but women are much less likely to do that, they're much more likely to develop code that does something for human causes.

(Carmin Karasic, EDT member: phone interview)

Karasic embodies the potential for hacktivism to broaden out the more purely technical focus of hacking. She programmed the hacktivist DOS tool Floodnet not for technical elegance but to encourage mass participation. Karasic described the negative response from Dutch hackers (who Ricardo Dominguez, also of the EDT, caricatures as the 'digitally correct'), neatly illustrating the contrasting hacker and hacktivist mentalities:

They have a notion of technical elegance above all else – they got annoyed that Floodnet just clogged up the Internet. This goes back to the pinging of servers, and issues like pinging the server on the way there rather than the channel on the way back…Dutch hackers want focused and targeted attacks to avoid clogging up like that'.

(phone interview)

In stark contrast to such attitudes is the much more artistic approach of hacktivists who seek to use technology as an art medium. Thus Karasic describes how a colleague, Lisa Javbret

Dabbled with 404[12] as an art medium. Within the first version of Floodnet there's a part that allows you to send a personal message to the server of your choice; for example, 'peace' to a bank server. The reply comes back 'peace is not found on this server'. That's the artistic bit.

(phone interview)

Karasic suggests that hacktivism retains 'true hacking's' desire to master the system, but opens up its focus to go beyond the more limited technical concerns of hackers who: 'aren't so much interested in social issues, they're much more interested in the human/machine interaction like the kid who unpicks the lock, so they're much more interested in things rather than people' (phone interview). Furthermore, echoing Paglia's concept of the Apollonian as an escape from the Dionysian, she complains about hackers' over-dependence on the abstract world of the former: 'you can't just resort to cyberspace and until it's our primary space we can't just ignore the flesh-space' (ibid.).

Conclusion

[A]ll cultural achievement is a projection, a swerve into Apollonian transcendence, and...men are anatomically destined to be projectors.

(Paglia 1990: 17)

Man is sexually compartmentalised. Genitally, he is condemned to a perpetual pattern of linearity, focus, aim, directedness. He must learn to aim.

(ibid.: 19)

Concentration and projection are remarkably demonstrated by urination, one of male anatomy's most efficient compartmentalizations. Freud thinks primitive man preened himself on his ability to put out a fire with a stream of urine. A strange thing to be proud of but certainly beyond the scope of woman, who would scorch her hams in the process. Male urination really is a kind of accomplishment, an arc of transcendence. A woman merely waters the ground she stands on.

(ibid.: 20–21)

The three basic criteria of the original hacking ethos were outlined by Turkle at the beginning of this chapter as *simplicity* (the act has to be simple but impressive); *mastery* (the act involves sophisticated technical knowledge); and *illicitness* (the act is 'against the rules'). These criteria have been re-engineered by both cypherphunks/technolibertarians and hacktivists. Thus the former adhere to a political neo-Darwinist political philosophy pared down of any recognition of social complexity. They maintain detailed technological knowledge as a distinguishing badge of honour, in this case particularly its commercial value, and they revel in the radical nature of their anti-communitarian ethos. Similarly, hacktivists have an agenda which, although diametrically opposed in its rationale, contains the same three basic elements. They retain the method of subverting a system or an artefact through relatively simple means (e.g. denial-of-service attacks that merely overload a server by requiring it to fulfil its function to excess). They, too, maintain detailed technical knowledge although this is much more as a means to an end rather than an end in itself. Finally, their *raison d'être* is very much against the political establishment's status quo.

The crucial difference between the two approaches, however, resides in their contrasting relationships to the concepts of hard and soft mastery.

Technolibertarian culture can be seen as a continuation of the hacker mindset with signs of the attributes Turkle associates with hard mastery evident in the three main conceptual representations of hacking (the psycho-sexual, the fictional and the Wild West). They associate their programming prowess with the imposition of sexual will in a receptive or passive environment and, aided by the leading role taken by fictional images of cyberspace, they have conceptualised new independent, 'objective' spaces as environments for programming. In relation to Turkle's schema, the rise of hacktivism marks the reassertion of soft-mastery. Instead of the libertarian monologue of the cyber-selfish with its socially monotone environment for high aspirers, hacktivism seeks to explore the basis for a much more 'conversationally' based and inclusive social agenda that reunites the abstract 'objective' world of cyberspace back with the physical world from whence it sprang.

In this chapter's discussion of the origins of hacking, we have seen the 'true hacker' distinguished from the programmer by their overriding interest in manipulating technological *systems* in general rather than any particular systems of computer code. They treat computer systems as something to be hacked rather than an end in itself. If the political status quo is understood in terms of the commonplace phrase 'the system', hacktivists' desire to *hack the system* represents a return to the original roots of hacking and a rescuing of its ethos from its drift to techno-libertarianism. With their willingness to re-engage with the messy contingencies of the world (increasingly eschewed by programmers who seek the 'crystalline purity' of code) hacktivists have reintegrated pro-gramming with the concerns of the real world. In Paglia's argot, they have served to re-ground technological ingenuity away from the pseudo-womb of the Appollonian matrix and back into the Dionysian, chthonic flux of day-to-day life and its refractory reality. Console cowboys might be surprised to learn that there is more than one way to put out the capitalist camp fire.

Appendix

The following quotations provide further evidence of a generally recognised gender gap in the number of female hackers compared to their male counterparts:

> A hallmark of the event [Hack-Tic computer club's 1993 summer conference] was the male to female ratio: running at roughly 100:1, it did not bode well for the demise of the anorak. Even so there was

some emergence of a hacker chic, with one of the few women sporting jewellery made from watch parts and hair decoration courtesy of an eviscerated floppy disk.

(Goodwins 1993: 11)

Not that many women frequent the underground, and most that do come into it as transients while they are dating a hacker or as press to do a one-time story. On IRC [Internet relay chat] about two dozen women hang out with hackers regularly...I have met more than a thousand male hackers in person but less than a dozen of the women.

(Gilboa 1996: 106)

In the course of a career in computing which spans 20 years in industry and academia in the United States and Great Britain I have met several people I would call hackers...I have never met a female hacker. No one I know with whom I have discussed hacking can recall an instance of meeting or hearing of a female hacker...The *Hacker's Handbook, 3rd Edition* mentions one [in a footnote] but at one point puts 'she' in quotes, as though to denote irony or uncertainty about that particular hacker's true gender.

(Keller 1988: 57)

We have met the enemy, and he is...well, just that: a He...In the wake of recent 'denial-of-service' attacks on some of the Web's largest e-commerce sites, the culprits have been called everything from packet monkeys to digital outlaws. But nobody is calling them anything but male. In fact, ask anybody who purports to know...and it's unanimous: hackers are male. Sophomorically, solipsistically, and scruffily male.

(Lynch 2000: unpaginated)

Given this shortfall in the number of female hackers, below are brief details collated by Sascha Segan of ABC News of the major female figures who in recent years have either been hackers, hacktivists or played an influential part in the subculture of computing:

1. Courtnee, a hacker based in the Pacific Northwest.

2. Carmin Karasic (her real name) of The Electronic Disturbance Theatre project, an online political performance-art group. She was a key figure in the development of Floodnet, a programming tool used by EDT to

bombard its opponents with access requests to servers that with sufficient mass participation of activists overloads them.

3. Susan Thunder, who was one of the early phone-phreakers and associated with Kevin Mitnick's phone-phreaking group of the 1970s.

4. Natasha Grigori (Net handle based upon a US cartoon character) who ran a bulletin board system for software pirates in the early 1990s and is now the founder of an anti-paedophile hacker group entitled antichildporn.org.

5. 'St.Jude' Milhon (her real surname), who helped found *Mondo 2000*, an influential cyber-lifestyle magazine of the late 1990s.

6. Jennifer Grannick, a lawyer active in the realm of hackers' rights.

7. ViXen900, a legal adviser to the HNC hackers' group.

In *Approaching Zero*, the authors describe another example: 'Leslie Lynne Doucette was once described as the "female Fagin" of the computer underworld...As a woman, she has the distinction of being one of only two or three female hackers who have ever come to the attention of the authorities' (Clough and Mungo 1992: 148).

Notes

1. This chapter was developed as part of an ESRC-sponsored seminar series on the theme of 'immateriality'.
2. Quoted with the permission of the author in Taylor (1999: 39–40).
3. See Taylor (1999: especially pp. 56–58) for a more specific discussion of the role power plays in the motivational aspects of hacking.
4. Weizenbaum describes the earliest generation of hackers and at this point there is little distinction between legitimate and illegal programming activity. Elsewhere (Taylor 1999) I have dealt at length with the issue of the fiercely contested nature of hacking, but for the purposes of this chapter I have kept faith with Weizenbaum's association of hacking with programming in general.
5. *Phone-phreakers* is the phrase used to describe people who use various electronic devices to hack into the telephone networks to explore the system and/or obtain free phone calls.
6. In *Hackers: Crime in the Digital Sublime* (1999), I explore in detail the social construction of the negative connotations of hacking.
7. See J. Peterson (1997) 'Everything a hacker needs to know about getting busted by the Feds' (available at: www.grayarea.com/agsteal.html).

8. In Paglia's 'Sexual Personae', the 'Dionysian' is used to refer to an aesthetic grounded in the material flux and shapes of the physical world, while the 'Apollonian' in contrast is an aesthetic based upon the non-physical purity of numbers, mathematics and clean lines. The former she intrinsically associates with the condition of being female while the latter is symptomatic of a male perspective. In Greek mythology, the god Dionysus was fond of earthly life. He was associated with sensual pleasures, inventing the orgasm and showing mortals how to farm bees for honey and make wine. Apollo, meanwhile, was aloof from mortals and was associated with the more immaterial delights of music.

9. Given the focus of the previous section, it is interesting to note that implicit in Gibson's zeitgeist-capturing approach is a strong psycho-sexual element. Hackers appear in the form of console cowboys who, as this quotation illustrates, 'jack themselves into' the womb-like space of the matrix. Resonating with Keller's claim that hacking is a subliminally masturbatory activity, Springer (1996: 72) points out that Gibson originally wanted to call his book not *Neuromancer*, but *Jacked In*, but was told that it sounded too much like 'jacked off'. The association of sex with the Matrix in *Neuromancer* has an ambivalent quality of both empowerment and death. The protagonist, Case, is the archetypally empowered console cowboy whose love of the bodily transcendence afforded by the Matrix is such that his body is described as a 'prison of his own flesh' and even his orgasm is couched in informational terms. The negative aspect is personified in the non-corporeal yet phallic-sounding figure of Dixie Flatline, who's consciousness became trapped inside the Matrix after his physical death and who therefore arguably represents the primordial male fear of the vagina dentata and mini-death of detumescence that inevitably follows the act of sexual penetration.

10. A denial-of-service attack (DOS) is designed to overload the servers of a targeted website by generating more requests for information than the server can fulfil. It provides a good example of the way in which hacktivism blends old-style hacking and new forms of political activism because, true to the nature of 'the hack', it simply uses the original purpose of technology against itself, while its novel political element derives from the way in which it allows simultaneous concerted mass action from otherwise physically isolated people.

11. For a more detailed account, see Taylor (2001).

12. The identifying number of the standard reply received when a requested piece of information is not available on a website.

Chapter 9

Digital counter-cultures and the nature of electronic social and political movements

Rinella Cere

Introduction

Like all major technological innovations the Internet has spurred numerous debates about its utility or futility, its accessibility and the direction in which it is going to take us. This chapter aims to be a small contribution to this debate by considering the relationship between computer-mediated communications (CMCs) and political activism (both specific struggles 'on the ground' and global contemporary social and political movements). It will refer to three case studies and relevant, related websites to highlight whether the relationship between CMCs and activism is a meaningful one, whether it is advancing the cause of the particular struggles discussed and whether it can continue as it has previously, circumventing the machinations of 'digital capitalism' and the 'unprecedented phenomenon of ideological contamination' (Virilio 2000: 110). Inevitably this will lead us into a short exploration of the 'new information technology paradigm' and the nature of the 'network society' (Castells 1996) in addition to some of the theoretical approaches to 'transnational social movements' and the way Internet technologies and alternative political activism (or 'hacktivism') are integral to one another. Certainly the Internet, with its 'young', Utopian and libertarian nature, clearly appeals to radical politics, but – as this chapter will demonstrate – that is only half the story of the Net's origins, which could equally be seen as rooted in the defence strategy of the US National Security Agency (Gillies and Cailliau 2000; Slevin 2000).

In this chapter I will distinguish between two main types of Internet political activists: Net-dedicated activists or 'hacktivists' and political *users* of the Net. Although the two categories are fluid and may share some features, I understand the former in terms of the description given by Jordan as people who 'from their individuality, their singularity ...build cultural and political places in cyberspace...the land of empowerment of individuals' (1999: 96). The latter refers to people whose main concerns are in the 'real' community but are none the less aware of the way in which political battles can be enhanced and linked at a global level through the Internet. In this chapter I am mainly concerned with political uses of the Net, but not in the comprehensive sense encompassing mainstream political parties *and* alternative political and pressure groups (Margolis and Resnick 2000). Here I will just be considering alternative political action and social movements, but with the added proviso that politics that affects the Net and political uses of the Net are not always clearly separable, especially in relation to questions of regulation and censorship and also in terms of allegiances and solidarities created within cyberspace. It is also worth pointing out that some alternative political struggles and social movements started making use of the Internet long before mainstream politics or established political parties did (Coleman *et al* 1999; Davis 1999). This is hardly surprising given that many of the people involved in radical or alternative politics have grown up with computer technologies and are completely au fait with their possibilities and potential.

I will be also be using the term 'political' and 'social' interchangeably, partly because the term social has replaced political in many cases. However, this is not an indication of an anti-political age but of the twofold paradox described by Melucci (1996: 117) as follows:

> On the one hand collective action is no longer separable from individual demands and needs, and is therefore constantly threatened by trends towards atomisation and privatisation; and on the other, the conflictual pressure brought to bear on the logic of the system does not operate through politics. Nevertheless, and precisely for this reason, it cannot do without politics.

Finally, although I will be referring to three specific case studies, the peoples and activities embraced by political activism are extremely diverse. Yet despite that diversity, the Internet has the propensity to unite people in a common global struggle against neoliberal economics. In this respect, the aims espoused at zeligConf[1] – a meeting of European digital counter-cultures in March 2000 – are worth quoting in full:

Around network practices, and on networks, during the last years many collective subjects, actors of practices, initiatives and confrontations have formed, which mark communication territories with a strong alternative presence. Whether it is a matter of experiences linked to struggles or social movements (illegal immigrants, unemployed and precarious workers, occupied social centers, etc), of embryonic alternative networks (Nodo 50, Sindimonio, ECN, Sherwood, Samizdat), of theoretical and cultural aggregations around virtual spaces of development and reflection (Nettime, Syndicate), of online publishing initiatives (Sherwood-Tribune, Active Territorial Network, agencia in permanent construccion, Hacktivist news service), or the effervescence around free software, a real richness has emerged from practices, contents and analysis which we want to consider as a common and collective inheritance.

(www.zeligconf/)

The 'network paradigm' and 'network politics'

One of the central features of anti-globalisation/anti-capitalist movements is their 'network-like' nature. This has increased and intensified through use of the Internet – a technology which itself has a 'network' structure. From the early days of Unix, Usenet and bulletin board systems (BBSs) to the recent expansion of the World Wide Web (WWW) and contemporary open source systems, the Net has established its place as a socio-technological formation 'with technologically and culturally embedded properties of interactivity and individualisation' (Castells 1996: 358). In the same way that a movement consists of 'diversified and autonomous units which devote a large part of their available resources to the construction and maintenance of internal solidarity' (Melucci 1996: 113), a communication and exchange network 'keeps the separate, quasi-autonomous cells in contact with each other' (ibid.). This interpretation is a useful way of conceptualising the nature of the thousands of politically and socially orientated 'webforms' to be found in the Net galaxy. As with many of the activities described in this volume, it is the global network structure of the Internet that serves contemporary political and social movements so very well both in organisational and informational terms. 'Alternative' websites are the lifeblood of counter-information, in spite of the growing commercialisation of the WWW and the concomitant changes brought about by what has been described as the 'process of normalisation' (Margolis and Resnick 2000). Furthermore, if the Internet is not only a 'revolution about *real information*' but is at the same time also 'a revolution about *virtual disinformation*' (Virilio 2000: 108), the importance of a global forum for counter-information, both real and virtual, has arguably never been so vital.

The Internet and 'new social movements'

Social movement theory has been around for some time and is abundant, but there is as yet very little systematically assembled information about the specific ways various social movements have adopted electronic networking as an instrument of mobilisation and resistance to excessive state repression. Some commentators have criticised the use of CMCs by activists, claiming that electronic communication in some sense negates the authenticity of the experience and dilutes participants' commitment to the struggle they are involved in. For example, Tarrow (1998: 193) somewhat submissively claims that '[a]s anyone who has caught the Internet virus can attest, virtual activism may serve as a *substitute* – and not as a spur – to activism in the real world'. For him electronic contacts 'cannot promise the same crystallisation of collective trust as…the live experience' (ibid.). This is a thought shared by Diani (whose study of the Italian environmental movement is used by Tarrow as an example of 'collective trust in lived experience') in his recent reflection on the value of CMCs to social movements: 'it is disputable whether the warmth and intensity of direct, face-to-face communications may be found in computer-mediated interactions' (Diani 2001: 121). What they both ignore, however, is the way in which such networking activities usually evolve into 'real life' experiences through meetings, festivals, support concerts, visits and many varied fund-raising activities (as the Chiapas and Porto Alegre websites mentioned later will incontrovertibly demonstrate).

Hacktivists and activists: politics and technology

Another aspect which cannot be ignored when discussing political activism and the use of the Net is the technological one of 'open source' software. This is as much a political issue as it is a technological one and it is 'organically' tied to the space and direction that alternative political activism and social movements may have in the future. This was no clearer than at the zeligConf where the aim of the organisers centred on ways to advance, co-ordinate and bring to fruition the different 'spirits' of the participants/speakers:

> It will be as much about conducting an inventory of fixtures in the experience of digital communication practises of NGOs, social movements, militant initiatives or activism, as about attempting to formalise hypotheses on a wide integration of the Internet, and on potentialities of free software in the development of alternative communication initiatives.
>
> (www.zeligconf/)

Free software and open source systems, such as Linux, Gnu/Linux and Freenet, have long been considered allies of alternative circuits of distribution and access, in spite of the fact that 'free' does not usually mean cost-free.[2] These kinds of ambiguities spell out the contradictions and problems at the heart of those alliances, all the more so recently with what are perceived as mounting commercial pressures on successful open source systems to compete against the Microsoft monopoly which has control of 95 per cent of the operating systems. Whether the perception spelled out by Richard Stallman of the Free Software Foundation – that free software today has enormous commercial value – is actually shared by groups which are trying to combat neoliberal capitalism is another matter, but I suspect not. Perhaps we should remember that all these 'radical programmers' and their allies are none the less part of 'the technopower elite...somewhere between the institutional giants and the underground hackers' (Jordan 1999: 140). The words 'freedom' and 'free' are inarguably abused and overused in most walks of life, but nowhere more so than in the 'cyberwalks' of life.

In the 'Philosophy behind the Freenet' project – 'an adaptive peer to peer network application that permits publication, replication, and retrieval of data while protecting the anonymity of its users' (www.freenetproject.org) – Ian Clarke suggests that we really need unlimited freedom of information and that there is no such thing as 'good censorship'. He brings a somewhat cryptic example to bear: 'There are already criticisms that the anti-racism censorship in many European countries is hampering legitimate historical analysis of events such as the Second World War' (ibid.). What this legitimate historical analysis might be is not actually spelled out, but more worrying is the notion that somehow racist views need to be in the open and that people need to be exposed to them in order to counteract them: 'Unfortunately, preventing people from being aware of the often sophisticated arguments used by racists, makes them vulnerable to those arguments when they do eventually encounter them' (ibid.). The assumption that racists use sophisticated arguments is dubious enough, but the logic of such a statement is truly alarming: i.e. that if people are not subjected to racist arguments then they will not be able to counter their force, a familiar empirical argument proven wrong time and time again. Put simply, it is akin to saying that human beings cannot understand or be critical about situations of which they do not have first-hand experience. Apart from the fact that this would probably lead to political inaction, web-based political activities and, more importantly, their follow-up in the real world disprove that point once and for all.

The hackers' culture

The other aspect I want to consider briefly before discussing specific case studies, as it is both closely tied to open source ideals and clearly overlaps with political activism online, is the hackers' culture. There are as many different hacker 'types' and typologies as there are Net-based political activities. However, two forms of hacking which draw from and contribute to alternative politics are undoubtedly those described by Ross (cited in Taylor 1999: 43) as follows: 'Hacking is an important form of watchdog counter-response to the use of surveillance technology and data-gathering by the state, and to increasingly monolithic communications power of giant corporations' and 'Hacking, as guerrilla know-how, is essential to the task of maintaining fronts of cultural resistance and stocks of oppositional knowledge as a hedge against a techno-fascist future.'

There is not sufficient space here to mention the many terms currently used for different types of hackers which range from the benign to the more criminally orientated element who are normally defined as 'crackers'. The latter may engage in a range of unlawful activities from trespassing to information warfare. The literature on the subject of hackers is certainly proliferating to the point where hacking is being seen as a veritable 'ethic' of our age (Himanen 2001). Yet interestingly, the alliances between 'benign' hackers and political activists hardly extend to women in the way that one would expect looking at the intense Internet activities of feminists, as well as at women's struggles being publicised online around the world. I visited about a hundred women's/feminist websites for the purposes of researching this chapter and found that the hacker's world is still, with very few exceptions, a very masculine environment.

Their gender composition aside, hackers have undergone much change in recent years, to the point of professionalising their activities

(Taylor 1999). This trend is going some way to counteract the processes of demonisation and stigmatisation to which hackers have been subjected since the inception of CMCs. Prominent hackers have even become part of Internet governance, as in the case of the (short-lived as it turned out) election to ICANN (Internet Corporation for Assigned Numbers and Names) of the head of a German hacker group, the Chaos Computer Club, which had been established to challenge anti-corporatist values.

Indigenous struggles and the Net: the case of the Zapatistas

The Internet has been linked with several indigenous populations around the world, fuelling debates about whether computer technologies and the medium of the Internet help to preserve or tend to destroy indigenous cultures and traditions. Indigenous peoples such as Native Americans have successfully used the Internet to circulate information about their political struggles and have used sites to teach their language, history and customs in a medium arguably more akin to the oral and pictographic tradition than the dominant written forms of communication (Arnold and Plymire, 2000), although there are counter-arguments to this view, which will be explored below. But in theory at least, the Internet has an advantage over traditional print media by facilitating the building of bonds of community across time and space while avoiding, or at least limiting, the degree of censorship from governments or federal agencies (ibid.).

One of the first political struggles to receive worldwide publicity and support via the Net (it has in fact become known as the first 'cyberwar') was the uprising of the indigenous people, the Zapatistas, against occupation by a tyrannical government in Chiapas, Mexico, which began on 1 January 1994:

> Even as the government mobilised its army to occupy the state of Chiapas and tried to deny the revolutionaries access to the mass media, they and their supporters were mobilizing words and images to disseminate ideas electronically...To begin with, it became the only way of posting the Zapatistas' concerns and programmes for economic and social reform which were being underplayed, ignored or suppressed by the mainstream media.
>
> (Vidal 1999: unpaginated)

As time went on, information was downloaded from the Net and transformed into flyers, pamphlets, newsletters, articles and books detailing the torture, rape, executions and other violence being perpetrated by the police and military. The material fuelled marches and vigils around the world (Cleaver, cited in Vidal 1999) and provoked new awareness, respect for and study of the much broader phenomenon of indigenous resistance in this period. In fact, the struggle has been described by the 'Zapatistas in Cyberspace' site as 'one of the most successful examples of the use of computer communications by grass-roots social movements' (www.eco.utexas.edu/homepages/faculty/cleaver/chiapas/). This site, compiled 'over the border' at Texas University includes details of all the political campaigns and activities (web-based and non web-based) surrounding the struggle of the people of Chiapas against the state's anti-worker/peasant policies. One of the debates to be found on the site and its interconnected links concerns the relationship between 'real life' politics and virtual politics and the effectiveness and value of electronic support to political struggles against capitalism around the world. This is undoubtedly an important new dimension, although reading some of the debates online one has the distinct impression that these are very much concerns generated among the left in the west (the USA in this case, but also parts of Europe) and not necessarily part of the concerns of the Zapatistas themselves, or of the Indian population of Chiapas.

This brings us to some of the criticisms of sites that claim to represent native peoples. At the most fundamental level, access to the Internet – while usually requiring less capital outlay than print media – is far from equally distributed and marked inequalities remain. Disparities along lines of race, class, gender and ethnicity are well documented elsewhere although it should be noted that the balances *are* changing: for example, it is now the case that the majority of Internet users (59.8 per cent) are from non-English speaking zones (www.nua.ie/surveys/index.cgi). However, regional growth in Internet use is not always smooth and continuous, but may be disrupted by war, disaster or displacement. For example, the digital divide in Bosnia and Herzegovina is widening as refugees and displaced people return to their pre-war homes. In 2000 the Internet population in the region was between 2 per cent and 3 per cent, but it has since dropped to 1.5 per cent. This compares with an Internet population of 30 per cent in Slovenia and 20 per cent in Croatia (ibid.).

Start-up costs of Internet access are still prohibitively high for the poorest people in the world, where many do not even have access to a telephone service. There are further technological difficulties for communities like those in Chiapas, not least because, as Belausteguigoitia (1999: 27) suggests: 'they are too busy moving from place to place...to protect their lives, and technologies such as computers and modems are not easy to preserve in the middle of the jungle.' More fundamentally, although Chiapas 'has been penetrated by the most diverse technologies to extract its wealth…the majority of its population and the entire Indian population still live in misery' (ibid.). Moreover, the Mexican state has tried to counter the Zapatistas' appropriation of cyberspace with its own intervention on the Net. It has been accused of tampering with computer communications, causing networks to 'go down' at critical moments, monitoring the Net closely for counter-insurgency and trying to de-legitimise the Zapatistas' arguments (Vidal 1999).

But despite difficulties of access and attempts at sabotage by the Mexican state, the Internet has succeeded in the promotion of passionate discussion not just about the struggle in Chiapas, but more widely about the failures of global capitalism and market-driven neoliberalism around the world. The EZLN (Ejército Zapatista de Liberación Nacional) has its own site – www.ezln.org – and the Zapatistas are clearly winning the battle of ideas. Eight years on, many of their concerns surrounding poverty, land rights, justice, exploitation, the environment and society are part of the vocabulary of new democracy movements in other parts of Mexico and in many other countries around the world (Vidal 1999).

Also worth a special mention here is the women's struggle within the context of the EZLN uprising and the peasants' and indigenous people's struggle over land. Mujeres Zapatistas (www.actlab.utexas.edu/~geneve/zapwomen/) is a website concerned specifically with the position of women within the overall movement, and it incorporates links to other women's movements in Latin America. The website contains important information about the position of women in rural societies and within the Zapatistas' struggle specifically, and is evidence that the web is one place (albeit not the only one) where 'missing' women have a voice (ibid.). Other activists' action through and on the web have included the organisation of intercontinental conferences (via the Inter-continental Network of Alternative Communication), the first of which took place in Chiapas in the summer of 1996 and brought together 3,000 grassroots activists and intellectuals from 42 countries on five continents 'to discuss the struggle against neo-liberalism on a global scale' (www.actlab.utexas.edu/~zapatistas).

This kind of political activity through the web has sparked re-percussions by US national security analysts who are starting to view alternative political activities online as a form of unlawful activity: 'What we view as new methods of collaborative self-activity, they view as threatening forms of "Netwar" or "information warfare"' (www.eco.utexas.edu/homepages/faculty/cleaver/chiapas95.html).

That national security view the development of a university-based site supporting the Chiapas 'campesinos' as a form of 'warfare' tells a long story about the interests the USA has in this area, and – in a broader context – about the attitudes of political and law enforcement authorities to counter-cultures generally. As the Internet undergoes a transformation of the kind we have witnessed with many media and communication technologies before – centralisation, commercialisation, over-regulation and unwarranted harassment from the police – moves to criminalise its users have become increasingly apparent. As all the anti-capitalist/anti-globalisation demonstrations of recent years have proved – the demonstration in Genoa in 2001 protesting against the meeting of the G8 states being but one recent example – heavy-handed intervention by police and other state-authorised agencies is common. But in addition to this intervention on the ground, there has also been extreme action taken with regard to activists' use of electronic communications systems. For example, earlier this year, the police tried to stop the Mayday website by threatening to shut down the service provider.

Undoubtedly counter-cultures are part and parcel of political resistance to capitalist forces. But their characterisation in much of the pro-US literature and on related web links as unlawful activities which should be subject to criminalisation is frequently overblown and hysterical in tone. The role of activist websites such as the Zapatistas sites mentioned earlier is principally to act as a forum to create international solidarity and support for the oppressed people of a state which has historically relinquished its land and people for US profit (Harvey 1998). To trace the history of some of these sites reveals three important issues for the elucidation of the relationship between social movements, political activists and the Net. The first is that many of these sites and links are part of the Zapnet project which involves activists, writers and artists representing all parts of the world where new technologies are available and part of everyday life, but principally from the USA. As we have seen in the past it is frequently from countries which 'lead the exploitation' that some of the resources to counteract it also come, particularly in relation to information technology. The second point to be made is that what is achieved in terms of sharing information, mobilisation and support via the Internet is not so very different from what was (and still is) accomplished in print form by activists. In that sense it may be more accurate to characterise the Internet, not as an entirely new means of co-ordination and communication, but simply as an additional and complementary instrument for struggle. The third important point to arise from this discussion is that, although the Internet might be used predominantly as an extension of existing activities, it none the less clearly gives activism a global reach and introduces people to social movements whose political activities they may not have previously known about or dreamt of taking part in. This is not *always* the case, and interest is often generated from existing networks: 'even transnational networks seem to take the form of "virtual extensions" rather than "virtual communities", given their reliance on a small élite of strongly connected activists' (Diani 2001: 126). However, younger generations are more attracted to 'new social movement' politics than mainstream political activities, and computer-mediated communications – especially 'postings' – give extra 'pull' to this new form of political activity. Unfortunately, as discussed in Chapter 2 of this volume, the same factors are similarly being used to attract youthful members to extreme right-wing organisations and hate movements.

Porto Alegre and the World Social Forum

On 4 February 2002, 'Net surfers of the world' were invited to go on an online demonstration with the people and participants of the World Social Forum in Porto Alegre, capital of the southernmost Brazilian state of Rio Grande do Sul. The World Social Forum (WSF) was established as a counter-movement to the World Economic Forum (WEF) which meets once a year in the luxurious Alpine resort of Davos in Switzerland and is composed of an élite club of chief executives representing more than a thousand powerful corporations (Juniper 2002). The WSF takes place around the same time but with contrasting aims. One of its key initiatives is to challenge the global economic institutions which have failed to narrow the poverty gap (the UN reports that between 1960 and 2000, the divide between the poorest fifth and richest fifth of the world's population has doubled) and to 'make another world possible' especially in countries of the Southern Hemisphere where widespread poverty is still rife. This new 'global social movement' is especially critical of issues concerning neoliberal economic processes and globalisation, and is in total opposition to liberalising agricultural markets. It also presses for the cancellation of third-world debt and the end of tax havens, and has special interests concerning environmental disasters, war, poverty, discrimination and many other issues involving a lack of social justice, equality and solidarity structural to the present system.

Although still in its infancy, the WSF has strong foundations. The anti-IMF riots of the mid-1970s marked the beginning of a movement which challenged the way that global economic institutions were turning southern countries into quarry for corporate predators (Wainwright

2002). The WSF's venue for meeting – Porto Alegre, Brazil – is clearly in contrast and in ideological opposition to the venue chosen by the WEF (which, for the first time in 2002, was transferred to the Waldorf Hotel in New York after the Swiss authorities refused to provide security). Not surprisingly, Latin America has always been a pivotal area for anti-imperialist, anti-capitalist movements and critiques, given that many of its countries have been at the receiving end of the worst excesses of capitalist exploitation and have suffered colluding military right-wing regimes to boot. Brazil was considered a particularly appropriate host because of its variety of social movements and experiments, and Porto Alegre was chosen as the location partly because of a sympathetic local government which contributed approximately £350,000 to the forum. In his opening speech, Olivio Dutra, the state governor, said: 'The World Social Forum is the opportunity we need to rescue history's most valuable asset: solidarity. It is the tool we need to assure ethics in politics and democracy in social action' (Bellos 2001: unpaginated). Dutra is a member of the Partidodos Trabalhadores (Brazilian Workers Party) which has pioneered an impressive experiment in participatory democracy by opening up the municipal and state investment budgets to a process of popular control. The result has been a rooting out of corruption, a significant redistribution of wealth and a degree of citizens' engagement with the political processes unprecedented in the west (Wainwright 2002).

The WSF's website (www.forumsocialmundial.org.br) is a good place to find all the details about the event and about how to use the Internet and other new media to reach people without the mediation of main-stream media or press agencies. The alternative online media also report from Porto Alegre on all the programmes and events organised by the various participants at the forum yet if one relied on the mainstream media in Britain one would hardly know that it was taking place as there were few reports, especially on television (the *Guardian* is a notable exception to this general disinterest). This in spite of the fact that the mainstream media usually consider major anti-global/anti-capitalist demonstrations as highly newsworthy events, and often report extensively in advance of them taking place, and usually with moral-panic-tinged predictions about their outcomes. It is precisely this kind of disinformation that renders alternative information websites even more vital. During the four days of the event there was extensive coverage by the Indymedia (www.indymedia.org), an international network of news now available in many continents and countries, and by contributors to several other anti-globalisation websites.[3] Moreover, the effective use of the Internet to organise and maintain activities around the world was addressed by some participants (see, for example, www.peacelink.it/portoalegre/).

Whether the WSF can be seen as one of the first 'transnational social movements' or simply as an umbrella organisation which encompasses disparate associations and groups is still to be decided. The WSF itself does not have homogeneous aims in mind and it certainly does not act as a unified international representative. It avoids using concepts like 'left wing' and 'right wing' and its participants claim that 'anti-capitalist' is no longer an adequate description for a social movement rich in practical solutions (Wainwright 2002). The impetus in 2001 was a strong belief that 'protest is not enough', as Filipino activist and intellectual Walden Bello stated, and that protesters *do* have effective alternatives. However, protest has not been completely abandoned as evidenced by the fact that more than 1,000 members of one of the organising groups, the Movement of Landless Rural Workers, invaded the nearby biotech plant of Monsanto during the event.

Feminism, women's liberation and the Net

Women are silly creatures who don't know how to use the Internet.
(quoted in Spender 1995: 223)

My neighbour is a Jazz singer who has her own web site as well as her quartet.[4]

Perhaps more than most, the feminist movement has been classified and discussed in terms of a 'new social movement' aligned to radical and alternative political processes and open to the adoption of political communicative strategies based on fundamentally different principles from those of the mainstream media, who always appear ready to pounce on any insignificant scrap of 'evidence' that what women *really* want is to take over the world. Like other social movements, the women's movement has a long history of dedicated 'networking' at a national and international level (Keck and Sikkink 1998) and today much activity is going on in cyberspace. This does not of course invalidate the central feminist tenet that patriarchy carries 'over and into' cyberspace its domination of women, especially in relation to representation. Wise (1997: 185–86) argues that one of the reasons for this is tied to the fact that even before the advent of cyberspace, women were already virtual:

> Women's very embodiment in the phallocentric imagery is the source of a perpetual virtuality: women are only useful as embodied presences by virtue of being perpetually virtualised...In the imagery of patriarchal colonisers of cyberspace, the conflated 'woman-object' is both in the machine and the machine itself...emergent virtual spheres are also replete with familiar features that suggest to many women just another extension of patriarchal hegemonics, regardless of some current theoretical analysis regarding the radical possibilities of a new, genderless, classless cybercitizenry.

New technologies may well prove to be a turning point for the re-formation of gender-constructed divisions and inequalities within society, but this will not happen automatically. The gender gap among Internet users is negligible in some parts of Europe, but that is not the case in all European countries, nor in countries around the world. According to Norris (2001: 82–84) 'the evidence about the gender gap remains inconclusive', not least because statistical data do not reveal the full extent of the different uses that women and men make of the Internet generally.

Feminist websites, as might be expected, are principally about issues which concern women, but many of them have links to wider organisations and websites of the kind mentioned throughout this chapter. However, it is also apparent that many of these sites have been created and developed in the countries of the rich world: North America, Australia and Europe. In addition, many are based in university women's studies departments. Some of them are very American centred and one could dispute the value of such sites for women in Africa, for example. Many are what I call 'mixed websites', which are both commercial and political (especially the North American ones). In other words, they are certainly women orientated, but invariably couple 'liberation' with shopping! Also in North America there have been many developments in women-only search engines which are of some use in finding specific websites/information about women's political struggles around the world, but at the same time they too have a 'national' and commercial component.[5]

There is however much useful feminist activity taking place via the Net, much of it directed towards solidarity and support. For example, the Australian Global Sisterhood Network (http://home/vicenet.au/) gathers support and funds from women around the world. It has a number of associated projects and groups, many in countries where women are still fighting for their survival and where direct action remains part of the struggle. Other examples include the Revolutionary Association of the Women of Afghanistan (RAWA), an organisation which has been more widely publicised in recent months following the war waged by the USA and its allies, but which has existed since 1977, and whose main aim has been to bring about social justice for women as well as to campaign for a secular society. RAWA's website (www.rawa.org) is rich both in terms of the history of the movement and of the women involved (one of its leaders was assassinated in 1987) and in the transnational activities of support surrounding it.

Another example I want to mention briefly is the website for Gramya, a resource centre for women in India in the district of Andhra Pradesh supported by the Global Sisterhood Network (http://home.vicenet.au/gramya/). This organisation is very active in trying to help women within the overall struggle for survival of the very impoverished tribal and dalit communities. It specifically works towards the eradication of female infanticide and the sale of girl children; education for tribal and dalit children, particularly girls; women's access to credit through self-help initiatives; setting up livelihood networks developing sustainable agriculture practices with women; and so on. The website itself is quite basic but it is nonetheless an important point of contact for support and funding activities.

One last project worth mentioning is Women on the Net, funded by Unesco and originally set up by the Society for International Development (Harcourt 1999). This has tried to address questions of how women of the south are to use Internet technologies as a political tool to empower them and many of the conclusions are clearly cautious about leaps of faith in relation to the Internet, and about the necessity to remain with one's feet firmly on the ground and 'map (out) virtual reality as closely as possible to (their) place-based politics' (ibid.: 223). Many women cannot afford access to cyberspace and/or live in areas which lack the technical infrastructure necessary to facilitate their participation (ibid.). Women frequently constitute the poor in poor countries and the poor in rich countries, and disproportionate levels of illiteracy among women remain a barrier to cyber-participation the world over (ibid.). Even women in relatively wealthy countries may feel hindered and intimidated within the relatively small areas of cyberspace they are permitted to inhabit (ibid.). Research is continuing about the uses that women are making of the Net but, despite the healthy and vibrant culture of alternative feminist networks and websites, much more remains to be done in terms of origination, design, access and use.

Conclusion

The conclusion I have reached through researching this chapter, my ongoing research and my own political activism, is that progressive political struggles are still very high on many people's agenda in spite of the death knell rung by many theorists and writers about the demise of politics and, more specifically, of party politics.[6] I certainly do not want to make the claim here that the Internet has completely 'revolutionised' the way society is organised or is capable of entirely undermining the worst excesses of global capitalism and bringing about world equality. None the less, some of the memorable anti-capitalist demonstrations in recent years, staged at key 'capitalist' events such as the IMF, World Bank, WEF, CMO and G8 meetings, promoted and supported by multifarious groups of people, and largely powered by the young, have made extensive use of the Internet and dedicated websites for the organisation of both day-to-day activities and for wider publicity. Similarly, many of the dedicated websites mentioned in this chapter are helping to further the cause of indigenous people, the fight against poverty and women's struggle for equality, in the east and south of the earth and at the same time strengthening transnational social movements, thus ensuring the survival of vital political alliances. With its almost limitless global out-reach, the Internet is encouraging communities to seek alliances beyond geographical boundaries and is empowering them in ways unimaginable in the pre-Internet age. As political and social movements grow in number and share information, knowledge and education, those in power are increasingly forced to reassess their views of minority and marginalised groups as passive and exploitable. The flourishing of counter-cultures that are using the Net to circulate information and gain support for causes ranging from the efforts of indigenous people to reclaim their identities, their heritage and their land, to the struggles by women against sexual oppression and exploitation, not only demonstrate that 'deviation' can have positive outcomes, but they demand fresh consideration of how we define 'deviance' and respond to processes of criminalisation. The concerns of counter-movements such as the World Social Forum are already starting to penetrate the agendas of their mainstream, oppositional, 'Establishment' cousins who are, in turn, increasingly feeling sufficiently defensive to proclaim their own concern for the social problems that drive the activists' agendas (Wainwright 2002). Times are changing fast. We may be 'flat earth activists', but we are 'wired' and the 'WTO, IMF and World Bank will meet somewhere. Sometime. And we will be there!' (www.resist.org.uk).

Notes

1. There have been many events/conferences around Europe concerning alternative uses of the Internet but perhaps zeligConf was the one that most successfully attempted to harness and unite alternative practices on and off the networks against neoliberal economics. I enclose a section of the text from two organisations who contributed to this conference, samizdat.net and sherwood.it which are based respectively in France and Italy: 'We believe that today it's possible, and necessary, to confront our experiences, and especially to consider the formalisation of effective levels of common initiative, of exchange of knowledges and competences, of theoretical debates and production. In other words, to conquer the means to be actors of our own communication, the capacity to be free producers of information services, to echo the richness of the initiatives of civil society against neo-liberalism' (Padua–Paris, 26 March 2000, English translation by Le Barde and Germinal, www.zeligconf/).

2. In an interview with La Repubblica both Richard Stallman and Richard Sterling have argued the case for free software: 'users should be free to study the workings of a program, modify it to their needs, distribute copies of it to other people and publish the improved copies. And if you are not programmers, you can charge somebody else for the task. This is what we mean when we talk about "free software": whether it is free in money terms doesn't influence its nature' (my translation. R. Staglianó, interview with Richard Stallman, 'Il software deve essere tutto libero' ('software must all be free'), *Repubblica.it* 8 April 2002).

3. The author is particularly familiar with websites in English and Italian which reported on Porto Alegre, in addition to Indymedia: respectively Globalise Resistance (www.resist.org.uk), Isole nella rete (www.ecn.org), Centri Sociali (www.ecn.org/cslist2.ipg).

4. My own quotation in answer to the first! (www.rosiebrown.co.uk).

5. See, for example, Womensnet, Feminist Internet Gateway, Virtual Sisterhood, etc.

6. There is an extensive literature on the subject. Of note are the debates which took place *circa* a decade ago led by Demos. See Mulgan (1994a, 1994b).

Chapter 10

Investigating cybersociety: a consideration of the ethical and practical issues surrounding online research in chat rooms

Andy DiMarco and Heather DiMarco

The advent and inescapable march of communication and information technologies have presented the social researcher with a whole new set of ideas, concepts and research fields that simply did not exist just a few years ago. Not only does the Internet enable social scientists to access information almost immediately that might previously have taken hours, days or even weeks of painstaking library research, and give us easy contact with other researchers around the world via email, but it also affords us access to numerous new areas of knowledge and experience available on a 24-hour-a-day, 365-day-a-year basis. Many argue that these processes and the opportunities they offer in the spheres of employment, education, commerce, leisure and crime are changing the face of society and of social science forever. Illingworth (2001: 5) sums up this revolution for the researcher: 'The rapid development of the World Wide Web has lifted the restrictions of geographical boundaries and opened new research horizons...In effect, the Internet provides the research community with the chance to interface with respondents in ways which may overcome some of the barriers imposed by conventional research approaches.' However, a research approach that transforms traditional modes of interaction and participation between researcher and respondent also inevitably raises new ethical dilemmas and as yet largely unaddressed practical research issues. It might thus be argued that current methodological and ethical guidelines – based in 'real world' research – are unsuited to the demands of the online researcher. Concepts such as informed consent and confidentiality are based in the research tradition of the last 150 years and may be unadaptable to the world of virtual research (in cyberspace, what is 'public' and what is 'private'? Is entering cyberspace equivalent to going 'into the field' or is it not 'real'?). In fact the rigid and dogmatic application of 'conventional' research methods may be a hindrance to online research rather than a positive feature. This final chapter will explore these issues, arguing that the dawn of a virtual society – with its different rules, language and culture – requires a fresh approach to research methods and methodology. The chapter will introduce this methodological minefield and offer some points for discussion and debate, before presenting a brief guide to the practicalities of researching in virtual meeting places such as chat rooms.

Unlike physical spaces, virtual spaces allow almost anyone with a computer to 'meet' with others in a virtual environment that has no borders, no exclusions to entry, and is truly global and equitable. Individuals can come together from all corners of the world and no gatherings or interactions (including those between researcher and respondent) need to be restricted to the spatially localised. The use of Internet spaces for collecting data is still a largely untapped resource, although there are a growing number of examples of discourse analyses of personal home pages (e.g. Miller 1995; Chandler 1998; Slevin 2000) and of what could be termed 'online ethnographies' of chat rooms, news groups and so on (Turkle 1995; Hamman 1997; Sannicolas 1997; Cavanagh 1999; Rutter, 2000). In much of this research, results have indicated that the Net offers a wide array of forums where 'users can experiment with identity, gender (re)construction, form friendships, and build virtual relationships' (Hamman 1997: 1). Virtual locations would therefore seem an ideal field of study for the online ethnographic researcher as they provide a unique insight into the ways in which individuals experiment with 'traditionally' determined identities. The use of the Internet as a research tool may be of particular use to those who are studying what could be termed 'sensitive' areas (as one of us does in Chapter 4), as the anonymity the Net provides ensures that those being researched remain, in effect, hidden from the gaze of the researcher and may be more candid than they would be in face-to-face interviews. Equally, the opportunities for the researcher to operate covertly are considerable. Just as a thief can move surreptitiously through cyberspace stealing others' identities or manipulating financial accounts and security systems, so the researcher can move obliquely through chat spaces silently observing and eavesdropping in the shadows. Our presence in cyberspace requires us to reveal little about ourselves; we are as ghosts in the machine.

This, of course, raises a number of methodological and ethical issues. Traditionally, ethnography is a research approach that requires extended observation of (and sometimes participation in) people's lives to gain insight into the social rules and patterns of cultural membership. This implies a level of physical contact and engagement that would, at first glance, seem incompatible with the virtual world. As Willis (1982: 78) observes, ethnography's advantage is the access it gives the researcher to 'real, solid, warm, *moving*, and *acting* bodies in actual situations'; a curious anomaly in an environment where participants effectively leave their bodies behind. But ethnography *is* compatible with online research, not least because it provides the researcher with access to a unique social world and a potential to uncover behaviour and activities that other methods might fail to disclose. It is particularly useful to the researcher attempting to gain insight into relatively 'closed' groups with complex layers of rules, distinctive behavioural codes and special language or 'argot'. While it is possible to interview respondents about their experiences in cyberspace, ethnography allows the researcher to immerse him or herself completely in the virtual world. In particular, what has been generally termed 'combinative ethnography' is a useful starting point for the online researcher.

Combinative ethnography attempts to investigate interactions of individuals and groups by examining their use of space or territory. Baszanger and Dodier (1997: 16) discuss this idea, suggesting that 'the main point [i]s to make an inventory of space by studying the different communities and activities of which it is composed, that is, which encounter and confront each other in that space'. The concept of 'space' in this case refers to familiar 'real life' spaces. Classrooms, the workplace, football matches and the local pub are all spaces that have commonly been observed by traditional ethnographers. But the spaces created for social interaction in cyberspace are, in fact, not as dissimilar to those in 'real life' as may first be assumed. 'Virtual pubs', for example, are common, and the social manners, rules and expectations of behaviour exhibited in these areas are recognisable as similar to those taking place in 'real' pubs. However, we are not suggesting that the research experience will be the same. Where online ethnography and 'real life' ethnography' differ most obviously is at the point of data collection. In 'real life' research, ethnographers use all their senses to acquire information and assess its accuracy. They can observe an event taking place, hear what is being said and, in some cases, even smell, taste and feel what is occurring around them. If ethnographic research was being undertaken in a real pub, the researcher would not only hear and see the interactions occurring in the social space, but would also feel the heat of the crowd, be jostled by passing drinkers, smell tobacco smoke, booze and the myriad of body smells emanating from the assembled drinkers. Such 'real life' experiential research has formed the basis of real-world ethnography, and allowed the researcher to see, react to and report on the social interaction in a particular environment or social space. However, when researching the 'virtual' pub, the ethnographer who attempts to use a 'traditional' ethnographical approach to examine this social area is metaphorically researching with both hands and one leg tied down! The 'virtual' pub has no physical manifestation: no smell, sound, vision – and no real beer! The researcher has to rely entirely on the very narrow communication method that is 'text' and the inclination and resourcefulness of those who are participating in the chat room to provide ambience and pseudo-reality.

As an example of this phenomenon, 'chatters' in virtual pubs regularly offer each other drinks, the nuance and meaning behind such symbolic gestures being offered and taken according to shared meanings and understandings based on prior experience in the physical world. But while it may be possible to observe or assess the motivation and agenda for such action in real pubs, in the virtual pub the researcher has to rely on action commands posted on the screen by the participants in this space. In a real pub a young man may buy a girl he finds attractive a drink as an icebreaker, or as a prelude to asking for a date. In the virtual pub the motive for this kind of action cannot be observed or interpreted. Further-more the 'young man' may in fact be a 60-year-old female who is having some fun online, and the 'young woman' who is the object of attention may in reality be a 40-year-old male lorry driver! In virtual reality the richness of data is enhanced by action commands such as 'girl smiles seductively at young man across bar – young man smiles back'. These action commands provide the participant-researcher with a simulation of real-world interaction and add depth and richness to the narrow-band nature of text-based social interaction.

Stone distinguishes this narrow-band/broad-band dichotomy by arguing that 'reality' is wide-band, because when people communicate face to face in real time, they use multiple modes of communication – speech, bodily gestures, facial expressions, the 'entire gamut of semantics' – simultaneously (1995: 93). Computer-mediated communi-cation, on the other hand, is narrow-band-width; in other words, it is restricted to lines of text on a screen. This does not necessarily mean that it lacks richness or texture, however. Howard Rheingold (1994: 182) asserts that chat-based interaction is a skill that requires 'creativity, quick thinking, imagination, and either a literary sensibility or the style of a stand-up comedian'. Elsewhere, Branwyn (quoting a cybersex en-thusiast) goes so far as to suggest that being able to type fast and write well is 'equivalent to having great legs or a tight butt in the real world'! (2000: 398).

None the less, 'narrow-band' interaction has been identified as problematic by some researchers due to the greater possibility of misinterpretation (Hamman 1997). An example of such misunder-standing occurred recently when a colleague was researching in a chat-room environment. When 'chatting' to a woman who stated she was from 'Jersey' it was assumed that this woman was in the Channel Islands. However, confusion arose when the responses being given to questions did not relate to familiarity with the Channel Islands and the con-versation steadily became more perplexing. When challenged by asking 'are you in the Channel Islands?' she replied 'Where is that?...I live in Jersey...New Jersey, USA'. This example demonstrates the confusion that can occur when the researcher is not part of the same physical environ-ment as his or her respondents. The 'real life' ethnographic researcher would be in the physical presence of the research participant and would pick up on verbal and non-verbal cues which would eliminate the need for such clarification. But equally they might be more predisposed to making subjective judgements about their respondent based on such signifiers.

As with all interpretative methods, questions relating to the role of the researcher and the ethical implications of this role require some thought and justification. Research in cyberspace is intrinsically different from 'real life' research, and these differences cover the full spectrum of the research process. One of the advantages of the anonymity provided by the Net is that topics which might usually be difficult to research in a face-to-face setting because of their potential to cause embarrassment or offence are much more openly discussed in the mediated virtual research context. For example, university researcher Robin Hamman notes that respondents are much more likely to reveal aspects of their cybersex lives (and issues such as solitary masturbation) online than they would be if interviewed in person. Indeed, willingness to speak about very intimate details of their sexual experiences to a complete stranger in interviews is 'almost immediate' (Hamman 1997: 3). In such research contexts, the establishment of ethical and moral boundaries becomes even more im-portant if the researcher is to avoid allegations of, for example, voyeurism. This is a subject largely unaddressed by those who write about their experiences of conducting online research, although Hamman (ibid.) refers to the dilemmas that can confront the online researcher who is also a devotee of chat rooms in their 'own' time. He notes that in his own research, problems occurred when his 'social' – that is, 'off duty' identity – and his 'professional researcher' identity were confused by a respondent, a situation which, if not immediately clarified, could lead to accusations of voyeurism and exploitation. More than one author in this book has caused eyebrows to be raised among colleagues when they discussed their research interests in university staff rooms and corridors!

Hamman (ibid.) also describes the awkwardness that can arise when personal details such as race, gender or age are misread by himself or a respondent. In 'real life' research, ethical considerations and research standards are usually expected to be applied in accordance with guidelines that are set down by professional bodies, such as the British Sociological Association. However, in the case of 'cyber' or 'virtual' research, many of these ethical guidelines and requirements become unworkable, irrelevant and at times may even be unethical in themselves. While this assertion may seem rather dramatic, there are arguments to indicate that by attempting to apply a set of ethical guidelines based on 'real life' research to research in cyber-sociology, researchers may be seen to be behaving in a heavy-handed and arrogant way. For example, anonymity is usually a key aspect of participation in chat rooms. In 'real life' research, the name, appearance and circumstances of respondents are usually known to the researcher, who may have access to a great deal of information about them which is not directly related to their inclusion in the research sample. Furthermore, the respondent will know, and be able to identify the researcher, and will probably have access to details regarding his or her institution or organisation, as well as having a contact number for him or her. To transfer this to research in cyberspace might be both reckless and unworkable. The reason that many people use virtual spaces such as chat rooms is precisely because they not only want to remain anonymous, but they want the people they are communicating with to be anonymous also (Sannicolas 1997).

As ethnographers in 'real life' we try to abide by the rules of the group we are observing, and be sensitive to their rituals and expectations of behaviour. If online ethnography is undertaken, it must similarly be undertaken with due regard to the rules of that arena or society (Cavanagh 1999). In addition, the personal safety of the researcher has to be considered. It should be remembered that people in chat rooms may well not be who or what they say they are. While there are doubtless many individuals who have 'genuine' motives for using chat rooms, there are also many who have more nefarious or predatory motives. The social spaces that are accessed via the Internet are still in effect 'open access' spaces, with very little in the way of control or policing. To offer personal information such as names, addresses or institutional affiliations would not only break the social rules of the chat room, but may also compromise the safety of the researcher and those being researched.

One of the biggest ethical considerations in this kind of research surrounds exactly what constitutes public and private material in chat rooms. This dilemma has been highlighted by several researchers in the social world of cyberspace. Homan (1991) argues that the ideas surrounding the definition of space as public or private are directly related to the definitions of those who occupy that space. The global, democratic nature of 'virtual' spaces suggests that those who use them are fully cognisant of the fact that what they discuss in chat rooms can be read by large numbers of people all over the world. It is partly for this reason that individuals anonymise themselves to protect their identity, but this has implications in terms of what is deemed to be private communication and what is considered to be in the public domain. In other words, as Homan suggests, any data gathered by a researcher in this environment cannot be said to be peculiar to any specific individual, and therefore do not require informed consent. The identity of individuals in the room is not known; they participate in chat without coercion; the space is, by its nature, a public one ergo it is a legitimate field for social research. Cavanagh (1999), using a Goffmanesque analysis, further argues that information gathered from chat rooms comes from the notion of self as an intersubjective construction of social interaction. Given the understanding of participants that everyone in chat rooms is not necessarily who or what they say they are, to seek informed consent to use data gleaned from them in social research would be a futile and pointless task.

However, matters are complicated further by the use of personal messages (PMs or 'whispers'). While interactions in the main chat room can be claimed to form part of the public domain, 'whispers' – that is, messages sent by one chatter to another in private as personal one-to-one messages – are another matter. They are not seen by any other members of the chat room and thus give rise to the kind of ethical dilemmas that arise in 'real life' research from the use of remarks made 'off the record' in private conversations between researcher and respondent. As when off-the-record confidences are shared, researchers who receive a 'whisper' from another chat room member have to make some difficult decisions about their inclusion in the write-up. If included, confidences may be betrayed, but if the researcher discloses their intentions and requests consent to use the information, it may well change the context and content of any further discussion with that individual. Given the 'clubby', intimate feel of most chat rooms, the risk of personal reactivity is surely greater in the virtual social world than it is in most physical research contexts.

Another problem facing the online ethnographer is the lack of control he or she has over his or her respondents, the data available or the usual physical parameters of research (location, timescale and so on). The covert observer can no more influence the subject of conversation in chat rooms than can any other participant, and it may prove difficult to steer the conversation towards his or her areas of interest on more than a couple of occasions. Problems may also arise in the recording or transcribing of data. Notes can be taken while chatting or observing other people's chat, and these can be formulated into short field reports at the end of each chat session, just as any raw data obtained from observational research are written up. Indeed, it may be possible for the researcher to cut and paste snippets of conversation. However, the premise of chat rooms is based on the implicit assumption that the contents of conversations on-screen are regarded as temporary and disposable text. The transcription of chat-room conversations would seem to conflict with the accepted protocol of chat rooms, and could be seen as an attempt to preserve something that was not necessarily intended for posterity by the originator of the text.

The spirit of chat rooms is democratic which means that everyone shares information without fear of it going beyond that time and space, but equally each person has the power to terminate the conversation at any time, to 'ignore' any other 'chatter' or to leave the room or network at any time. It is also possible for any chatter to have someone who makes him or her feel uncomfortable expelled from the room by informing the 'host' who will subsequently 'kick' the offender out of the chat room, or alternatively participants may combine to 'flame out' the offending party. In this sense the covert ethnographer researching in chat rooms has very little control over the research process, as to try to exert any influence over the proceedings would almost certainly raise suspicions among other users and could lead to the researcher's own expulsion. To some extent, then, in the grand tradition of ethnographic fieldwork, this involves the researcher 'playing it by ear' (Patrick 1973) and 'going with the flow' of conversation; a situation which might be to the disadvantage of the researcher in some respects, but which does mean that the actions observed are not compromised by the presence of a known ethnographer.

We should emphasise that it is *not* our intention to advocate that online research be undertaken without any ethical guidelines or thought. As discussed earlier, attempting to impose 'real life' ethical practice and guidelines to another, entirely different dimension, is largely unworkable, and to do so may well contaminate or compromise much of the information being sought. As there appears to be no firm precedence for this kind of research, we would suggest that the following ethical guidelines may provide a platform for conducting (especially covert) research in chat rooms in a safe and responsible manner:

1. When entering a chat room give the information asked for by the host, and observe the 'chat' that is occurring. It may be useful occasionally to make 'natural' comments to avoid being 'kicked' out of the room.

2. Only ask questions that occur as a natural part of the interaction, and do not attempt to direct or lead the conversation in any specific way.

3. Do not instigate 'whispers' with any other person but if anyone should whisper you it is acceptable to respond. Some of the most 'rich' information may be obtainable in this way, but bear in mind our previous comments concerning privacy and consent.

4. Under no circumstances should you, as a researcher, feel obliged to engage in any interaction you do not feel comfortable with. A polite refusal will usually deter any further approaches, but if not the 'ignore' tab in the chat room will block messages from any particular chatter.

5. Whenever possible, chat rooms should only be entered when the researcher is alone, and in a place where he or she cannot be observed. It is important that the information received is used for research and only for that purpose, and not for titillation or recreation.

6. If at any time you feel uncomfortable with the conversation, or you feel that others are uncomfortable or intimidated by your presence, the conversation can be terminated or you can simply exit the chat room.

7. If you are using a computer owned by a university or other institution, make your research intentions clear to your tutor or supervisor and follow the institution's guidelines regarding online activity.

(Adapted from Hamman 1997)

While these guidelines are very basic, they provide what we would argue to be an ethical and responsible basis for research on the Internet. The use of chat rooms, although still in its infancy, is an exciting and richly textured forum for research, and the lack of an 'official' code of ethics should not deter researchers from exploring and developing our understanding of this area of the social world.

Having discussed some of the methodological and ethical considerations that should be taken into account when undertaking research on the Net, it would now seem pertinent to address some of the more practical issues concerning the characteristics of online spaces, and the specifics of how to analyse data and report findings that arise from research in the virtual field.

The practicalities of researching online

Although we are primarily concerned with research in chat rooms, there are other virtual 'chat' spaces that are worth brief consideration. First, electronic mail discussion lists may be fruitful arenas for online researchers, although they contain inherent difficulties of access. Email discussion lists are popular precisely because they afford a level of protection and privacy not available in newsgroups and chat rooms. Communication is distributed to a list of subscribers only, which restricts the amount of intrusion from voyeurs or those who are not sympathetic to the aims of the group. This level of gatekeeping makes discussion lists popular as spaces for those wishing to exploit criminal, deviant or otherwise stigmatised aspects of their identity, although it raises obvious questions about who has the power to define or negotiate identity online (Wakeford 1997). Newsgroups are less 'safe' in that respect, but are of great value to the researcher who is seeking information or interested parties potentially to research. In essence, newsgroups allow participants to stick messages – the equivalent of an electronic Post-It note – on a bulletin board (that is, bulletin board system or BBS). They can be read by anyone who has access to the system which gives them a wide outreach, but makes material of a sensitive (that is, deviant or criminal) nature less likely to be exchanged on the more mainstream versions. However, BBSs aimed specifically at, for example, groups promoting hatred and in-tolerance, or with a specifically 'adult content' theme, are common locally and nationally.

Chat rooms are where groups of people can engage in asynchronous or 'real time' discussions with each other via their personal computer. This is known as Internet relay chat (IRC) and it allows you to see what others type, as they type. A variation of the chat space is the multi-user domain (MUD) in which users can create their own textual objects which are saved within the computer system itself (Wakeford 1997). Over recent years it has become possible to use both web cameras and microphones in chat rooms, but most currently feature text-based interaction only.

Anyone can set up a chat room in some 'chat areas' (for example on Microsoft network) by clicking on the 'create a chat' icon in the chat menu. This process usually takes only a few seconds, and the person who creates the room then becomes its host. They set the subject and agenda for discussion in that room, and can also specify the type of chatter that is welcome in the room, for example 'all male', 'teenagers' and so on. Once a chat room has been created, others can join it by clicking on the 'join a chat' icon and selecting the type of chat they are seeking. This means that from a technological viewpoint, access is simple and requires very little skill. On a user's first visit to a chat room, a small program is downloaded to the user's PC, which contains all the necessary software to chat in the selected area. At this time, the user is given information about security, chat 'manners' (sometimes referred to as 'chatiquette') and is asked to choose a chat 'handle' or nickname. Once all this is completed, interaction can begin.

The choice of a handle is often critical, as it gives an impression of you to others. Genderless handles predominate, and in fact the police advise that users choose genderless screen names as a safety precaution (www.lancashire.police.uk/chatrooms.html). But security worries aside, the choice of handle is important in determining how well you will 'fit into' the chat environment (and, if you are conducting research covertly, or pretending to be something that you are not, how likely you are to be exposed). If you are – or want to portray yourself as – a female looking to chat with other females, nicknames that contain male connotations would be inadvisable. For example, the handle 'hot rod' would be unlikely to be perceived as female by others in the chat room. Once a name has been chosen, it is important (although not always essential) to set up a 'profile' by clicking on the 'create a profile' icon on the chat menu. This gives a brief description of yourself to other chat users, and lets them know a little bit about you and your interests. It is advisable to avoid putting any information into your handle or profile that could identify you or your exact whereabouts. It should be remembered that when chatting, we simply don't know who the other person is or what their motives are! Your profile might, however, indicate what type of inter-action you are looking for in the chat room. The profile does not have to portray the 'real' you, but rather how you want those you are interacting with to perceive you. As Turkle (1995) notes, individuals regularly change their profiles and use multiple identities when participating in different chat rooms and areas, but omitting to give a profile often raises suspicions in close-knit chat communities. It is important to remember that, when joining an established chat room, many of those present may have been chatting together for a considerable time and have developed long-standing ongoing relationships. These people are often very wary of anyone who does not create a profile that indicates their status and intentions.

On entry to any chat room it is likely that your first interaction will be with the 'host' or a nominated co-host. The host or co-host can eject any 'chatter' from the room at any time, and exclude them for up to 24 hours, usually as a result of some infringement of the 'rules' or failure to observe chat protocol. When first entering a chat room a newcomer is usually asked to state their age, sex and location (A/S/L). This gives the host and other chatters an idea of who is entering the room, and at this point many chatters check the profile of the newcomer to ensure he or she is 'room-friendly'. If the entrant is felt to be acceptable he or she is usually allowed to participate. However, if there are discrepancies between what the person announces to the main chat room and their profile, the user will usually be either further questioned or ejected. It is therefore imperative that a user's profile matches what he or she states in the room. If the profile agrees with the description and fits the 'character' of the room he or she will usually be allowed to participate. Once accepted into a chat room, participants communicate via text-based interactions usually in the kind of shorthand that is becoming increasingly familiar to users of mobile phones. However, despite our growing familiarity with abbreviations and acronyms, those who are new to the specific linguistic codes of chat frequently experience difficulty in deciphering the meanings of abbreviated text. An example of two terms regularly used in chat are 'lol' and 'rofl' which mean respectively 'laughs out loud' and 'rolls on floor laughing' (a more comprehensive list of these abbreviations can be found in the glossary at the end of this chapter).

In addition to this, chatters frequently embellish their textual conversation with small picture symbols to demonstrate feelings and actions. For example, if in text someone types :) a smiley face appears thus ☺, demonstrating that the chatter is happy about what has been said. Similarly, if unhappy, they simply type in :(which demonstrates sadness: ☹. The use of these symbols acts in the virtual world in the same way that bodily and facial expressions communicate in the real world, and can be seen as a way of adding depth to the narrow-band textual medium of chat.

Those who wish to chat privately can do so, usually by clicking on the name of the person they want to chat privately to, and by then clicking on the 'whisper', 'PM' (personal message) or 'IM' (instant message) icon. As long as no one causes any offence to others in the room, and adheres to the basic rules of 'chatiquette', they can then remain in that room for as long as they wish, or until everyone else has left the room. The room only closes when there are no chatters left in the domain. This form of communication requires some practice as there are numerous problems that the 'new chatter' may encounter. These include the unwritten rules of the room, the special language and how to use chat software. Participating in any new social space can be daunting, and most new entrants to the field find the best way to start is simply to observe what is going on. This is known as 'lurking' and it has been suggested that for newcomers 'lurking' is part of the expected ritual in chat rooms: 'lurkers often receive a warm welcome from communities [and] when changing status [from lurker] to participant' (Correll 1997: 280). In short, most rooms will allow people to observe chat-room interaction to learn the basic rules of engagement, and it is also acceptable for newcomers to ask about anything they don't understand (see Chapter 4 of this volume for examples of novices' experiences of chat rooms for bisexual and bi-curious women). Experienced chatters are usually happy to give advice on protocol and explain what different symbols and shorthand messages mean. It may also be a good idea for the novice online researcher to visit a variety of different chat rooms on different networks in order to familiarise him or herself with the workings of chat across a range of domains.

Rheingold (1994) emphasises the importance of mastering the 'rules' of chat. He argues (ibid.: 178) that IRC is what you get when '[Y]ou strip everything that normally allows people to understand the unspoken shared assumptions that surround and support their communications, and thus render invisible most of the web of socially mediated definitions that tells us what words and behaviours are supposed to mean in our societies'. He claims that words can still have an elegance of expression and timing even when they exist in a purely disembodied state, but hints that chat is best suited to the extrovert, gregarious or attention-seeking: 'You know when you've arrived in the social hierarchy of an IRC channel when the regulars begin to greet you heartily when you arrive…Personal attention is a currency in IRC: everyone is on stage who wants to be, everyone is the audience, and everyone is a critic' (ibid.: 182).

It is important for any researcher to show respect for other chatters and to ensure his or her presence does not spoil the enjoyment of those participating in the room. It is therefore advisable to avoid language that may be offensive to others and reply to anyone who attempts conversation in a courteous way, even if his or her interaction has no relevance to the research aim. When chatting it is generally advisable to avoid using bold text and capital letters as this is construed as the equivalent of shouting, or being overbearing. These are only basic rules of 'chatiquette', however, and it is incumbent on the researcher to use his or her skills of perception, interpretation and evaluation and to conduct his or her investigations in a ' chat-room friendly' manner.

It is essential to reiterate that personal safety and security should remain paramount when using chat rooms for social research. As in 'real life', there are dangers and, as a general rule, it is *never* a good idea to give out a home address or phone number, or agree to meet someone you have encountered on the Internet. Remember also that you can exit the program at any time – departure is just a click away! As a final note of caution, it should be remembered that the privacy of chat and other Internet-based communication is an illusion. Tsang (2000: 432) counsels that it pays to have a 'healthy sense of paranoia' and treat every message as public. The basic rule is that, unless you are happy to let the whole world see what you are writing, don't write it!

While on the subject of cautions, although we would strongly advocate the use of chat rooms to gain data for research purposes, we would also warn that in certain areas of research there is a need for extreme vigilance on the part of the researcher. Investigating interactions between children in online chat rooms, for example, may bring about a multitude of problems for the adult covert researcher. At the very least it is possible that genuine research may be misconstrued as something more sinister or potentially criminal. As many of the other chapters of this book have demonstrated, criminal activities – including not only paedophilia, but also fraud, pornography, abuse, harassment and stalking – plague the Internet and there are numerous agencies investigating them. Researchers could easily come to the attention of these agencies should they attempt to research 'sensitive', controversial or illegal issues and environments.

Another problem facing the online ethnographer is anti-academic sentiment. Internet spaces are frequently characterised by a radical, anti-establishment agenda in which participation by 'outsiders' is seen as akin to trespass. Zickmund (2000: 250) describes the experience of a university researcher who posted a request for information for her doctoral thesis from female skinheads on an 'alternative' newsgroup. It was written in sophisticated, 'academic' language and concluded with a cheery 'thanks for your time and I look forward to your response'. The query was met with hostile and mocking responses, including the following:

She iz EzTABLIzHMENT. IgnoR her sizterz. she iz Evl.

The newsgroup participants positioned the academic as 'foreigner'; she represented the outsider from a culture that was alien to the previously established parameters of the newsgroup and sought to define the skinhead movement, 'gaze' upon it and redefine it in academic terms (ibid.: 251).

This example illustrates the problems inherent in trying to impose 'real world' research conventions on a cyber-community (although arguably the eager researcher would have met with similar – if not so immediate – responses had she posted her request in a traditional medium). It is tempting to enter the virtual realm with a different set of expectations and 'rules' of conduct in mind. Cyberspace is usually characterised as a play-ground of limitless boundaries and opportunities; an 'anything goes' environment where the usual rules of behaviour do not apply, and it would be easy for the online ethnographer to relax his or her moral standards and 'go with the flow'. Just as those who have appropriated the Internet for criminal or deviant ends can believe themselves untouchable, so the social science researcher might be tempted to abandon many of the principles that govern the research community. The dangers of 'going native' are arguably greater in a realm which seems to promise none of the restrictions on speech, behaviour or presentation of self that shape social interaction in the physical world. Online ethnography is a valuable means of gathering data on subjects that are, in the real world, sensitive or taboo but most ethnographers would argue that participant observation of cybersex is unethical, and that even exchanging personal information and photographs with online respondents is morally dubious. We must therefore be aware of the methodological flaws and moral pitfalls that await us in cyberspace, adapting and adhering to the ethical principles that govern our research elsewhere.

Chat room glossary

A/S/L?	age/sex/location?
ASAP	as soon as possible
B4N	bye for now
BBL	be back later
BBS	be back soon
BF	boyfriend
BRB	be right back
BTW	by the way
CU	see you
CYA	see you (seeya)
CYAL8R	see you later (seeyalata)
F2F	face to face
GF	girlfriend
IRL	in real life
L8R	later
LHO	laughing head off
LMAO	laughing my arse off
LOL	laugh out loud
LTNS	long time no see
MP	my pleasure
OIC	Oh, I see
OL	old lady (partner)
OM	old man (partner)

OMG	Oh my God
PM	private message
PML	pissing myself laughing
RL	real life
ROFL	rolling on floor laughing
ROFLMAO	ROFL my arse off
ROTFL	rolls on the floor laughing
RT	real time
S^	S'UP – what's up?
SO	significant other
TNT	till next time
TNX	thanks
TTFN	ta ta for now
TY	thank you
WB	welcome back
WTG	way to go
YW	you're welcome

Source: Adapted from www.SteveGrossman.com

References

Abercrombie, N. and Longhurst, B. (1998) *Audiences*. London: Sage.

Adam, A. and Green, E. (1998) Gender, agency, location and the new information society. In B. Loader (ed.) *Cyberspace Divide: Equality, Agency and Policy in the Information Society*. London: Routledge.

Aggleton, P. (ed.) (1999) *Men Who Sell Sex: International Perspectives on Male Prostitution and HIV/AIDS*. London: UCL Press.

Agustin, L. (1999) They speak but who listens? In W. Harcourt (ed.) *Women@Internet*. London: Zed.

Annandale, E. and Clarke, J. (1996) What is gender? Feminist theory and the sociology of human reproduction. *Sociology of Health and Illness* 18(1): 17–34.

Arizpe, L. (1999) Freedom to create: women's agenda for cyberspace. In W. Harcourt (ed.) *Women@Internet*. London: Zed.

Arnold, E.L. and Plymire, D.C. (2000) The Cherokee Indians and the Internet. In D. Gauntlett (ed.) *Web.studies: Rewiring Media Studies for the Digital Age*. London: Arnold.

Ashurst, P. and Hall, Z. (1989) *Understanding Women in Distress*. London: Routledge.

Ault, A. (1999) Ambiguous identity in an unambiguous sex/gender structure: the case of bisexual women. In M. Storr (ed.) *Bisexuality: A Critical Reader*. London: Routledge.

Barlow, J.P. (1990) Crime and puzzlement. *Whole Earth Review*, Fall: 44–57.

Barney, D. (2001) Say good-bye to privacy. *www.networkcomputing.com*, 29 October: unpaginated

Baszanger, I. and Dodier, N. (1997) Ethnography: Relating the part to the whole. In D. Silverman (ed.) *Qualitative Research Theory Methods and Practice*. London: Sage.

Becker, H. (1963) *Outsiders: Studies in the Sociology of Deviance*. New York: Free Press.

Belausteguigoitia, R.M. (1999) Crosssing borders: from crystal slippers to tennis shoes. In W. Harcourt (ed.) *Women@Internet*. London: Zed.

Bell, D. and Kennedy, B.M. (eds.) (2000) *The Cybercultures Reader*. London: Routledge.

Bellos, A. (2001) Alternative views find their place in the sun. *Guardian Unlimited*, www.guardian.co.uk/archive 27 January: unpaginated.

Bendle, M.F. (2002) The crisis of 'identity' in high modernity. *British Journal of Sociology* 53: 1–18.

Boorsook, P. (2000) *Cyberselfish: A Critical Romp through the Terribly Libertarian World of High-Tech*. London: Little Brown & Co.

Born, M. (1999) Country's first email stalker is convicted. *Electronic Telegraph* issue 1398, 24 March (www.intelsec.demon.co.uk/index.htm?ref=stalking/litigate/pha/index.htm).

Bostock, R. (1993) *Consumption*. London: Routledge.

Branwyn, G. (2000) Compu-sex: erotica for cybernauts. In D. Bell and B. Kennedy (eds.) *The Cybercultures Reader*. London: Routledge.

Bright, M. (1999) They're watching you. *Observer* (*Guardian Unlimited*) www.guardian.co.uk/archive 29 August: unpaginated.

Brooks, J. and Boal, I. (eds.) (1995) *Resisting the Virtual Life: The Culture and Politics of Information*. San Franciso, CA: City Lights.

Brooks, L. (1999) Private lives. *Guardian Unlimited* www.guardian.co.uk/archive 2 November: unpaginated.

Buba, N.M. (2000) Waging war against identity theft: should the United States borrow from the European Union's battalion? *Suffolk Transnational Law Review* 23: 633–65.

Budd, T. and Mattinson, J. (2000) *The Extent and Nature of Stalking: Findings from the 1998 British Crime Survey*. London: Home Office Research, Development and Statistics Directorate.

Butterworth, D. (1993) Wanking in cyberspace. *Trouble & Strife* 27, Winter: 33–37.

Cant, S. (2001) Courts wrangle over cyberstalking. *E-Commerce News* 26 March (http://it.mycareer.com.au/e-commerce/20010326/A32026-2001Mar26.html).

Carroll, J.M. (1991) *Confidential Information Sources* (2nd edn.). New York: Butterworths.

Castells, M. (1996) *The Rise of the Network Society*. Malden, MA: Blackwell.

Cavanagh, A. (1999) Behaviour in public? Ethics in online ethnography. *Cybersociology* 6 (www.socio.demon.co.uk): unpaginated.

Chandler, D. (1998) *Personal Home Pages and the Construction of Identities on the Web* (available at www.aber.ac.uk/media/Documents/short/webident.html).

Chapkis, W. (1997) *Live Sex Acts: Women Performing Erotic Labour*. London: Cassell.

Clarke, R. (1994) Human identification in information systems: management challenges and public policy issues. *Information Technology and People* 7: 6–37.

Clough, B. and Mungo, P. (1992) *Approaching Zero: Data Crime and the Computer Underworld*. London: Faber & Faber.

Cloughlan, S. (2000) Fraud's on the cards. *Guardian Unlimited* (www.guardian.co.uk/archive) 15 July: unpaginated.

CNET Networks (2000) *Cyberstalkers* (http://coverage.cNet.com/Content/Features/Dlife/Dark/ss01a.html).

Cohen, A. (2001) Internet insecurity. *Time* 2 July: 44–52.

Coleman, S., Taylor, J. and van de Donk, W. (1999) *Parliament in the Age of the Internet*. Oxford: Oxford University Press.

Congress 106th (2000) *Just Punishment for Cyberstalkers Act of 2000*, s. 2991 (available at http://thomas.loc.gov/cgi-bin/bdquery/z?d106:s.02991).

Conley, V. (1993) *Rethinking Technologies*. Oxford, OH: Miami University Press.

Connell, R. (1987) *Gender and Power: Society, the Person and Sexual Politics*. Sydney: Allen & Unwin.

Corea, G., Klein, R.D., Hanmer, J., Holmes, H.B., Hoskins, B., Kishwar, M., Raymond, J., Rowland, R. and Steinbacker, R. (eds.) (1985) *Man-Made Women: How New Reproductive Technologies Affect Women*. London: Hutchinson.

Cornwell, R. (2002) Intercepted email traffic points to new al-Qa'ida grouping in remote Pakistan. *Independent* 7 March: 3.

Correll, S. (1997) The ethnography of an electronic bar: the lesbian café. *Journal of Contemporary Ethnography* 24(3): 270–98.

Coupland, D. (1995) *Microserfs*. London: Flamingo.

Curran, J. and Seaton, J. (1991) *Power without Responsibility: The Press and Broadcasting in Britain* (4th edn.). London: Routledge.

Curzon-Brown, D. (2000) The teacher review debate part II: the dark side of the Internet. In D. Gauntlett (ed.) *Web.studies: Rewiring Media Studies for the Digital Age*. London: Arnold.

Cyber-Rights and Cyber-Liberties (UK) Report (1998) Who watches the watchmen part II: accountability and effective self-regulation in the information age. September (available at www.cyber-rights.org.watchmen-ii.htm).

Danet, B. (1996) Text as mask: gender and identity on the Internet. Paper presented at the Masquerade and Gendered Identity conference, Venice, Italy, 21–24 February (available at http://atar.mscc.huji.ac.il/~msdanet/mask.html).

Dann, J. and Dozois, G. (1996) *Hackers*. New York: Ace Books.

Davies, S.D. (1994) Touching Big Brother: how biometric technology will fuse flesh and machine. *Information Technology and People* 7(4) (available at www.privacy.org/pi/reports/biometric.html): unpaginated.

Davis, K. (1971) Prostitution. In R.K. Merton and R. Nisbet (eds.) *Contemporary Social Problems*. London: Hart-Davies.

Davis, R. (1999) *The Web of Politics. The Internet's Impact on the American Political System*. Oxford: Oxford University Press.

Diani, M. (2001) Social movement networks: virtual and real. In F. Webster (ed.) *Culture and Politics in the Information Age: A New Politics?* London: Routledge.

Di Filipo, J. (2000) Pornography on the web. In D. Gauntlett (ed.) *Web.studies: Rewiring Media Studies for the Digital Age*. London: Arnold.

Di Giovanni, J. (1996) Losing your voice on the Internet. In P. Ludlow (ed.) *High Noon on the Electronic Frontier: Conceptual Issues in Cyberspace*. Cambridge, MA: MIT Press.

Dobash, R. and Dobash, R. (1980) *Violence against Wives*. Shepton Mallet: Open Books.

Dunne, M. (1997) Southall black sisters. *Third World Network* (www.hartford-hwp.com/archives/61/061.html).

Dworkin, A. (1981) *Pornography: Men Possessing Women*. London: The Women's Press.

Edwards, S.S.M. (1993) Selling the body, keeping the soul: sexuality, power, the theories and realities of prostitution. In S. Scott and D. Morgan (eds.) *Body Matters: Essays on the Sociology of the Body*. London: Falmer Press.

Ellis, H.H. (1936) *Studies in the Psychology of Sex. Vol. 3*. New York: Random House.

Ellison, L. and Akdeniz, Y. (1998) Cyber-stalking: the regulation of harassment on the Internet. *Criminal Law Review* 29 (special edition, December): 29–48.

Epstein, S. (1997) A queer encounter: sociology and the study of sexuality. In S. Seidman (ed.) *Queer Theory/Sociology*. Oxford: Blackwell.

Exley, C. and Letherby, G. (2001) Managing a disrupted lifecourse: issues of identity and emotion work. *Health* 5(1): 112–32.

Federal Trade Commission (2000) *Identity Theft*. Washington, DC: Federal Trade Commission.

Federal Trade Commission (2002) *Identity Theft: The FTC's Response*. Washington, DC: Federal Trade Commission.

Fiddy, A (2001) The Internet twins. *Childright* 173 (January/February): 12–13 (available at www2.essex.ac.uk/clc/hi/childright/article/002.htm).

Foucault, M. (1979) *Discipline and Punish: The Birth of the Prison*. New York: Vintage.

Fox, N. and Roberts, C. (1999) GPs in cyberspace: the sociology of a 'virtual community'. *The Sociological Review* 47(4): 643–71.

Franklin, S. (1990) Deconstructing 'desperateness': the social construction of infertility in popular representations of new reproductive technologies. In M.V. McNeil and S. Yearley (eds.) *The New Reproductive Technologies*. London: Macmillan.

Freundlich, M. and Phillips, R. (2000) Ethical issues in adoption. *Adoption and Fostering* 24(4): 7–17.

George, S. (1999) Extracts from women and bisexuality. In M. Storr (ed.) *Bisexuality: A Critical Reader*. London: Routledge.

Gibson, W. (1984) *Neuromancer*. London: Grafton.

Gibson, W. (1986) *Burning Chrome*. London: Grafton.

Giddens, A. (1990) *Consequences of Modernity*. Cambridge: Polity Press.

Gilboa, N. (1996) Elites, lamers, narcs and whores: exploring the computer underground. In L.L. Cherny and E.R. Weise (eds.) *Wired Women: Gender and New Realities in Cyberspace*. Seattle, WA: Seal Press.

Gillespie, T. (2000) Virtual violence? Pornography and violence against women on the Internet. In J. Radford *et al* (eds.) *Women, Violence and Strategies for Action: Feminist Research, Policy and Practice*. Buckingham: Open University Press.

Gillies, J. and Cailliau, R. (2000) *How the Web was Born: The History of the World Wide Web*. Oxford: Oxford University Press.

Gleason, P. (1983) Identifying identity – a semantic history. *Journal of American History* 69: 910–31.

Glodava, M. and Onizuka, R. (1994) *Mail-Order Brides: Women for Sale*. Fort Collins, CO: Alaken.

Goffman, E. (1959) *The Presentation of Self in Everyday Life*. London: Penguin Books.

Goffman, E. (1963) *Stigma: Notes on the Management of Spoiled Identity*. Englewood Cliffs, NJ: Prentice-Hall.

Goffman, E. (1974) *Frame Analysis*. New York: Harper & Row.

Goodwins, R. (1993) Motley bunch hack at the end of the universe. *The Independent* 13 August: 11.

Grafx-Specs Design and Hosting (1997) *Cyberstalking: A Real Life Problem* (http://grafx-specs.com/News/Cybstlk.html).

Greene, T. (2001) *Australia Outlaws Email Forwarding* (www.theregister.co.uk/content/6/).

Gregorie, M.T. (2001) *Cyberstalking: The Dark Side of the Information Superhighway*. National Center for Victims of Crime (www.ncvc.org/newsltr/networks).

Hamelink, C.J. (2000) *The Ethics of Cyberspace*. London: Sage.

Hamman, R. (1997) The application of ethnographic methodology in the study of cybersex. *Cybersociology* 1 (www.socio.demon.co.uk): unpaginated.

Hanmer, J. (1997) Women and reproduction. In V. Robinson and D. Richardson (eds.) *Introducing Women's Studies*. Basingstoke: Macmillan.

Harcourt, W. (ed.) (1999) *Women@Internet*. London: Zed.

Harvey, N. (1998) *The Chiapas Rebellion: The Struggle for Land and Democracy*. Durham, NC: Duke University Press.

Haywood, T. (1998) Global networks and the myth of equality: trickle down or trickle away? In B. Loader (ed.) *Cyberspace Divide: Equality, Agency and Policy in the Information Society*. London: Routledge.

Heikkila, P. (2001) Defacements increase five-fold in 2001 (www.silicon.com) 11 January: unpaginated

Hillyard, P. and Percy-Smith, J. (1988) *The Coercive State: The Decline of Democracy in Britain*. London: Fontana.

Himanen, P. (2001) *The Hacker Ethic and the Spirit of the Information Age*. London: Vintage.

HMSO (1998) *Supporting Families*. London: HMSO.

Holderness, M. (1998) Who are the world's information-poor? In B. Loader (ed.) *Cyberspace Divide: Equality, Agency and Policy in the Information Society*. London: Routledge.

Homan, R. (1991) *The Ethics of Social Research*. Harlow: Longman.

Hopper, I. (2000) Pirated software subject of suit. *Associated Press* 13 November (available at www.bsa.org).

Hothschild, A.R. (1983) *The Managed Heart*. Berkeley, CA: University of California Press.

Houghton, D. and Houghton, P. (1984) *Coping with Childlessness*. London: Unwin Hyman.

Hughes, D. (1998/9) Men@Exploitation.com. *Trouble & Strife* 38 (Winter): 24.

Hyde, S. (1999) A few coppers change. *Journal of Information, Law and Technology* (available at http://elj.warwick.ac.uk/jilt/99-2/hyde.html).

Illingworth, N. (2001) The Internet matters: exploring the use of the Internet as a research tool. *Sociological Research Online* 6(2) (www.socresonline.org.uk): unpaginated.

Jacobs, S., Jacobson, R. and Marchbank, J. (eds.) (2000) *States of Conflict: Gender, Violence and Resistance*. London: Zed.

Jordan, T. (1999) *Cyberpower: The Culture and Politics of Cyberspace and the Internet*. London: Routledge.

Juniper, T. (2002) It's your shout. *Guardian Unlimited* 13 February (www.guardian.co.uk/archive): unpaginated.

Kaloski, A. (1997) Extracts from bisexuals making out with cyborgs: politics, pleasure, con/fusion. In M. Storr (ed.) *Bisexuality: A Critical Reader*. London: Routledge.

Karp, H. (2000) Angels online. *Reader's Digest*: 34–40.

Katz Rothman, B. (1994) Beyond mothers and fathers: ideology in a patriarchal society. In E. Nakono Glenn *et al* (eds.) *Mothering, Experience and Agency*. New York: Routledge.

Keck, M.E. and Sikkink, K. (1998) *Activists beyond Borders: Transnational Advocacy Networks in International Politics*. Ithaca, NY: Cornell University Press.

Keller, L.S. (1988) Machismo and the hacker mentality: some personal observations and speculations. Paper presented to the WiC (Women in Computing) conference.

Kemp, A. (1999) Dark side of the Net is forced into the light. *Observer* (*Guardian Unlimited*) (www.guardian.co.uk/archive) 17 October: unpaginated.

Kitzinger, J. (1999) The ultimate neighbour from hell? Stranger danger and the media framing of paedophiles. In B. Franklin (ed.) *Social Policy, the Media and Misrepresentation.* London: Routledge.

Kofman, E., Phizacklea, A., Raghiram, P. and Sales, R. (2000) *Gender and International Migration in Europe: Employment, Welfare and Politics.* London: Routledge.

Kolko, B., Nakamura, L. and Rodman, G.B. (2000) Race in cyberspace: an introduction. In B. Kolko *et al* (eds.) *Race in Cyberspace.* New York: Routledge.

Krafft-Ebing, R. von (1901) *Psychopathia Sexualis.* London: Rebman.

Krueger, M.W. (1991) *Artificial Reality II.* Reading, MA: Addison-Wesley.

Laing, R. (1960) *The Divided Self.* Harmondsworth: Penguin Books.

Langford, D. (1998) Ethics @ the Internet: bilateral procedures in electronic communication. In B. Loader (ed.) *Cyberspace Divide: Equality, Agency and Policy in the Information Society.* London: Routledge.

Lathouwers, R. and Happ, A. (2000) The teacher review debate part I: just what the Internet was made for. In D. Gauntlett (ed.) *Web.studies: Rewiring Media Studies for the Digital Age.* London: Arnold.

Laughren, J. (2000) *Cyberstalking Awareness and Education* (www.ucalgary.ca/ ~dabrent/380/webproj/jessica.html).

Left, S. (2002) Casting the net for paedophiles. *Guardian Unlimited* (www.guardian.co.uk/archive) 24 April: unpaginated.

Lenk, K. (1997) The challenge of cyberspatial forms of human interaction to territorial governance and policing. In B. Loader (ed.) *The Governance of Cyberspace: Politics, Technology and Global Restructuring.* London: Routledge.

Letherby, G. (1994) Mother or not, mother or what: the problem of definition. *Women's Studies International Forum* 17: 524–32.

Letherby, G. (1999) Other than mother and mothers as others: the experience of motherhood and non-motherhood in relation to 'infertility' and 'involuntary childlessness'. *Women's Studies International Forum* 22(3): 359–72.

Letherby, G. and Williams, C. (1999) Non-motherhood: ambivalent auto-biographies. *Feminist Studies* 25(3): 719–28.

Levy, S. (1984) *Hackers: Heroes of the Computer Revolution.* New York: Bantam Doubleday Dell.

Loader, B. (1997) The governance of cyberspace: politics, technology and global restructuring. In B. Loader (ed.) *The Governance of Cyberspace: Politics, Technology and Global Restructuring.* London: Routledge.

Loader, B. (1998) Cyberspace divide: equality, agency and policy in the information society. In B. Loader (ed.) *Cyberspace Divide: Equality, Agency and Policy in the Information Society.* London: Routledge.

Lynch, D. (2000) Wired women: it's a guy thing – why are there so few female hackers? *ABCNEWS.com* (available at: http://abcnews.go.com/sections/ tech/WiredWomen/wiredwomen000223.html).

Marchbank, J. (2000) *Women, Power and Policy: Comparative Studies of Childcare.* London: Routledge.

Margolis, M. and Resnick, D. (2000) *Politics as Usual: The Cyberspace Revolution*. Thousand Oaks, CA: Sage.

Marx, G.T. (1990) Fraudulent identification and biography. In D. Altheide (ed.) *Law and Social Control: New Directions in the Study of Justice*. New York: Plenum Publishing.

Marx, G.T. (2001) Identity and anonymity: some conceptual distinctions and issues for research. In J. Caplan and J. Torpey (eds.) *Documenting Individual Identity*. Princeton, NJ: Princeton University Press.

McGibbon, A. (2001) Beware the security enemy within. Network News 13 June (www.vnu.com).

McKeganey, N. and Barnard, M. (1996) *Sex Work on the Streets: Prostitutes and their Clients*. Buckingham: Open University Press.

McLaughlin, M.L., Osborne, K. and Smith, C. (1994) Standards of conduct on *Usenet*. In S.G. Jones (ed.) *Cybersociety: Computer-mediated Communication and Community*. London: Sage.

Melucci, A. (1996) *Challenging Codes: Collective Action in the Information Age*. Cambridge: Cambridge University Press.

Meyrowitz, J. (1985) *No Sense of Place: The Impact of Electronic Media on Social Behaviour*. Oxford: Oxford University Press.

Meyrowitz, J. (1989) The generalised elsewhere. *Critical Studies in Mass Communication* 6(3): 326–34.

Middleton, J. (2000) EC calls for end of anonymous email. *Network News* 18 April (www.vnunet.com).

Middleton, J. (2001) Hacking could become an act of terrorism. *Network News* 26 September (www.vnunet.com).

Miller, H. (1995) The presentation of self in electronic life: Goffman on the Internet. Paper presented at the Embodied Knowledge and Virtual Space conference, Goldsmiths' College, University of London, June (available at www.ntu.ac.uk/soc/psych/miller/goffman.html).

Moreiras, A. (1993) The leap and the lapse: hacking a private site in cyberspace. In V. Conley (ed.) *Rethinking Technologies*. Oxford, OH: Miami University Press.

Morley, D. and Robins, K. (1995) *Space of Identity, Global Media, Electronic Landscapes and Cultural Boundaries*. London: Routledge.

Mulgan, G.J. (1994a) *Politics in an Antipolitical Age*. Cambridge: Polity Press.

Mulgan, G.J. (1994b) *After the End of Politics. Occasional Paper* 2. Sheffield: University of Sheffield.

Murray, N. (2001) Hyper-nationalism and our civil liberties. Paper presented at the After September 11: Paths to Peace, Justice and Security conference, organised by the American Friends Service Committee and Tufts University's Peace and Justice Studies Program and Peace Coalition, 7–8 December, Medford, MA (available at www.afsc.org/nero/pesp/murray.htm).

National Center for Victims of Crime (2001) *Cyberstalking* (www.nvc.org/special/cyber).

Naughton, J. (1999) *A Brief History of the Future: The Origins of the Internet*. London: Phoenix.

Newman, J.Q. (1999) *Identity Theft: The Cybercrime of the Millennium*. Port Townsend: Loompanics.

Norris, P. (2001) *Digital Divide: Civil Engagement, Information, Poverty and the Internet Worldwide*. Cambridge: Cambridge University Press.

O'Connell Davidson, J. (1998) *Prostitution, Power and Freedom*. Cambridge: Polity Press.

Ogilvie, E. (2000) *Cyberstalking* 166. Canberra: Australian Institute of Criminology.

Paglia, C. (1990) *Sexual Personae: Art and Decadence from Nefertiti to Emily Dickinson*. London: Penguin Books.

Patrick, J. (1973) *A Glasgow Gang Observed*. London: Eyre Methuen.

Perry, B. (2001) *In the Name of Hate: Understanding Hate Crimes*. New York: Routledge.

Perry, J. (ed.) (1975) *Personal Identity*. Berkeley, CA: University of California Press.

Petchesky, R. (1987) Fetal images: the power of visual culture in the politics of reproduction. In M. Stanworth (ed.) *Reproductive Technologies: Gender, Motherhood and Medicine*. Cambridge: Polity Press.

Peterson, J. (Agent Steal) (1997) Everything a hacker needs to know about getting busted by the feds (available at www.grayarea.com/agsteal.html).

Petherick, W. (1999) Cyber-stalking: obsessional pursuit and the digital criminal. *The Crime Library* (www.crimelibrary.com/criminology/cyberstalking/index.html).

Pettman, J.J. (1996) *Worlding Women: A Feminist International Politics*. London: Routledge.

Pfeffer, N. (1993) *The Stork and the Syringe*. Cambridge: Polity.

Pheterson, G. (1993) The whore stigma: female dishonour and male unworthiness. *Social Text* 37: 39–54.

Phizacklea, A. (1996) Women, migration and the state. In S. Rai and G. Lievesley (eds.) *Women and the State: International Perspectives*. London: Taylor & Francis.

Plant, S. (2000) On the matrix: cyberfeminist simulations. In D. Bell and B.M. Kennedy (eds.) *The Cybercultures Reader*. London: Routledge.

Plummer, K. (1975) *Sexual Stigma*. London: Routledge & Kegan Paul.

Plummer, K. (1997) Symbolic interactionism and the forms of homosexuality. In S. Seidman (ed.) *Queer Theory / Sociology*. Oxford: Blackwell.

Plumridge, E. (2001) Rhetoric, reality and risk outcomes in sex work. *Health, Risk and Society* 3(2): 199–215.

Plumridge, E., Chewynd, J., Reed, A. and Gifford, S. (1997) Discourses of emotionality in commercial sex: the missing client voice. *Feminism and Psychology* 7: 228–43.

Pryce, A. (2001) Caught in a web of dangerous liaisons (www.independent.co.uk) 1 February: unpaginated.

Ramsay, K. (1998) Electronic stalkers at large: tracking down harassment in cyberspace. *Technological Crime Bulletin* (www.rcmp-grc.gc.ca/html/te-crime2x.htm).

Ravetz, J. (1998) The Internet, virtual reality and real reality. In B. Loader (ed.) *Cyberspace Divide: Equality, Agency and Policy in the Information Society*. London: Routledge.

Reid, E.M. (1996) Text-based virtual realities: identity and the cyborg body. In P. Ludlow (ed.) *High Noon on the Electronic Frontier: Conceptual Issues in Cyberspace*. Cambridge, MA: MIT Press.

Rheingold, H. (1994) *The Virtual Community: Surfing the Internet*. London: Minerva.

Roberts, C., Kippax, S., Waldby, C. and Crawford, J. (1995) Faking it: the story of 'Ohh!' *Women's Studies International Forum* 18(5/6): 523–32.

Robertson Elliot, F. (1986) *The Family: Change or Continuity*. Basingstoke: Macmillan.

Rose, D. (2001) Resentful West spurned Sudan's key terror file. *Observer* (*Guardian Unlimited*) (www.guardian.co.uk/archive) 30 September: unpaginated.

Roseneil, S. (2000a) *Towards an Understanding of Postmodern Transformations of Sexuality and Cathexis* (www.leeds.ac.uk/cava/files/).

Roseneil, S. (2000b) Queer tendencies: towards an understanding of post-modern transformations of sexuality. *Sociological Research Online* 5(3) (www.socresonline.org.uk): unpaginated.

Ross, A. (1991) *Strange Weather: Culture, Science and Technology in the Age of Limits*. London: Verso.

Rowland, D. (1998) Cyberspace – a contemporary utopia. *Journal of Information, Law and Technology* 3 (available at www.law.warwick.ac.uk/jilt/98-3/rowland.html): unpaginated.

Rutter, J. (2000) Identity is ordinary: presentations of self in everyday life online. Paper presented to the Virtual Society? Get Real! conference, University of Oxford, 4–5 May (available at http://virtualsociety.sbs.ox.ac.uk/).

Safir, H. and Reinharz, P. (2000) DNA testing: the next crime-busting breakthrough. *City Journal* 10: 49–57.

Sagan, S. (1995) Sex, lies and cyberspace. *Wired Magazine* 3.01 (www.wired.com/wired/archive/3.01/sex.lies.typing).

Sannicolas, N. (1997) Erving Goffman, dramaturgy, and online relationships. *Cybersociology* 1 (www.socio.demon.co.uk).

Sansam, M. (1992) Bi-o-logical. In P. McNeil *et al* (eds.) *Women Talk Sex: Auto-biographical Writing on Sex, Sexuality and Sexual Identity*. London: Scarlett Press.

Saunders, K.M. and Zucker, B. (1999) Countering identity fraud in the information age; the Identity Theft and Assumption Deterrence Act. *International Review of Law Computers and Technology* 13: 183–92.

Savill, R. (2001) Internet stalker gets seven years. *Electronic Telegraph* issue 2119 (available at www.telegraph.co.uk/).

Scambler, G. and Scambler, A. (1997) Afterword: rethinking prostitution. In G. Scambler and A. Scambler (eds.) *Rethinking Prostitution: Purchasing Sex in the 1990s*. London: Routledge.

Scambler, G. and Scambler, A. (1999) Health and work in the sex industry. In N. Daykin and L. Doyal (eds.) *Health and Work: Critical Perspectives*. London: Macmillan.

Scannell, P. (1996) *Radio, Television and Modern Life*. Oxford: Blackwell.

Schofield, J. (2002) Can the spam. *Guardian Unlimited* (www.guardian.co.uk/archive) 25 April: unpaginated.

Scholes, R.J. (1999) The 'mail-order bride' industry and its impact on US immigration. Appendix A, INS (Immigration and Naturalization Service) (available at www.ins.usdoj.gov/graphics/aboutins/repsstudies/mobappa.htm).

Sedgwick, E.K. (1991) *Epistemology of the Closet*. Hemel Hempstead: Harvester Wheatsheaf.

Segan, S. (2000a) Part I: hacker women are few but strong (available at: http://abcnews.go.com/sections/tech/DailyNews/hackerwomen000602.html#top).

Segan, S. (2000b) Part II: female hackers face challenges (available at: http://abcnews.go.com/sections/tech/DailyNews/hackerwomen000609.html).

Seidman, S. (ed.) (1997) *Queer Theory/ Sociology*. Oxford: Blackwell.

Seidman, S., Meeks, C. and Traschen, F. (1999) Beyond the closet? The changing social meaning of homosexuality in the United States. *Sexualities* 2(1): 9–34.

Sider, T. (2001) *Four Dimensions: An Ontology of Persistence and Time*. Oxford: Clarendon Press.

Slattery, M. (1992) *Key Ideas in Sociology*. London: Macmillan.

Slevin, J. (2000) *The Internet and Society*. London: Routledge.

Smelik, A. (2000) Die virtuele matrix: het lichaam in cyberpunkfilms. *Tijdschrift voor Genderstudies* 3(4): 4–13.

Smith, J. (1989) *Misogynies*. London: Faber & Faber.

Spallone, P. (1989) *Beyond Conception: The New Politics of Reproduction*. London: Macmillan.

Spender, D. (1995) *Nattering on the Net: Women, Power and Cyberspace*. Melbourne: Spinifex Press.

Spring, T. (1999) Hacker tool targets windows NT. *PC World.com* (www.pcworld.com/pcwtoday/article/).

Springer, C. (1996) *Electronic Eros: Bodies and Desire in the Postindustrial Age*. Austin, TX: University of Texas Press.

Stanko, E.A. (1985) *Intimate Intrusions*. London: Routledge & Kegan Paul.

Stanley, L. and Wise, S. (1993) *Breaking out again: Feminist Ontology and Feminist Epistemology*. London: Routledge.

Stanworth, M. (ed.) (1987) *Reproductive Technologies: Gender, Motherhood and Medicine*. Cambridge: Polity Press.

Stone, A.R. (1995) *The War of Desire and Technology at the Close of the Mechanical Age*. Cambridge, MA: MIT Press.

Strathern, M. (1992) The meaning of assisted kinship. In M. Stacey (ed.) *Changing Human Reproduction: Social Science Perspectives*. London: Sage.

Suler, J. (1996) *The Psychology of Cyberspace* (www.rider.edu/users/suler/psycyber/disinhibit.html).

The Sunday Times (2000) Invisible man faked death in Paddington rail crash. 6 February: 9.

Sutherland, J. (2000) How the other you could ruin your life. *Guardian Unlimited* (www.guardian.co.uk/archive) 19 June: unpaginated.

Tang, P. (1997) Multimedia information products and services: a need for 'cybercops'? In B. Loader (ed.) *The Governance of Cyberspace: Politics, Technology and Global Restructuring*. London: Routledge.

Tarrow, S. (1998) *Power in Movement: Social Movements and Contentious Politics*. Cambridge: Cambridge University Press.

Taylor, P.A. (1998) Hackers: cyberpunks or microserfs? *Information Communication and Society* 1(4): 401–19.

Taylor, P.A. (1999) *Hackers: Crime in the Digital Sublime*. London: Routledge.

Taylor, P.A. (2001) Hacktivism: in search of lost ethics? In D.S. Wall (ed.) *Crime and the Internet*. London: Routledge.

The Communications Act of 1996, 47. U.S.C. 223.

Theobald, S. (1999) Modern lovers. *Guardian Unlimited* (www.guardian.co.uk/archive) 28 June: unpaginated.

Theobald, S. (2000) To bi or not to bi. *Guardian Unlimited* (www.guardian.co.uk/archive) 30 March: unpaginated.

Torpey, J. (2000) *The Invention of the Passport: Surveillance, Citizenship and the State*. Cambridge: Cambridge University Press.

Toxic Shock Group (1990) The evil that hackers do. *Computer Underground Digest* 2(6): file 4.

Tran, M. (2001) Identity crisis. *Guardian Unlimited* (www.guardian.co.uk/archive) 5 July: unpaginated.

Triseliotis, J. (2000) Intercountry adoption, global trade or global gift? *Adoption and Fostering* 24(2): 45–54.

Tsang, D. (2000) Notes on queer 'n' Asian virtual sex. In D. Bell and B.M. Kennedy (eds.) *The Cybercultures Reader*. London: Routledge.

Turkle, S. (1984) *The Second Self: Computers and the Human Spirit*. London: Granada.

Turkle, S. (1995) *Life on the Screen: Identity in the Age of the Internet*. New York: Simon & Schuster.

Turkle, S. (1996) Who Am We? *Wired Magazine* 4.01 (www.wired.com/archive/4.01/turkle).

Ullman, E. (1997) *Close to the Machine: Technophilia and its Discontents*. San Francisco, CA: City Lights Books.

Usher, J.M. (1997) *Fantasies of Femininity: Reframing the Boundaries of Sex*. Harmondsworth: Penguin Books.

US Justice Department (1999) *1999 Report on Cyberstalking: A New Challenge for Law Enforcement and Industry.* Washington, DC: US Justice Department.

van Zoonen, L. (2002) Gendering the Internet: claims, controversies and cultures. *European Journal of Communication* 17(1): 5–23.
Vidal, J. (1999) Anatomy of a very nineties revolution. *Guardian Unlimited* (www.guardian.co.uk/archive) 13 January: unpaginated.
Virilio, P. (2000) *The Information Bomb.* London: Verso.

Wainwright, H. (2002) Ante upped. *Guardian Unlimited* (www.guardian.co.uk/ archive) 13 February: unpaginated.
Wajcman, J. (1991) *Feminism Confronts Technology.* Cambridge: Polity Press.
Wakeford, N. (1997) 'Networking women and grrrls with information/ communication technology: surfing tales of the world wide web', in J. Terry and M. Calvert (eds) *Processed Lives: Gender and Technology in Everyday Life.* London: Routledge.
Waldby, C., Kippax, S. and Crawford, J. (1993) Heterosexual men and 'safe sex' practice: research note. *The Sociology of Health and Illness* 15: 246–56.
Walkowitz, J.R. (1980) *Prostitution and Victorian Society: Women, Class, and the State.* Cambridge: Cambridge University Press.
Wall, D. (1997) Policing the virtual community: the Internet, cyberspace and cybercrime. In P. Francis *et al* (eds.) *Policing Futures: The Police, Law Enforcement and the Twenty-First Century.* Basingstoke: Macmillan.
Wall, D. (1999) On the politics of policing the Internet: striking the right balance. Paper presented at the Cyberspace 1999: Crime, Criminal Justice and the Internet Bileta conference, College of Ripon and York St John, York, 29–30 March (available at www.bileta.ac.uk/99papers/wall.html).
Wall, D. (2001) Cybercrimes and the Internet. In D. Wall (ed.) *Crime and the Internet.* London: Routledge.
Wall, D. (2002) Insecurity and the policing of cyberspace. In A. Crawford (ed.) *Crime and Insecurity.* Cullompton: Willan.
Wegar, K. (1997) In search of bad mothers: social constructions of birth and adoptive mothers. *Women's Studies International Forum* 20: 77–86.
Weizenbaum, J. (1976) *Computer Power and Human Reason.* San Francisco, CA: Freeman.
Westin, A.F. and Baker, M.A. (1972) *Databanks in Free Society.* New York: Quadrangle.
Whine, M. (1997) The far right on the Internet. In B. Loader (ed.) *The Governance of Cyberspace: Politics, Technology and Global Restructuring.* London: Routledge.
Williams, R. (2001) *Making Identity Matter – Identity Society and Social Interaction.* Durham: Sociology Press.
Willis, P. (1982) Male school counterculture. In *U203 Popular Culture.* Buckingham: Open University Press.
Wilton, T. (1999) Selling sex, giving care: the construction of AIDS as a workplace hazard. In N. Daykin and L. Doyal (eds.) *Health and Work: Critical Perspectives.* London: Macmillan.

Wise, P. (1997) Always already virtual: feminist politics in cyberspace. In D. Holmes (ed.) *Virtual Politics: Identity and Community in Cyberspace*. London: Sage.

Working to Halt Online Abuse (2001) *Online Harassment Statistics for 2000* (www.haltabuse.org/resources/laws/).

Worsnop, J. (1990) A re-evaulation of 'the problem of surplus women' in 19th century England, the case of the 1851 Census. *Women's Studies International Forum* 13(1/2): 21–31.

Wright Mills, C. (1956) *The Power Elite*. Oxford: Oxford University Press.

Zickmund, S. (2000) Approaches to the radical other: the discursive culture of cyberhate. In D. Bell and B.M. Kennedy (eds.) *The Cybercultures Reader*. London: Routledge.

Zizek, S. (1999) *The Plague of Fantasies*. London: Verso.

Index